Lecture Notes in Computer Science 12499

Preface

We are pleased to present in this LNCS volume the scientific proceedings of the 17th EuroVR International Conference (EuroVR 2020), organized by the Immersive Neurotechnologies Lab (LabLENI) of the Polytechnic University of Valencia (UPV), Spain, during November 25–27, 2020. Due to the COVID-19 pandemic, EuroVR 2020 was a virtual conference, to guarantee the best audience while maintaining the maximum-security conditions for the attendees.

Prior to this year, the EuroVR conferences were held in Bremen, Germany (2014); Lecco, Italy (2015); Athens, Greece (2016); Laval, France (2017); London, UK (2018); and Tallinn, Estonia (2019). This series was initiated in 2004 by the INTUITION Network of Excellence in Virtual and Augmented Reality, supported by the European Commission until 2008, and imbedded within the Joint Virtual Reality Conferences (JVRC) from 2009 to 2013. The focus of the EuroVR conference series is to present, each year, novel Virtual Reality (VR) up to Mixed Reality (MR) technologies, also named eXtended Reality (XR), including software systems, immersive rendering technologies, 3D user interfaces, and applications. These conferences aim to foster European engagement between industry, academia, and the public sector, to promote the development and deployment of XR in new and emerging, but also existing fields.

Since 2017, the EuroVR association has collaborated with Springer to publish the papers of the scientific track of our annual conference. To increase the excellence of this applied research conference, which is basically oriented toward new uses of XR technologies, we established a set of committees, including scientific program chairs, leading an International Program Committee (IPC) made up of international experts in the field.

12 scientific full papers were selected to be published in the scientific proceedings of EuroVR 2020, presenting original and unpublished papers documenting new XR research contributions, practice and experience, or novel applications. 6 long papers and 6 medium papers were selected from 35 submissions, resulting in an acceptance rate of 34%. Within a double-blind peer-review process, three members of the IPC with the help of some external expert reviewers evaluated each submission. From the review reports of the IPC, the scientific program chairs took the final decision. The selected scientific papers are organized in this LNCS volume according to three topical parts: Perception, Cognition and Behaviour; Training, Teaching and Learning; and Tracking and Rendering.

Moreover, with the agreement of Springer and for the second year, the last part of this LNCS volume gathers scientific poster/short papers, presenting work in progress or other scientific contributions, such as ideas for unimplemented and/or unusual systems. Within another double-blind peer-review process, based on two review reports from IPC members for each submission, the scientific program chairs selected 6 scientific poster/short papers from 17 submissions (acceptance rate of 35%).

Along with the scientific track, presenting advanced research works (scientific full papers) or research work in progress (scientific poster/short papers) of this LNCS volume, several keynote speakers were invited to EuroVR 2020. Additionally, an application track, subdivided into talk, poster, and demo sessions, was also organized for participants to report on the current use of XR technologies in multiple fields.

We would like to thank the IPC members and external reviewers for their insightful reviews, which ensured the high quality of the papers selected for the scientific track of EuroVR 2020. Furthermore, we would like to thank the application chairs, the demo and exhibition chairs, and the local organizers of EuroVR 2020.

We are also especially grateful to Anna Kramer (Assistant Editor, Computer Science Editorial of Springer) and Volha Shaparava (Springer OCS Support) for their support and advice during the preparation of this LNCS volume.

EuroVR 2020 is the last issue of this international conference under this name. As highlighted above, the scope of this conference and its related association is globally XR technologies and their applications. Thus, the EuroVR association recently became EuroXR (https://www.euroxr-association.org/), and our next international conference will follow this renaming. Our wish is that future EuroXR conferences will pursue and enhance this unique human-dimension framework, interconnecting European and international XR communities, for knowledge cross-fertilization between researchers, technology providers, and end users.

September 2020

Patrick Bourdot
Victoria Interrante
Regis Kopper
Anne-Hélène Olivier
Hideo Saito
Gabriel Zachmann

Organization

General Conference Chairs

Mariano Alcaniz Raya   Universidad Politécnica de Valencia, Spain
Frank Biocca   New Jersey Institute of Technology, USA
Yoshifumi Kitamura   Tohoku University, Japan

Scientific Program Chairs

Patrick Bourdot   Paris-Saclay University, CNRS, VENISE team, France
Victoria Interrante   University of Minnesota, USA
Regis Kopper   The University of North Carolina at Greensboro, USA
Anne-Hélène Olivier   University of Rennes 2, Inria, France
Hideo Saito   Keio University, Japan
Gabriel Zachmann   University of Bremen, Germany

Application Program Chairs

Angélica de Antonio   Universidad Politécnica de Madrid, Spain
Jorge D. Camba   Purdue University, USA
Kaj Helin   VTT, Finland
Jérôme Perret   Haption, Germany
Christoph Runde   VDC, Germany
Krzysztof Walczak   Poznań University of Economics and Business, Poland

Demo and Exhibition Chairs

Jaime Guixeres   Universidad Politécnica de Valencia, Spain
Giannis Karaseitanidis   ICCS, Greece
Matthieu Poyade   GSA, UK
Arcadio Reyes-Lecuona   University of Malaga, Spain

International Program Committee

Mariano Alcañiz Raya   Universidad Politécnica de Valencia, Spain
Toshiyuki Amano   Wakayama University, Japan
Daniel Andersen   Purdue University, USA
Pierre Boulanger   University of Alberta, Canada
Patrick Bourdot   Paris-Saclay University, CNRS, VENISE team, France
Andrea Bönsch   RWTH Aachen University, Germany
Weiya Chen   Huazhong University of Science and Technology, China

External Reviewers

Sandra Malpica   Universidad de Zaragoza, Spain
Kenan Niu   University of Leuven, Belgium
Vladimir Poliakov   University of Leuven, Belgium
Jeanne Vézien   Paris-Saclay University, CNRS, VENISE team, France

Organization Team

Alejandra Del Valle   Universidad Politécnica de Valencia, Spain
Jaime Guixeres   Universidad Politécnica de Valencia, Spain
Elena Parra   Universidad Politécnica de Valencia, Spain
Carla De Juan   Universidad Politécnica de Valencia, Spain
Alice Chicchi   Universidad Politécnica de Valencia, Spain
Javier Marín   Universidad Politécnica de Valencia, Spain
Marco Sacco   EuroVR
Beatrice Palacco   EuroVR
Patrick Bourdot   EuroVR

Contents

Perception, Cognition and Behaviour

Effect of Social Settings on Proxemics During Social Interactions in Real and Virtual Conditions

Tristan Duverné[1], Théo Rougnant[1], François Le Yondre[2], Florian Berton[3],
Julien Bruneau[3], Katja Zibrek[3], Julien Pettré[3], Ludovic Hoyet[3],
and Anne-Hélène Olivier[4(✉)]

[1] ENS, Univ. Rennes, Rennes, France
[2] Laboratoire VIPS2, Univ. Rennes, Rennes, France
[3] Univ Rennes, Inria, CNRS, IRISA, Rennes, France
[4] Univ Rennes, Inria, CNRS, IRISA, M2S, Rennes, France
anne-helene.olivier@univ-rennes2.fr

Abstract. Virtual Reality (VR) offers unlimited possibilities to create virtual populated environments in which a user can be immersed and experience social interactions with virtual humans. A better understanding of these interactions is required to improve the realism of the interactions as well as user's experience. Using an approach based on Interactionist Sociology, we wondered whether the social settings within which the individual interact has an impact on proxemics norms in real conditions and if these norms apply in VR. We conducted an experiment in real and virtual conditions where individuals experienced a transgression of proxemics norms at a train station and in a sports fan zone. Our results suggest that proxemics norms vary according to the subjective relationship of the individual to the social settings. This variation would translate directly into a modulation of bodily sensitivity to the proximity of the body of others. While we were able to show that social norms still exist in VR, our results did not show a main effect of the social settings on participants' sensitivity to the transgression of proxemics norms. We discuss our results in the frame of the cross-fertilization between Sociology and VR.

Keywords: Virtual Reality · Proxemics · Social settings

1 Introduction

Immersion in populated environments is an essential requirement in many Virtual Reality (VR) applications, including entertainment, education, security, but also for the study of human behavior during person-to-person interactions. In this context, social interactions between a user and virtual human characters

Supported by the ANR OPMoPS project (ANR-SEBM-0004) and the Inria associate team BEAR.

moving in the same environment need to be better understood to improve the realism of the interactions as well as users' experience. When considering social interactions, body norms were shown to be very important metrics [24]. As one of them, proxemics norms can be very influential on bodily interactions especially in the current context of COVID-19 pandemic. The proximity of one body to another may indeed appear excessive and lead to physical displacement even when this proximity is not mechanically constraining.

Proxemics is the study of people's perception and use of space [25]. The exploration of this field of study emerged in the 1960's as an interdisciplinary approach to understanding complex human behaviour in crowds. Proximity was shown to be influenced by cultural aspects [25], as well as by gender [13], behaviour [2] or attractiveness [31]. Among variables that influence proxemics norms, the subjective relationship that the individual maintains with the social setting was rarely considered. However, interactionist sociology showed that body norms vary depending on the subjective relationship with the social setting [29]. The amount and variety of social settings users can be immersed into with VR therefore raises the following questions: does changing the social setting of the environment have an impact on proxemics norms? Do these norms still apply in VR?

To answer these questions, we used a transdisciplinary approach relying on Sociology, Movement Sciences and Computer Sciences. We first aimed at verifying that the same transgression of proxemics norms provokes different reactions in individuals undergoing this transgression in real situations, according to the subjective relationship they have with the social setting in which they are interacting. To manipulate social settings, we used the concept of "non-place", proposed by the anthropologist Marc Augé [4], and which designates excessively standardized places such as shopping malls or stations. In contrast, anthropological places are social settings that make sense for individuals and in which they engage their identities, their affiliations, their tastes, etc. We then compared proxemics norms in a train station where individuals have to stand in front of the departure board to get information about the train (the presence in this specific location is constrained by the need to get information) and a sports fan zone, where individuals stop because they are attracted by an event of interest. Our second objective was to evaluate the ability of VR to study the influence of the subjective relation to social settings on proxemics by replicating the real experiment in a virtual environment. In real conditions, results showed that the subjective relation to social setting has an influence on proxemics, which results in an increased sensitivity to the transgression of proxemics norms in a non-place in comparison to an anthropological place. Proxemics norms still exist in VR, but the difference in sensitivity to social settings was not observed.

2   Related Work

Social rules have a main influence on human behavior during non-verbal interactions. In that context, interactionist sociology offers a reading framework that can help understanding norms. This section presents related work in this field, as well as studies exploring proxemics norms in VR.

2.1 Social Norms as a Determinant of the Individual Behavior

In populated environments, individuals form a coherent whole that makes them interdependent with one another [19,20]. This implies behaving according to the norms, which are the basis of the process of civilization [19,20]. A norm is defined here as a tacit rule which is constantly regulated in the course of daily life interactions [24] and is part of the socialization process during which each individual incorporates the normative behaviours of the social group to which he or she belongs to [12]. Any deviation to the norm is anticipated by the individual and, if necessary, sanctioned by consequences that can range from mere reprobation to exclusion. According to Goffman [24], the reason why the collective disapproves individuals' deviance from the norm is twofold: deviant behaviours challenge the norms that regulate the foundations of the course of interactions, and it makes the collective lose face insofar as it highlights the unnatural character of socially constructed reality. This is why each interactor has to play his or her role correctly.

2.2 The Body Proximity as a Social Norm

Proxemics norms require the interactants to maintain interpersonal distance [25]. They can be considered as determinants of individuals' motor conduct during unfocused interaction. This interaction refers to a co-presence of the interactors, without direct contact but while still influencing each other normatively [24,28]. Individuals' non-verbal reactions in terms of body posture, motion, interpersonal distance as well as gaze behaviour in such an interaction were extensively studied in the literature (see [26] for a review).

Proxemics studies identified 3 types of distances: intimate, personal and extra-personal ones [25]. Transgressing personal distance is a deviant behaviour that causes significant discomfort. The individual who transgresses is, in this case, doubly at fault: he or she does not respect the minimum distance imposed by the situation and he or she does not correctly practice socially constructed norms [24].

Social distances vary according to cultures [16,37], speed of movement and density [40], lighting condition [1], indoor or outdoor locations [17], obstacle movements [23] as well as gender and age [34,37]. Studies also investigated social distances by people's perception of crowding. McClelland and Auslander [33] found that crowdedness is associated with both the number of persons, as well as the social setting and the amount of space available. Social density was found to be more positive in specific settings, such as bars and discos, which are associated with pleasant, hedonic experiences, whereas density was negative in utilitarian settings [8]. Interestingly, the same settings can be perceived differently by individuals. Baker and Wakefield [7] found that shoppers with higher need for control tend to perceive social density in shopping malls as stressful, while shoppers with a higher need for intimacy, perceived density as exciting. Despite the amount of work on that topic, little is known about the influence of the subjective interpretation of social settings. For example, socially acceptable uses of the body are not the same in a football stadium, on a beach or in a railway station hall [18] and Interactionist Sociology showed that body norms vary by the subjective relationship to social settings [29]. Body would act as a sensory barometer of social status [30]. This is precisely why the transgression of proxemics norms causes a feeling of discomfort even when it does not mechanically limit movement. But could this discomfort, linked to excessive proximity, vary according to the subjective relationship to the social settings?

2.3 Subjective Relationship to Social Settings: Non-place and Anthropological Place

The subjective relationship between one individual and the place where he or she evolves is infinitely variable. According to Augé [4] we can however identify two main types of places according to their level of symbolization and sociality, namely "anthropological places" and "non-places".

An "anthropological place" is highly charged with symbols, such as a football stadium. Colours, individual placement, behaviour, clothing, words and songs are all symbols that manifest the identities, affiliations, antagonisms and history of the place. Interactions are focused [24] and individuals have expectations which act as foundations of the collective experience in which they come to participate. Other places are poorly charged with symbols, such as shopping malls or train station halls, which have been highly standardised by urbanisation to the extent that they all look alike and their utilitarian function overwhelms their social dimension. These places are called "non-places" [4]: individuals remain more anonymous and solitary. The subjective relationship that individuals maintain with these non-places is marked by distances and constraints. Interactions in such a non-place correspond to a logic of necessity to which everyone is accustomed. The distinction between non-place and anthropological places is not systematic and exists in the subjective representation made by individuals as well as the task they have to perform. For example, an individual can perceive the station in a very positive way if it reminds a happy encounter. Conversely, a professional steward will have a more functional and constrained relationship with the stadium. Moreover, we can wonder whether that distinction between theses two main sensitive and subjective social settings still apply in VR.

2.4 Virtual Reality and Social Interactions

VR is a powerful tool to study human social interactions [36]. VR offers new experimental perspectives since it enables experimental control while preserving a high ecological fidelity [10,32,36] which is an important challenge when considering interactions between individuals. In addition, a main advantage is to enable to manipulate any characteristics of the virtual environment the user is interacting with and to then design new experimental contexts [36]. The growing interest of Social Sciences for VR can be illustrated by the recent surveys about methodological guidelines for using VR and its benefits and drawbacks in this context [21,36,38,43,44].

The persistence of proxemics norms in VR in comparison to real conditions has been extensively evaluated. Bailenson et al. [5] designed a task where users have to approach a virtual human to find some elements on its clothes. In such a condition, users always preserve a distance threshold (40 cm) with the virtual human. As previously demonstrated in real conditions, this study also demonstrated that users maintained a larger distance when the virtual human was engaged in a constant mutual gaze. They also highlighted that users left more distance when approaching a virtual human from the front than from the back. Observing the behaviour of users' avatar playing the Second life game, Yee et al. [45] showed that male-male dyads maintain larger interpersonal distances than female-female dyads. They also reported a preservation of the Equilibrium Theory [3,6] where mutual gaze was inversely correlated with interpersonal distance. They concluded that social interactions in such a virtual environment follow the same social norms than in the physical world. Iachini et al. [27] used a paradigm where users have to press a button as soon as they feel uncomfortable with the interpersonal distance between them and a virtual human (interpersonal space), or as soon as they can reach the virtual human with their hands (periper-sonal space). They performed this task while walking towards the virtual human (active) or standing and observing the virtual human walking towards them (passive). The gender and the age of the virtual human was manipulated. They also replicated the experiment in real conditions. Their results showed a similar effect of factors manipulated in both environments: the interpersonal distance was larger in passive than in active conditions, interpersonal and peripersonal spaces were similar in the active condition but interpersonal space was larger than peripersonal space in the passive condition. Both in real and virtual conditions, the distances were larger when participants formed a dyad with a male than with a female and larger when a young adult interacted with an older adult in comparison to a young adult or a child. Finally several studies used a collision avoidance paradigm where a user has to avoid a virtual human while walking. Collision avoidance consists in regulating the interpersonal crossing distance, which is not only a contact distance but includes social norms too. In line with this idea, Gérin-Lajoie et al. [22] showed that the elliptical shape of personal space demonstrated in real conditions is preserved in VR, even if its dimensions are slightly increased. An increase of the crossing distance but a preservation of the main characteristics of the avoidance behaviour have also been reported in several studies either while walking with a HMD [9,14] or using various locomotion interfaces and control laws [35]. Similar effects were also demonstrated for both environments regarding the effect of interacting with an anthropomorphic obstacle (i.e., a human) as opposed to inanimate objects as well as the effect of anthropomorphic obstacle orientation [39].

All these studies, while using different approaches, converge to the same conclusion that social norms are preserved in VR, even though quantitative differences sometimes exist. This is an important result which encourages researchers to consider VR as a relevant tool to study human social behaviour but also to consider social rules when designing virtual populated environments. While many factors were investigated in VR such as the influence of age and gender [27], gender and attractiveness of motion [46], emotion [11], interpersonal attitude [15], there was no investigation of the effect of the subjective meaning of the virtual social setting on proxemics norms.

3 Experimental Design

3.1 Objectives

This study had two main objectives. First, we were interested in evaluating the effect of the subjective meaning of social settings on proxemics. Specifically, we investigated whether a similar transgression of proximity norms implies similar body reactions depending on the subjective relation the individual undergoing the transgression has with the social settings. To this end, we compared two types of spaces: a "non-place" (a train station) and an "anthropological place" (a sports fan zone). Secondly, we evaluated the persistence of these results in VR by replicating this experiment with participants immersed in a virtual environment. From an applicative point of view, the aim is both to grasp the extent to which virtual reality preserved the bodily sensitivity involved in social interactions, and to understand to which extent VR must integrate the social dimensions of the space when designing virtual crowded environment.

3.2 Social Settings

We considered two social environments, both in real and virtual conditions (cf. Fig. 1), that differ in term of the subjective relation they can infer to individuals:

- **An anthropological place:** A symbolized and social place where people choose to come to interact and share an experience with others. A place around a soccer game was chosen, where people observe others playing for pleasure.
- **A non-place:** A very common place that cannot be defined as identity, relational or historical and which is often transitory [4]. For this purpose, we chose a train station hall, as it is a transitory space where the individuals' presence is constrained by the obligation to wait for the necessary information to be displayed on a screen.

These two environments share similar physical properties: the density is close, individuals stand still to get an information displayed on a screen or to watch a soccer game, their position is determined by the screen being the only common focal point.

Non-place   Anthropological place

Fig. 1. Illustration of the four social environments used in the experiment.

The four environmental conditions were then the followings:

- **Real "non-place":** a train station hall where individuals are constrained to wait in front of the train display board (Fig. 1 top-left).
- **Real "anthropological place":** a stand in a fan zone in front of the soccer stadium on match days, where individuals watch other people having fun (Fig. 1 top-right).
- **Virtual "non-place":** a train station hall where individuals are constrained to wait in front of the train display notice board (Fig. 1 bottom-left).
- **Virtual "anthropological place":** a giant screen broadcasting a football match in a fan zone (Fig. 1 bottom-right).

We then formulated two hypotheses:

- **H1:** the transgression of proximity norms induces less discomfort in a highly symbolized and social place (i.e. an anthropological place), such as a sport event where individuals come to spend a good time, than in a non-place, such as a train station where presence is constrained. In particular, we expect larger reactions in the non-place condition. According to [4], we hypothesize that individuals will feel more at ease in anthropological places and then tolerate more easily a transgression of proxemics norms.
- **H2:** In line with the results of the studies presented in Sect. 2.4, we hypothesize that the transgression of proximity norms in VR induces similar reactions than in real conditions.

3.3 Participants

In order to minimize confounding individual factors, since it has been previously shown that proxemics is influenced by gender and age [37], inclusion criteria have been defined. Individuals had to be male, aged between 20 to 40 years, and their self-reported blood alcohol concentration below the legal limit for driving, since it is known that alcohol affects social behavior [42]. In real conditions, 17 subjects meeting these criteria from the post-experiment discussion were studied at the station and 13 in the fan zone. In virtual conditions, the experiment involved 22 participants in the fan zone and 22 participants in the station. In virtual conditions, we conducted experiments at the Sports Sciences University: participants were all in their twenties and male students in their 2nd year of Sport sciences bachelor's degree. They had no previous experience with VR.

3.4 Task

We designed a between-subjects experiment, which involved different participants in the four conditions considered (non-place vs. anthropological place × real vs. virtual environments).

In real conditions, a male confederate identified an unknown and uninformed male individual within a crowd of people. He then approached him and stood excessively close (15 cm away) in front of him in the same direction during 10 s (cf. Fig. 2). The confederate tried not to obstruct the subject's view of the screen to ensure that the reactions caused were not due to a mechanical impediment.

Fig. 2. Illustration of the proxemics norms transgression task used in this study: a confederate (red) approaches an individual (blue) and stops just in front of him at a very close distance so as not to occlude his view of the screen he is looking at. (Color figure online)

In virtual conditions, male participants were immersed in the virtual environment using a FOVE HMD (70 Hz, 100° field of view). A soundtrack specific to each space was played through headphones. Participants were able to move in a 2 m × 2 m space. In the train station condition, they had to stand and look at a screen until the track of the train going to a specific destination *(Dourdain-La-Forêt)* would appear. In the fan zone condition, participants stood in front of a screen where a soccer game was displayed, but were not given any specific instruction. We voluntarily provided participants with different instructions in the two virtual environments to reproduce the situation observed in real conditions: the constrained task of waiting for the information to be displayed on a screen in a train station versus a non-constrained task of watching at will a football game in a fan zone. In both virtual conditions, 30 s after the beginning of the immersion, a virtual human moved towards them, then stood in front of the participant, in order to reproduce the same stimuli as in the real conditions. In each environment, we made sure that the transgressor did not interfere with the subject's vision (by a slightly shifted position in front of him) in order to ensure that the transgressor's potential movement was related to a normative and not a visual disturbance.

Observation and Interview. For each condition, an experimenter observed the scene from a distant point of view and reported participants' reaction over the invasion of their interpersonal space. Then a post-observational interview was conducted at the end of the experiment to find out the degree of awareness expressed by subjects regarding the transgression of the proxemics norms that just occurred, their feelings, as well as the reasons that pushed them to react when they did. This explanation interview completed the observations performed by the experimenter and allowed each individual to verbalize their reactions. The interview also enabled us to confirm the subjective relationship (constrained/desired) of the individual to the social setting.

4   Analysis

We used an ethnographic method, often used in Interactionist Sociology, to describe the individuals' behaviour following the transgression of proxemics norms both in real and virtual conditions. Additionally, in virtual conditions, we recorded participant and virtual humans positions. At the end of all observations, an explanatory interview was also performed.

4.1   Ethnographic Data

Using an ethnographic approach, i.e. an observational method, we rated individuals' non verbal reactions to the transgression of proxemics norms using a 7-point scale from 1-None, 3-Minimal, 5-Moderate to 7-Frank. This rating was based on 3 indicators that were shown to be important when considering interpersonal interactions and proxemics namely, gaze, body posture and movement [26].

A minimal reaction corresponds, for example, to an increased surveillance on the confederate through the gaze, a straightening of the chest, a small displacement. A moderate reaction corresponds to a transfer of body weight from one foot to the other or micro-displacements both creating distance, accompanied by visual surveillance. Finally, a frank reaction results in a displacement increasing interpersonal distance.

4.2 Position Data in Virtual Reality

We studied the interaction as the time period in which participant's proxemics norms were violated, starting when the virtual confederate stood in front of the individual (T0) and ending when the confederate left. We computed the interpersonal distance (IPD) between the participants and the virtual confederate (center to center distance) at T0 to control the initial conditions of the interaction. We also computed the maximum IPD and the time to reach this distance during the interaction. It represents the IPD reached by participants after (more or less) motion adaptation in response to the transgression of proxemics norms.

4.3 Statistical Analysis

The statistical tests were performed using R software and the significance threshold was set at 0.05. The normality of data distribution for IPD and time variables in VR was assessed using the Shapiro-Wilk test. We evaluated the effect of the social settings using a Mann-Whitney test since data did not follow a normal distribution. Regarding ethnographic data, because our sample size was small to conduct a χ^2 test of association, we reported only descriptive statistics.

5   Results

5.1 Real Conditions

Results of the ethnographic analysis in real condition are reported in Fig. 3 in plain colours (train station in blue and stadium in green). In the train station, 47% of the individuals (8/17) had a frank embarrassed reaction to the obstruction of the proxemics standards, such as a displacement, and only 12% (2/17) did not exhibit any embarrassment-related reaction. At the stadium fan zone, 8% of the individuals (1/13) had a frank embarrassed reaction and 38.5% (5/13) did not show any embarrassment. The other intermediate reactions between those two extremes, like eye surveillance or weight transfer from one support to another, were observed in similar ranges, as shown in Fig. 3.

In the train station, 65% of the individuals (11/17) accompanied their reaction with a demonstration or a body attitude mobilized as a pretext for not revealing the transgression of the norm: turning to the other side of the confederate and pretending to search someone, for example. These "bodily excuses", dissimulating the embarrassment were found in individuals who had 'frank',

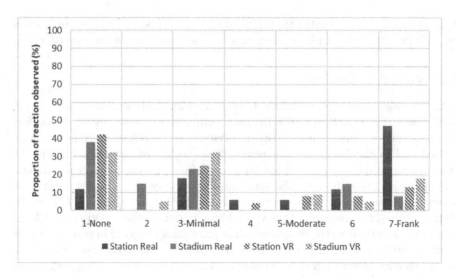

Fig. 3. Ethnographic observations during transgression of proxemics norms. The figure reports the proportion of bodily reaction and discomfort intensity observed in each conditions.

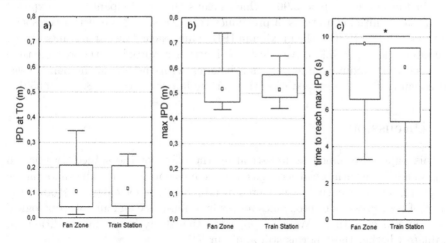

Fig. 4. Box plots of a) Interpersonal Distance (IPD) between participants and the virtual human at the beginning of the interaction b) maximum value of IPD during the interaction and c) the time to reach maximum IPD depending on the social setting. Significant differences between social settings are highlighted using a * (p < 0.05).

'light' and 'minimal' reactions. At the stadium fan zone, only 15% of the individuals (2/13) had this type of behaviour that could be interpreted as diversion strategies, but the interviews revealed that it was not a pretext and that the bodily attitudes were well justified by a practical reason. On the other hand, the explanatory interviews confirmed these diversion strategies in the train station.

The interviews also revealed that 47% of the individuals (8/17) at the station vs. 15% (2/13) at the stadium were aware of the proximity of the experimenter.

5.2   Virtual Conditions

Ethnographic observations (hatched colors in Fig. 3) showed that only 13.5% (3/22) and 18% (4/22) of the individuals exhibit frank reactions of discomfort when the virtual human invaded their personal space respectively in the train station and in the fan zone. Conversely, 42% (10/22) of the individuals in the train station and 32% (7/22) in the fan zone did not show any reaction. Minimal and moderate reactions were also quite similar between the 2 spaces. Interviews showed that all the individuals in the fan zone (22/22) and 95.5% (21/22) in the station noticed the presence of the virtual human during the experiment. A large part of the reactions to the transgression of proxemics observed in real conditions (body weight transfer, displacement by trampling...) were also observed in VR. Some behaviours were however not observed in real conditions: laughing, trying to touch the virtual human, a strong surprise manifested by a burst.

Distance and time metrics are reported in Fig. 4. Initial IPD, i.e., when the virtual human stopped in front of the participants was similar in the train station and in the fan zone ($p = 0.96$), which means that participants were exposed to the same initial conditions of proxemics transgression. No effect of the social settings was reported on the maximum IPD value reached by participants during the interaction ($p = 0.92$). An effect was however reported for the average time to reach the maximum interpersonal distance with the virtual human: it was significantly shorter in the station than in the fan zone ($U = 168$, $p = 0.032$).

6   Discussion

In this paper, we aimed at investigating the effect of the subjective relation individuals have with social settings on proxemics norms. Using an ethnographic method from a conceptual basis offered by interactionist sociology, we studied the effect of transgression of proxemics norms in a non-place and an anthropological place in real conditions. We also replicated this study in virtual conditions to evaluate whether these norms still apply in VR.

6.1   Proxemics in Non-place and Anthropological Place in Real Conditions

The ethnographic results in real-life situations indicated a tendency for individuals to be more sensitive to the proxemics norms in a constraining and perceived non-place space such as a train station compared to a meaningful anthropological place [4] such as a stadium. These results support our first hypothesis about the influence of the subjective relation between an individual and the social settings on proxemics norms: individuals showed more discomfort and tried to dissimulate more their discomfort in the train station than in the stadium.

As suggested by the interviews, individuals would possess a sensitive - more than reflexive - skill in reading and adapting to the normative context of the space in which they interact. The fan zones around the stadium are visited voluntary to share a collective identity around a local team, wearing jerseys and emblems, or at least a passion for the sport. These elements distinguish the football stadium as an anthropological place where people share the same social codes [4]. At the opposite, the train station can be considered as a transitory and temporary non-place that individuals do not appropriate, isolating them from the others. Individuals do not share an identity community linked to the space they pass through, so they are less inclined to accept the proximity of others. More generally, individuals are also less accommodating towards transgressions of norms and more sensitive to the "theatre of appearances" [24] because they do not share a collective identity.

6.2 Proxemics in Non-place and Anthropological Place in Virtual Conditions

As previously described in the literature [5, 22, 27], our results showed that social norms exist in VR and the violation of interpersonal space induces discomfort which leads individuals to perform adaptive motions to increase this distance, which is in line with our second hypothesis. We measured male-male interpersonal distances around 50 cm, which is consistent with the ones obtained in previous studies [5].

While proxemics norms apply in VR in our experiment, our results did not show main differences in sensitivity to deviance from proxemics norms depending on the social settings, which qualifies our conclusions regarding the validation of hypothesis 2. Nevertheless, we were able to show that the time to reach maximum distance after the invasion of interpersonal space was smaller in the train station than in the fan zone. Individuals reach a comfortable interpersonal distance quicker in the station, which suggests that they tend to be more sensitive to proxemics norms transgression in the virtual non-place than in the virtual anthropological place. Let us note that the dispersion of the timing to reach maximum interpersonal distance between individuals and the virtual human, was large both in the fan zone and the station. This high interindividual variability underlines the highly variable nature of the bodily reactions linked to the transgression of personal space by the virtual human. It also strengthens the interest of a transdisciplinary approach combining Movement Sciences and Social Sciences to fully comprehend the complexity of social interactions.

6.3 Limitations and Future Works

Several factors may explain the differences observed between real and virtual conditions, where the fundamental difference between anthropological place and non-place was decreased in VR.

First, individuals knew *a priori* that they are participating in an experiment in VR, which was revealed to individuals *a posteriori* in real conditions. For that reason, their level of awareness but also the control of their behavior was higher than in reality (every participant reported in the interviews the transgression of the virtual human which was not the case in reality). Although the precise research question was not explained to participants in VR, they knew that they were observed by an experimenter physically present in the same room, which may have modified their spontaneous behaviour. Being in co-presence with the experimenter may have added a constraint (a non-verbal real interaction) that tends to increase the impersonal character of the situation, bringing the two spaces closer together. The virtual interaction with the virtual human is part of a real interaction with the experimenter in the laboratory. This superposition of social settings (real and virtual) may produce two sources of potentially contradictory interactive rules and norms. It would be of interest, when performing experiments in VR related to social settings only, to decrease as much as possible the impact of the real interaction with the experimenter on the sensitive relationship individuals establish with their virtual environment. This could be performed by isolating them in a place with limited interactions with the real setting. Also, designing a distractor task to help enhancing PI and Psi could help to more firmly establish the ecological validity of the depicted social settings to participants prior to the invasion of their personal space by the virtual human. Moreover, for mainly organizational and practical needs, our participants in VR were students in Sports Sciences without any past experience with virtual reality.

Second, immersion in virtual reality, before the appearance of the virtual human, lasted only about thirty seconds, which is perhaps insufficient for the subjects to integrate and adapt to their new context. This possibly too short duration, as well as the discovery of virtual reality experiences, may make individuals feel more in a "virtual reality" situation than in a "station" or "fan-zone" situation. Indeed, several subjects told us in the interview that they did not react because they "were in virtual reality". This finding also highlights the fact that all subjects do not react in the same way to the virtual reality situation, some being fully aware of the fictitious nature of the situation while others show a much higher degree of immersion by going into the interviews to find reasons to justify the virtual human's behaviour. In future works, the level of individual engagement in the virtual environment could be tested by evaluating "Place Illusion" (PI) and "Plausibility" (Psi) [41] to better understand people's responses in virtual reality. It might also be useful to distinguish participants according to their level of familiarity with virtual reality which may affect their level of sensitivity to virtual social settings, and to extend the study with a larger sample size, including the analysis of other variables such as gaze behaviour, which was shown to be an important feature of social interactions.

Third, we acknowledge that, even if we have tried to minimize them (e.g., dedicated soundtrack, situation chosen), some differences exist between the studied conditions. The level of noise, the light or the fact that the movement was more restricted in VR as well as the point of view was more standardized in VR could have impacted participants' reactions. Future work should address the influence of such factors so as to fully understand the effect of social settings.

Lastly, it is obvious that the recent health crisis has upset the standards of proxemics by imposing a preventive distance from the bodies. Although this increased distance has a significant effect on the flow within crowds (in places for sports shows for example), the most important effect is certainly the transition from a sensitive and physical control of these distances to a reflexive and conscious control. Individuals no longer react only according to the level of perceived discomfort but according to awareness of the health risk assessed in a reflexive manner. It would be of interest to repeat this study in order to compare differences in reaction between the pre- and post-covid19 contexts.

7 Conclusion

Virtual reality offers unlimited possibilities to create virtual populated environments in which a user can be immersed and experience social interactions with virtual humans. Our study confirms the previously established evidence that VR can produce ecologically valid social responses. Furthermore, we presented an example of how VR can be used to study more complex anthropological concepts.

Our approach was based on the combination of Social Sciences and Computer Sciences, which we believe can benefit from each other. Interactionist sociology helps to understand some limitations of virtual reality in restoring the levels of sensitivity to the proxemics norms: it can be assumed that the experimental situation produces a superposition of two interactions (real and virtual) with potentially contradictory rules. Virtual reality offers highly controlled conditions as well as the possibility to measure additional quantitative variables regarding human behaviour during social interactions which is of main interest to study anthropological concepts. Future research is needed to refine the current protocols in VR to allow capturing more subtle effects of factors involved in social interactions.

References

1. Adams, L., Zuckerman, D.: The effect of lighting conditions on personal space requirements. J. Gen. Psychol. **118**(4), 335–340 (1991)
2. Argyle, M.: Social Interaction. Tavistock publications (1969)
3. Argyle, M.: Bodily Communication, 2nd edn. Methuen, London (1988)
4. Augé, M.: Non-places: an introduction to anthropology of supermodernity, le seuil (1992)
5. Bailenson, J.N., Blascovich, J., Beall, A.C., Loomis, J.M.: Equilibrium theory revisited: mutual gaze and personal space in virtual environments. Presence: Teleoper. Virtual Environ. **10**(6), 583–598 (2001)
6. Bailenson, J.N., Blascovich, J., Beall, A.C., Loomis, J.M.: Interpersonal distance in immersive virtual environments. Pers. Soc. Psychol. Bull. **29**(7), 819–833 (2003)
7. Baker, J., Wakefield, K.L.: How consumer shopping orientation influences perceived crowding, excitement, and stress at the mall. J. Acad. Mark. Sci. **40**(6), 791–806 (2012)

8. Bateson, J.E., Hui, M.K.: The ecological validity of photographic slides and video-tapes in simulating the service setting. J. Consum. Res. **19**(2), 271–281 (1992)
9. Berton, F., Olivier, A.H., Bruneau, J., Hoyet, L., Pettré, J.: Studying gaze behaviour during collision avoidance with a virtual walker: influence of the virtual reality setup. In: 2019 IEEE Conference on Virtual Reality and 3D User Interfaces (VR), pp. 717–725. IEEE (2019)
10. Blascovich, J., Loomis, J., Beall, A.C., Swinth, K.R., Hoyt, C.L., Bailenson, J.N.: Immersive virtual environment technology as a methodological tool for social psychology. Psychol. Inq. **13**(2), 103–124 (2002)
11. Bönsch, A., et al.: Social VR: How personal space is affected by virtual agents' emotions. In: 2018 IEEE Conference on Virtual Reality and 3D User Interfaces (VR), pp. 199–206. IEEE (2018)
12. Bourdieu, P.: The Logic of Practice. Stanford University Press, Palo Alto (1990)
13. Brady, A.T., Walker, M.B.: Interpersonal distance as a function of situationally induced anxiety. Br. J. Soc. Clin. Psychol. **17**(2), 127–133 (1978)
14. Bühler, M.A., Lamontagne, A.: Circumvention of pedestrians while walking in virtual and physical environments. IEEE Trans. Neural Syst. Rehabil. Eng. **26**(9), 1813–1822 (2018)
15. Cafaro, A., Ravenet, B., Ochs, M., Vilhjálmsson, H.H., Pelachaud, C.: The effects of interpersonal attitude of a group of agents on user's presence and proxemics behavior. ACM Trans. Interact. Intell. Syst. (TiiS) **6**(2), 1–33 (2016)
16. Chattaraj, U., Seyfried, A., Chakroborty, P.: Comparison of pedestrian fundamental diagram across cultures. Adv. Complex Syst. **12**(03), 393–405 (2009)
17. Cochran, C.D., Hale, W.D.e.H.C.P.: Espace personnel requis dans les emplacements intérieurs "et extérieurs". J. Psychol. **117**, 121
18. Di Méo, G.: L'individu, le corps et la rue globale. Géogr. Cult. **71**, 9–23 (2009)
19. Elias, N.: What is Sociology?. Columbia University Press, New York (1978)
20. Elias, N., Dunning, E., et al.: Quest for Excitement: Sport and Leisure in the Civilising Process. University College Dublin Press (2008)
21. de Gelder, B., Kätsyri, J., de Borst, A.W.: Virtual reality and the new psychophysics. Br. J. Psychol. **109**(3), 421–426 (2018)
22. Gérin-Lajoie, M., Richards, C.L., Fung, J., McFadyen, B.J.: Characteristics of personal space during obstacle circumvention in physical and virtual environments. Gait Posture **27**(2), 239–247 (2008)
23. Gérin-Lajoie, M., Richards, C.L., McFadyen, B.J.: The negotiation of stationary and moving obstructions during walking: anticipatory locomotor adaptations and preservation of personal space. Mot. Control **9**(3), 242–269 (2005)
24. Goffman, E.: The Presentation of Self in Everyday Life. Harmondsworth, London (1978)
25. Hall, E.T.: A system for the notation of proxemic behavior. Am. Anthropol. **65**(5), 1003–1026 (1963)
26. Harrigan, J.A.: Proxemics, kinesics, and gaze (2005)
27. Iachini, T., Coello, Y., Frassinetti, F., Senese, V.P., Galante, F., Ruggiero, G.: Peripersonal and interpersonal space in virtual and real environments: effects of gender and age. J. Environ. Psychol. **45**, 154–164 (2016)
28. Isaac, J.: La ville sans qualités. La Tour d'Aigues, Éditions de l'Aube, p. 62 (1998)
29. Kaufmann, J.C.: Corps de femmes, regards d'hommes: sociologie des seins nus. Nathan Paris (1995)
30. Kaufmann, J.C.: L'invention de soi. Une théorie de l'identité, Nathan Paris (2005)
31. Kmiecik, C., Mausar, P., Banziger, G.: Attractiveness and interpersonal space. J. Soc. Psychol. **108**(2), 277–278 (1979)

32. Loomis, J.M., Blascovich, J.J., Beall, A.C.: Immersive virtual environment technology as a basic research tool in psychology. Behav. Res. Methods Instr. Comput. **31**(4), 557–564 (1999)

33. McClelland, L., Auslander, N.: Perceptions of crowding and pleasantness in public settings. Environ. Behav. **10**(4), 535–553 (1978)

34. Mehrabian, A.: Orientation behaviors and nonverbal attitude communication. J. Commun. (1967)

35. Olivier, A.H., Bruneau, J., Kulpa, R., Pettré, J.: Walking with virtual people: evaluation of locomotion interfaces in dynamic environments. IEEE Trans. Visual Comput. Graph. **24**(7), 2251–2263 (2017)

36. Pan, X., Hamilton, A.F.D.C.: Why and how to use virtual reality to study human social interaction: the challenges of exploring a new research landscape. Br. J. Psychol. **109**(3), 395–417 (2018)

37. Remland, M.S., Jones, T.S., Brinkman, H.: Interpersonal distance, body orientation, and touch: effects of culture, gender, and age. J. Soc. Psychol. **135**(3), 281–297 (1995)

38. de la Rosa, S., Breidt, M.: Virtual reality: a new track in psychological research. Br. J. Psychol. **109**(3), 427–430 (2018)

39. Sanz, F.A., Olivier, A.H., Bruder, G., Pettré, J., Lécuyer, A.: Virtual proxemics: locomotion in the presence of obstacles in large immersive projection environments. In: 2015 IEEE Virtual Reality (VR), pp. 75–80. IEEE (2015)

40. Seyfried, A., Steffen, B., Klingsch, W., Boltes, M.: The fundamental diagram of pedestrian movement revisited. J. Stat. Mech: Theory Exp. **2005**(10), P10002 (2005)

41. Slater, M.: Place illusion and plausibility can lead to realistic behaviour in immersive virtual environments. Philos. Trans. Roy. Soc. B: Biol. Sci. **364**(1535), 3549–3557 (2009)

42. Steele, C.M., Southwick, L.: Alcohol and social behavior: I. The psychology of drunken excess. J. Pers. Soc. Psychol. **48**(1), 18–34 (1985). https://doi.org/10.1037/0022-3514.48.1.18

43. Vasser, M., Aru, J.: Guidelines for immersive virtual reality in psychological research. Curr. Opin. Psychol. **36**, 71–76 (2020)

44. Yaremych, H.E., Persky, S.: Tracing physical behavior in virtual reality: a narrative review of applications to social psychology. J. Exp. Soc. Psychol. **85**, 103845 (2019)

45. Yee, N., Bailenson, J.N., Urbanek, M., Chang, F., Merget, D.: The unbearable likeness of being digital: the persistence of nonverbal social norms in online virtual environments. CyberPsychol. Behav. **10**(1), 115–121 (2007)

46. Zibrek, K., Niay, B., Olivier, A.H., Hoyet, L., Pettre, J., McDonnell, R.: Walk this way: evaluating the effect of perceived gender and attractiveness of motion on proximity in virtual reality. In: 2020 IEEE Conference on Virtual Reality and 3D User Interfaces Abstracts and Workshops (VRW), pp. 169–170. IEEE (2020)

Influence of Dynamic Field of View Restrictions on Rotation Gain Perception in Virtual Environments

Hugo Brument[1]([✉]), Maud Marchal[2], Anne-Hélène Olivier[3], and Ferran Argelaguet[1]

[1] Inria, Univ. Rennes, CNRS, IRISA, Rennes, France
{hugo.brument,ferran.argelaguet}@inria.fr
[2] Univ. Rennes, INSA, IRISA, Inria, CNRS - France and IUF, Rennes, France
maud.marchal@inria.fr
[3] Univ Rennes, Inria, CNRS, IRISA, M2S, Rennes, France
anne-helene.olivier@inria.fr

Abstract. The perception of rotation gain, defined as a modification of the virtual rotation with respect to the real rotation, has been widely studied to determine detection thresholds and widely applied to redirected navigation techniques. In contrast, Field of View (FoV) restrictions have been explored in virtual reality as a mitigation strategy for motion sickness, although they can alter user's perception and navigation performance in virtual environments. This paper explores whether the use of dynamic FoV manipulations, referred also as vignetting, could alter the perception of rotation gains during virtual rotations in virtual environments (VEs). We conducted a study to estimate and compare perceptual thresholds of rotation gains while varying the vignetting type (no vignetting, horizontal and global vignetting) and the vignetting effect (luminance or blur). 24 Participants performed 60 or 90° virtual rotations in a virtual forest, with different rotation gains applied. Participants have to choose whether or not the virtual rotation was greater than the physical one. Results showed that the point of subjective equality was different across the vignetting types, but not across the vignetting effect or the turns. Subjective questionnaires indicated that vignetting seems less comfortable than the baseline condition to perform the task. We discuss the applications of such results to improve the design of vignetting for redirection techniques.

Keywords: Virtual Reality · Perception · Rotation gains · Vignetting

1 Introduction

Navigation is essential for exploring Virtual Environments (VEs). Then, it is important to provide to the users easy and comfortable navigation techniques for Virtual Reality (VR) experiences. While literature showed that real walking is

© Springer Nature Switzerland AG 2020
P. Bourdot et al. (Eds.): EuroVR 2020, LNCS 12499, pp. 20–40, 2020.
https://doi.org/10.1007/978-3-030-62655-6_2

the most ecological approach to navigate in VEs as it increases presence [59] and performance [32,48], the limitations of physical workspace in VR setups do not always enable users to walk. To encounter this constraint, numerous navigation techniques have been designed to freely navigate in VEs regardless of the size of the physical workspace [28]. Some encourage the physical movement of the user (e.g. redirected walking or walking-in-place), while others require minimal user motion, such as virtual steering techniques and teleport-based. However, virtual techniques lack of vestibular and proprioceptive feedback.

Among the different navigation techniques, redirection techniques try to compensate the limited physical workspace while maintaining real walking to navigate in the VE [35]. Therefore they enable real walking while requiring minimal training to be used. They are based on (1) manipulating the users virtual and real paths and/or (2) manipulating the VE itself by changing its internal structure. One solution to achieved infinite walking in the VE in a limited work space was proposed by Razzaque [44] and named *redirected walking*. They added imperceptible yaw rotational gain (i.e. scaling the mapping between real and virtual motion) to user's view point in the Head Mounted Display (HMD) in order to subtlety reorient the user in the real environment.

Redirection techniques rely on detection thresholds (DTs) gains, which define the limit the user can detect or not the rotation gain. Numerous studies have been done to estimate the DTs of different types of gains such as rotation [11, 19,54], translation [17,33,34] or curvature gains [5,54]. In this paper, we will only focus on rotation gains. Imperceptibility of rotation gains for redirected walking implementations is a challenge and active topic of research in VR. When using rotation gains, VR designers have to be careful in their implementations of redirection techniques: they have to use gains that would be subtle enough in order to not not disturb users experience (high gains might be noticeable or make the navigation more difficult) and comfort (high gains may provoke more cybersickness). While research focused on how to increase the DTs without breaking presence, it is also important to consider the usability and factors that could influence the perception of rotation gains.

For instance, modern HMDs, such as the HTC Vive or the Oculus Rift, offer Field of Views (FoVs) up to 100°. Recent work conducted with these HMDs has shown that FoV can alter motion perception [20,36]. However, related studies mostly focused on visually induced illusory self-motion known as vection [46,47]. Little is known about the relation between the FoV and the perception of rotations gains in VEs. Some recent work showed differences between large and narrow FoV [61] on DTs, but no one explored the impact of dynamic FoV modifications on the perception of rotation gains. Such results could be important for VR developers to design new redirection techniques considering FoV restrictions for a wide audience since the FoVs vary between HMDs.

In this paper, we present a perceptual study assessing participants ability to discriminate changes between virtual and real rotations under different FoV restrictions, hereinafter referred as vignetting. Participants had to perform rotations in a virtual forest with different vignetting configurations (see Fig. 1).

Two factors were considered, the shape of the restriction (horizontal, global) and the visual effect (darkning and blur). We evaluated the participants perception of rotation gains by computing the Point of Subjective Equality (PSE) and the DTs for each condition. Our main hypothesis was that vignetting could reduce participants ability to determine whether a rotation gain was applied or not, therefore increasing the DTs. Our results contribute to the understanding of human perception in VEs and discuss the usability of vignetting for redirection techniques.

2   Related Work

2.1   Rotation Gains and Detection Thresholds

In general, redirection techniques are required to scale users real movements in order to maintain them in the workspace. This intensity of the scaling is typically referred as gain. A rotation gain $g_r \in \mathbb{R}$ for head rotations is defined by the quotient between the virtual rotation $R_{virtual}$ and the physical (real-world) rotation R_{real}: $g_r = \frac{R_{virtual}}{R_{real}}$. Applying a rotation gain g_r to R_{real} will result to rotate the virtual camera by $R_{virtual} \times g_r$ instead of R_{real}. It means that if $g_r = 1$, the virtual rotation remains the same than the real one. Otherwise, when $g_r > 1$ or $g_r < 1$, the virtual camera rotates respectively faster or slower than the user's head rotation. For example, applying a gain $g_r = 2$ when the user rotates its head 90° in the real world, the virtual camera rotates by 180° [54]. Rotation gains can be applied for each angle of the rotation (i.e. pitch, yaw and roll). However, in redirection techniques, the gain is generally applied only on yaw rotations [19,41,44,52]. Besides, the gain is mostly applied constantly during the whole rotation, but there exist also other implementations if the final rotation is known in advance [14,49,63]. In this paper, we will only focus on amplified rotations with constant gains for yaw head rotations, excluding pitch or roll rotations [6].

Typically, perceptual studies to estimate detection thresholds (DTs) use two-alternative force-choice (2AFC) protocol, where different gains are applied, and estimate the detection thresholds by fitting a psychometric function to the percentage of positive answers. The gain at which the subject responds positively to the stimuli in 50% of the trials is defined as the Point of Subjective Equality (PSE), at which the user perceives the physical and the virtual rotations as identical. DTs are defined as the value of the gain at which the user has either 25% or 75% probability of choosing one item of the 2AFC question. DTs interpretation can vary based on the gains used in the protocol. DTs then represent the boundaries at which the portion of incorrect (25% DT) or correct (75% DT) answers is significantly different from chance.

Amplified head rotations have been widely studied in VR [19,54] including different experimental conditions such as varying the amount of rotation to perform [11] (ranging from 10° to 180°); adding visual effects [9,39] (e.g. contrast inversion or sinus gratings); varying the gain implementation [14,63] (delaying the gain rotation based on the amount of rotation performed); using auditory cues [37,53] (specialized sound to redirected users) or distractors [41,61] (to lose focus on the gains); using different FoVs [6,61] (e.g 40° vs 110°); comparing perception of gain between a CAVE and a HMD [43] or different locomotion interfaces [10] (walking and wheelchair steering). These studies resulted in different PSE and thresholds values but in general, 25% and 75% thresholds ranged respectively between 0.59-0.93 (25% DT) and 1.10-1.27 (75% DT), where the gains tested were between 0.5 and 1.5. Readers can refer to [25,35] for further information about detection threshold of head rotation gains.

Literature showed that modifications of the FoV can alter motion perception. Yet, most of the presented studies did not restrict the participants' FoV. In the following section, we will introduce FoV restrictions in VR and studies its influence on participants' behavior.

2.2 Field of View and Vignetting in VR

In human vision, the term "Field of View" (FoV) refers to the world that can be seen at any moment. It is defined as "the number of degrees of visual angle during stable fixation of the eyes" [55]. Humans effective visual field of view is 200° horizontally and 150° vertically [62]. Since vision is a fundamental cue for navigating, several research works conducted experiments to determine the effects of FoV restrictions on navigation performances. For instance, in Real Environments (REs), restricting both horizontal or vertical FoV increases the time to perform an obstacle course [18,57]. Besides, the walking speed linearly decreases when the FoV is restricted [58].

In VR applications, the FoV refers rather to what is visible while wearing additional apparatus. Most of HMDs have limited FoVs ranging from 40° to 110° diagonal, which are considerably smaller than human FoV. There exist several ways in VR to restrict users virtual FoV by applying visual effects. The most common technique is called vignetting and consists in reducing the virtual camera's brightness or saturation toward the periphery compared to the virtual camera's center. Hence, it gradually reduces the users FoV by applying mostly a black color or some blur effects in the peripheral vision [12,24]. Several vignetting models have been designed, either using a constant restriction [22], based on controller-based inputs [15,50], head movements [38] or ocular activity [1].

User studies have been conducted to determine whether vignetting could be a promising solution for decreasing cybersickness while preserving presence. However, the conclusions remain different across authors. Fernandes and Feiner assessed vignetting during navigation with a hand-held controller and they showed that vignetting can reduce cybersickness and improve users comfort [15]. Budhiraja et al. proposed a vignetting where mouse acceleration increased or decreased the Gaussian blur applied to the virtual camera [12]. Their vignetting allowed participants to experience less cybersickness during a first person shooter game in VR than the baseline group. Norouzi et al. studied the effect of vignetting during an exploration task in a virtual forest where head rotations gains were applied [38]. They found that most of the participants experienced more cybersickness with vignetting than without. These results could be explained by the difference in how users explored a VE using head movements (resulting in higher exploration) or a hand-held controller (resulting in slower exploration). Furthermore, vignetting seems not to have a negative effect on path integration [2], or spatial awareness [50]. Yet, some studies revealed that vignetting techniques are less preferred for navigation tasks [38,50] where participants tend to prefer conditions without FoV restrictions and could lead to lower presence [29].

Rotation gains and vignetting have been widely studied but mostly separately. While the study of rotation gains was achieved to improve redirection techniques, and vignetting for improving user comfort and decrease cybersickness, little is known about the influence of vignetting on human perception. While Williams and Peck found that participant's ability to discriminate 90° turn was more difficult (i.e. higher PSEs and DTs) with a wider FoV (110°) than a restricted one (40°) [61], we believe that restricting participants FoV could increase the DTs of rotation gains during turns. Indeed, Bolte et al. found that participants tend to underestimate pitch and roll gains when the FoV is reduced [6]. The objective of our study is therefore to use dynamic vignetting to explore its influence on rotation gain perception. We want to assess whether vignetting could increase DTs of rotation gains or not. Our main hypothesis is that FoV restrictions would alter participants ability to detect rotation gains. Our study aims at contributing to the improvement of redirection techniques.

3   Dynamic Field of View Restrictions Design

3.1   Description

In our experiment, we wanted to investigate the effect of several FoV restriction types. To design each vignetting, we followed models already designed to dynamically modify the FoV with respect to users head angular speed [4,38], but we adapted them in order to propose a generic vignetting model that allows any type of FoV restrictions and visual effects. Two different design choices were considered: (1) the restriction shape (i.e. the area of the FoV which is affected by the vignetting); (2) the effect type (i.e. the visual effect applied to the restricted area).

Regarding the restriction shape, most of studies used a circular restriction (an annulus defined by an inner and outer circles, hereafter referred as **Global** vignetting). In this paper, we also propose an **Horizontal** vignetting that reduces the users FoV to the opposite head rotation direction. The horizontal mode is inspired by the human anticipation behaviours in REs in which gaze will anticipate the head rotation during a turn [3]. Therefore, the Horizontal vignetting only hides the peripheral vision to the opposition gaze direction. The motivation to design this Horizontal vignetting is to reduce the amount of information and being more subtle than the Global one since the restriction is not applied in both eyes.

Regarding the effect type, we considered two methods that reduce the optical flow in the restricted area. A **Luminance** effect which decreases the contrast in the restricted area and a gaussian **Blur** effect which decreases visual saliency in the restricted area. While Luminance effect is the most widely used in VR applications using vignetting, we wanted to see whether Blur could provide similar perceptual results while less disturbing. This resulted in 4 different configurations: *Global Luminance, Global Blur, Horizontal Luminance and Horizontal Blur* (see Fig. 1).

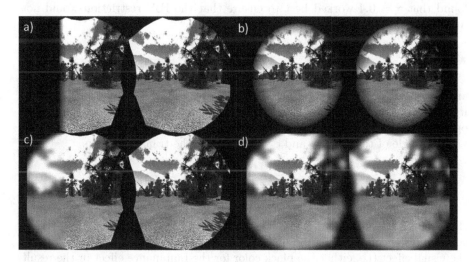

Fig. 1. Illustration of the 4 different FoV restrictions (vignetting) during the same rightwards rotation: (a) Horizontal Luminance; (b) Global Luminance; (c) Horizontal Blur; (d) Global Blur.

3.2   Implementation Details

Given a pixel position p in normalized screen coordinates and the current restriction angle (R_t), we first define whether the pixel falls within the restriction area:

$$Shape(p, R_t) \in [0, 1] \tag{1}$$

Zero means that the pixel is outside the restriction zone, one that the pixel is in the restriction zone and $]0, 1[$ is transition zone. R_t is defined by the yaw head rotation w and Eq. 1 has to be defined both for the Global, and the Horizontal restriction shapes.

The amount of restriction, R_t, is calculated using Eq. 2 were α_{max} and α_{min} respectively represent the maximum and minimum values to apply the restriction. When $R_t(\omega) = \alpha_{max}$ there is no restriction applied, and when $R_t(\omega) = \alpha_{min}$ the restriction is maximal. Users FoV is reduced as ω increases.

$$R_t(\omega) = \alpha_{max} - Min(\omega, \alpha_{max} - \alpha_{min}) \tag{2}$$

In our model, α_{max} and α_{min} were respectively set to 56 and 18° for the Horizontal restriction and 64 and 30 for the Global restriction. α_{max} was defined considering the HMD used in the study (HTC Vive), while α_{min} was defined empirically. For the Global restriction the minimum FoV was 60 ($\alpha_{min} \times 2$) while for the Horizontal restriction the minimum horizontal FoV was 74° (asymmetric).

In order to decrease jitter for the head rotations speed, an hysteresis was applied based on the instantaneous head rotation speed (ω_t). We empirically found that $\gamma = 0.4$ worked best to ensure that the FoV restriction would not jitter due to small head movements.

$$\omega = \gamma * \omega_t \tag{3}$$

Then, the cut-off of is defined by an inner and outer radius that together form an annulus for the Global type, and a rectangle for the Horizontal one. The opacity of the cut-off increases linearly from completely transparent to completely opaque (mask). The mask is calculated using Eq. 4, while $angle(p)$ defines the viewing angle of the pixel p, and $\epsilon_\alpha = 10$ defines the transition zone.

$$Shape(p, R_t) = \frac{R_t - angle(p)}{\epsilon_\alpha} \in [0, 1] \tag{4}$$

Finally, we apply the restriction effect to the pixel, where $Shape(p, R_t)$ defines the strength of the applied effect. The color of the pixel p in normalized screen coordinates is computed as the linear interpolation between the pixel color and the visual effect (i.e. either the black color for the Luminance effect or the result of the gaussian blur for the Blur one) where the interpolant is the result of $Shape(p, R_t)$.

4   User Study

The goal of this experiment was to investigate the effect of vignetting on the detection threshold of amplified head rotations. We considered the previously defined vignetting types and effects. This experiment was inspired from similar protocol already performed to assess perception of rotation gains without [54] or with FoV restriction [61].

4.1   Design and Hypotheses

We conducted a 3 (**Vignetting Type:** none, horizontal, global) × 2 (**Vignetting Effect:** luminance, blur) × 2 (**Rotation:** 60°, 90°) user study to estimate the perception threshold depending on the FoV restrictions. Vignetting Type and Rotation were within-participants factors whereas Vignetting Effect was a between-participant factor. We decided to test two different rotations because most of the studies only assessed 90° turns, and Bruder et al. showed that perception of rotation gains can differ depending on the amount of rotation performed [11]. Besides, in navigation, shorter rotations than 90° can occur and it is important to understand how participants could perceive gains during a shorter exposition.

For each Vignetting Type and Rotation, we tested 9 times each gain used in the experiment. The gains used in the experiment ranged from 1 (90° physical rotation resulted in a 90° virtual rotation) to 1.4 (54° physical rotation resulted in a 90° virtual rotation), incremented in steps of 0.1. We only applied gain on the yaw axis. Excluding practice session, this resulted in 3 vignetting × 2 rotations × 5 gains × 9 trials, totaling 270 trials per participant. The trials were randomized per block for each participant.

Note that, unlike similar protocols [11,54,61], we did not assess gains below than 1. These gains were not tested because our interest was to assess whether FOV manipulations could provide higher gains perception threshold. The task trials were a stimuli (gain applied) two-alternative forced choice (2AFC) task. 2AFC tasks avoid participant response bias as participants are forced to guess even when they are unsure of virtual head amplification. On average, when participants do not know the answer, if participants answer randomly, they will be correct 50% of the time. Our hypotheses for this experiment were:

- [H1] Detection thresholds would be higher when applying vignetting.
- [H2] Detection thresholds would differ depending on the vignetting effect.
- [H3] Detection thresholds would be higher for the 60° turn than the 90° one.
- [H4] Users would report no discomfort while using the FoV vignetting.

These hypotheses were motivated by our suggestions that vignetting could alter participants perception and therefore allow to add more imperceptible rotational gains. It means that we want to determine whether dynamic modification of FoV with different effects or restrictions could influence the way users perceive rotation with or without head amplifications.

4.2   Participants and Apparatus

24 participants (18 males and 6 females) aged between 22 and 37 years old (26.67 ± 3.62, mean ± SD) without any ocular or locomotion disorders volunteered to this study. 14 participants reported using VR on a weekly or daily basis, 6 few times and 4 never. All participants except 4 had regular experiences with videos games. They were naive to the purpose of the experiment and signed an informed consent form. The study was conformed with the standards of the declaration of Helsinki.

We developed the application with Unity3D and we use a Vive Pro HMD, that has a resolution of 1440×1600 pixels per eye and a 110° diagonal FoV. The reference coordinate system was defined by the HTC Vive tracking system. During the whole experiment we guaranteed the maximum frame-rate of the HTC Vive HMD (90 Hz). We use the Vive Wireless Adapter[1] in order to prevent users from being bothered by cables, as it could potentially influence users behavior during their rotations.

---

[1] https://www.vive.com/eu/accessory/wireless-adapter/.

The VE was a large outdoor forest with grass, trees and rocks. We designed it with the Green Forest Unity 3D asset[2]. This VE was chosen to generate motion flow from participants' while physically rotating. We also added a black cross located on the ground and a virtual sphere for calibration purposes.

4.3   Procedure

First, participants read and signed the consent form which provided detailed information regarding the experiment. They had a training session to get familiar with the task, the rotation gains, and the different vignetting conditions. Then, the experiment consisted in 9 randomized blocks, 3 for each vignetting (none, horizontal, global). Each block consisted in 30 trials (3 trials × 5 gains × 2 rotations), with a break after every 3 blocks completed. The experiment therefore resulted in a total of 270 trials (9 repetitions × 3 vignetting type × 5 gains × 2 rotations) per participants. At the beginning and the end of the experiment, participants filled a Simulator Sickness Questionnaire (SSQ) [21]. After filling the first demographic questionnaire (age, gender, amount of experience playing video games an exposure to VR), we assessed their dominant eye and measure their interpupillary distance (IPD). Then, they were placed at the center of the physical workspace and were equipped with the HMD and the controller.

A trial consisted of rotating the whole body in place (not just the head or the torso but also the feet) either 60 or 90° clockwise or counter-clockwise. We randomly ordered clockwise and counter-clockwise rotations during the experiment. Participants could visualize the turn to perform thanks to an arrow indicating the rotation direction. Before starting the trial, they had to calibrate by looking at a red sphere that was displayed in front of them. Once they were staring at it, the sphere turned green and participants could press the controller's trigger to start the trial. Then, participants rotated until a red sphere appeared at the center of their vision, signaling that they should end their rotation by facing at this sphere until it turned green indicating successful trial completion. Participants had to confirm the trial by pressing the controller's trigger. If the participant rotated past the virtual rotation, the green sphere's color changed to red and participants had to correct and maintain their orientation such that the sphere changed to blue green. At the end of the trial, the VE faded to black and participants had to answer the following 2AFC question: "My movement in the virtual world was greater than my physical movement: (yes or no answer)".

To prevent unintentional positional drift during the experiment, we ensure that the user started each trial around 50 cm to the center of the physical workspace, if the participants were not located nearby, they had to move towards a black cross displayed on the VE floor. Trials where the participants turned too quickly, slowly or inconsistently were rejected. For speed, participants were required to turn physically at between 45 and 180° per second averaged across the entire turn. Trials were tested to ensure participants did not turn against

---

[2] https://assetstore.unity.com/packages/3d/environments/fantasy/green-forest-22762.

the desired direction of motion. If a turn had failed, the trial would have been rejected and the 2AFC question would have been skipped and the participant got a feedback about the failure.

After a block of 30 trials, we asked participants to answer the following question "On a scale of 0–10, 0 being how you felt coming in, 10 is that you want to stop, where are you now?" [45]. This question ensured that participants did not feel severe sickness during the experiment, since doing a series of rotations with gains could lead to cybersickness. After every three blocks, the users took off the VR equipment and had a 5 min break to minimize potential negative effects of cybersickness.

At the end of the experiment, we asked participants to rate the comfort of each Vignetting Type to perform the task from 1 (not comfortable at all) to 7 (very comfortable). We also asked them to rank the Vignetting Type by their preferences (the one they preferred the most ranked 1st and the one they least preferred ranked 3rd). In total, the experiment took approximately an hour. At any time, users could ask for a break or stop the experiment.

4.4   Data Analysis

We recorded 6 480 trials (24 users × 2 Vignetting Effects × 3 Vignetting Types × 5 Gains × 9 Repetitions) during this experiment. Practice trials before the experiment and between blocks were not included in the analysis. Preliminary data analysis revealed that there were no side effects between leftwards and rightwards rotations. We therefore mirrored the leftwards turns in order to remove the side factor from the analysis.

We computed for each participant the probability $P(g_n; yes)$ of responding "Yes" for a given gain to the question "My movement in the virtual world was greater than my physical movement", for each gain, turn and vignetting type. Then, a psychometric curve was fit to each participant's data and the Point of Subjective Equality (PSE), 25% and 75% threshold gains were computed with the Quickpsy package in R [30]. It fits by direct maximization of the likelihood psychometric functions of the form $\psi(g_n) = \gamma + (1 - \gamma) * F(x)$, where γ is the guess rate and F the cumulative normal distribution function. We excluded 4 participants from the analysis because we were unable to fit a psychometric curve from their data (they mostly never answered "yes").

Before analyzing the positions and orientations of head and shoulders, we first resampled them and then applied a butterworth low-pass filter with a cutoff frequency of 1 Hz to remove oscillations due to the potential users displacements in the RE. We temporally normalized the evolution angular speed over the trials in order to analyze rotation behavior regarding the experimental conditions. We used the Statistical Parametric Mapping (SPM) method [16] to analyze the angular speed across the experimental conditions. This analysis allows comparing time-series data of different trials taking into account their variability at each time-step. In order to evaluate the effect of the Vignetting Effect, Vignetting Type, Rotation on PSEs and DTs, we performed a three-way analysis of variance (ANOVA) with repeated measures. We tested normal distribution of the data with the Shapiro-Wilk test. Greenhouse-Geisser adjustments to the degrees of freedom were applied, when appropriate, to avoid any violation of the sphericity assumption. Post-hoc analysis was based on pairwise t-tests with Bonferonni corrections. Only significant post-hoc comparison are reported in the next section. Finally, to analyse subjective data from the questionnaires, we used the Friedman test and post-hoc pairwise Wilcoxon tests with Bonferroni corrections.

4.5 Results

We found no significant effect of the vignetting type or gain on the evolution of the angular speed during a trial ($p > 0.05$). This means that participants rotation behavior remained similar across experimental conditions and trials (Fig. 2). Besides, we noticed no effect of SSQ scores between the luminance and blur effects, and no fast SSQ average answers remained below 3 for each blocks during the experiment. These results are important for a fair comparison of DTs since the way participants perform the rotation and cybersickness could alter the perception of the rotation gains.

Psychometric curves were fit to the pooled results of participants data by Vignetting type, Vignetting Effect, and Rotation (Fig. 3). Table 1 summarizes the PSEs and DTs computed for each experimental conditions based on participants individual fits. We compared $P(g_n; yes)$, the probability of responding "yes" at a given gain g_n, with a 4-way ANOVA (Vignetting Type x Vignetting Effect x Rotation x Gain). There was a significant main effect of Gain ($F(2.32, 51.05) = 177.68, p < .0001, \eta^2 = .89$), where post-hoc analyses showed that the higher the gain, the higher the probability of answer "greater" ($p < 0.05$).

To evaluate the effect of experimental conditions on PSEs, we performed a 3-way ANOVA (Vignetting Type x Vignetting Effect x Rotation). We found a significant effect of the Vignetting Type on the PSEs ($F(1.90, 30) = 3.99, p < 0.05, \eta^2 = .20$) and DTs ($F(1.45, 23.25) = 8.11, p < 0.01 \eta^2 = .34$), where post-hoc analyses showed that PSEs and DTs where higher with the Global vignetting than the baseline one (None). We found neither effect of Vignetting Effect ($p = 0.41$) nor Rotation ($p = 0.13$) on the PSEs and DTs.

A 2-way (Vignetting Type x Vignetting Effect) ANOVA showed an effect of the Vignetting Type on comfort ($F(1.30, 20.74) = 5.00, p < 0.05, \eta^2 = .24$), where Global vignetting was less comfortable than the None and the Horizontal ones ($p < 0.05$). Figure 4 shows the number of votes regarding vignetting type preferences (the most preferred ranked 1st and the least preferred ranked 3rd). A chi-square test showed that the Vignetting Effects were not independent ($\chi^2(8) = 18.595, p < 0.05$). In overall, participants ranked the baseline (None, no vignetting) as the most preferred then the Horizontal and finally the Global.

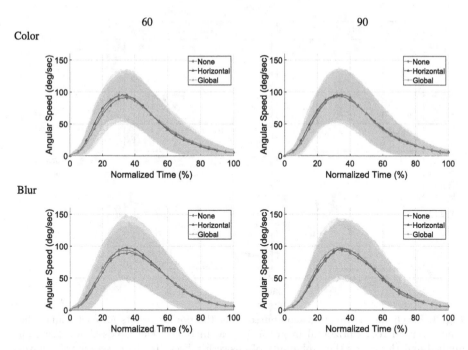

Fig. 2. This figure shows typical temporal evolution of mean and standard deviation of angular speed for each Vignetting type (None in red, Horizontal in blue and Global in green), Vignetting Effect (Color on first row and Blur on second) during 60° and 90° turns. Each sample of the temporal sequence is a dependant variable. No effect was found across the conditions. (Color figure online)

Table 1. The 25%, PSE, and 75% threshold gains derived from the psychometric curves. Results are grouped by Vignetting Effect, Type and Rotation.

Effect	Type	Rotation					
		60			90		
		25%	PSE	75%	25%	PSE	75%
Color	None	1.13 (0.11)	1.23 (0.10)	1.32 (0.11)	1.15 (0.05)	1.24 (0.05)	1.33 (0.06)
Blur	None	1.11 (0.08)	1.20 (0.07)	1.29 (0.06)	1.15 (0.11)	1.22 (0.08)	1.30 (0.07)
Color	Horizontal	1.13 (0.13)	1.23 (0.08)	1.32 (0.09)	1.12 (0.08)	1.25 (0.04)	1.40 (0.09)
	Global	1.13 (0.06)	1.25 (0.08)	1.38 (0.12)	1.16 (0.07)	1.26 (0.06)	1.35 (0.08)
Blur	Horizontal	1.10 (0.10)	1.20 (0.09)	1.29 (0.07)	1.13 (0.08)	1.24 (0.05)	1.35 (0.07)
	Global	1.08 (0.11)	1.20 (0.07)	1.35 (0.06)	1.12 (0.12)	1.24 (0.07)	1.33 (0.07)

5   Discussion

Our main objective was to assess whether vignetting (either its type or its effect) could alter the perception of rotation gains in virtual environments. More precisely, we designed an experiment where participants had to perform a 60 or 90° turns where we applied different rotation gains (from 1 to 1.4) and vignetting (None, Horizontal, Global). We analyzed participants ability to detect or not

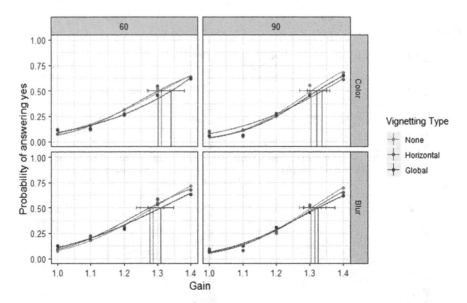

Fig. 3. Psychometric functions computed from the pooled results for each vignetting type (none in red, Horizontal in green, Global in blue). The x-axis shows the gain applied and the y-axis the probability of answering "yes" to the question "My movement in the virtual world was greater than my physical movement". Results are grouped by Rotation (60, 90) and Vignetting Effect (Color, Blur). (Color figure online)

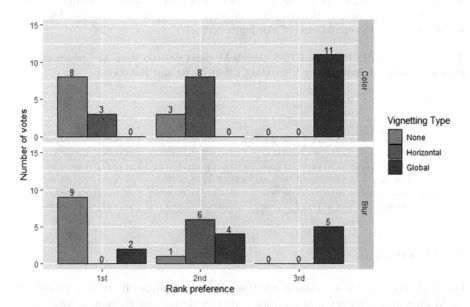

Fig. 4. Distribution of participants vignetting preferences (grouped by Vignetting Effect). At the end of the experiment, we asked participants to rank from their most to their least preferred vignetting.

the gains by computing their PSEs and DTs. While we observed an effect of the Vignetting Type on the PSEs variable of the experiment, our results showed that the average values remain similar.

Regarding [**H1**], we were expecting that restricting the participants FoV by applying a vignetting would make the detection of rotation gains more difficult, resulting in higher PSEs and DTs. This hypothesis was motivated by the fact that peripheral vision could help to disambiguate the perception of self motion [27]. We extended this statement by supposing peripheral vision could also help detecting or not a rotation gain. We wanted therefore to check how users would be able to determine a rotation gain with less information of the VE. Even though we found an effect of the Vignetting Type on the PSEs and DTs, Table 1 shows that the average PSEs per condition remained quite similar (around 1.20 and 1.26). We guaranteed in our vignetting model that the amount of restriction between the Horizontal and Global was similar, but the restricted regions were different. Restricting both eyes (Global vignetting) seemed be more efficient for disturbing the detection of rotation gains than restricting the eye opposite to the participant's rotation (Horizontal vignetting). One explanation could be that, during the rotation, the eyes were staring at the opposite direction of the region where the Horizontal vignetting was applied, while the Global one also covered peripheral region opposite to the rotation's direction. Then, Global vignetting tended to be more efficient in disturbing the detection of rotation gains than the others conditions.

In our experiment, we had the Vignetting Effect as a between group variable. Half of participants tested the Luminance effect and the other half the Blur one. We wanted to see whether different visual effects could alter perception of gains, as it was demonstrated that they can alter users self motion perception [9]. We did not see differences between both effects, rejecting [**H2**]. While most of the vignetting effects used in VR applications are based on a black texture decreasing the contrast in the restricted area, we wanted to see whether a blurring effect, that could be less noticeable to the user, could provide similar or higher PSEs and DTs. Finally, our experiment showed that both visual effects were similar. We could therefore consider different effects with respect to users preferences.

While most studies on the perception of rotation gains considered mainly 90° rotations, we wanted to see if the detection of rotation gains could be more difficult with a shorter rotation (60° in our experiment). With [**H3**], we expected differences in PSEs and DTs between both turns. Bruder et al. showed that participants were better at discriminating rotations when the virtual turning angle is rather large [11]. Even though we did not find a significant effect of Rotation on PSEs and DTs, Fig. 3 shows that, for 60° turns, the PSEs for the Global Vignetting Type is higher than the two others for both Vignetting Effects (the blue curve is slightly shifted to the right compared to the others). Thus, the use of vignetting and rotation gains might be interesting to manipulate user rotations during shorter rotations than 90°.

Subjective questionnaires showed that users preferred to perform the rotation task without vignetting. While some research work showed the benefits of vignetting to reduce cybersickness [15], participants did not prefer the use of vignetting to perform navigation tasks [38,50]. Thus, it is hard to determine the benefits of vignetting regarding user preferences and we believe that vignetting based on head movements is not appropriate for all users in VR. For instance, all participants that reported using VR on a weekly or daily basis noticed both vignetting effects, while the participants that experienced VR for the first time did not notice them. Besides, most of the "expert" participants did not recommend the vignetting effects, reporting that it was too constraining and uncomfortable. Few of them also reported that they were not affected by the vignetting since they were focused on the detection task. Thus, it could be interesting to consider the vignetting with respect to the user VR experience. Our results demonstrated the opposite of our hypothesis [**H4**]. We could have expected that the blurring effect (that mimicries the natural blurring in the peripheral vision) would be more comfortable than the luminance one (that hides the peripheral vision). However, the Horizontal vignetting seemed more appreciated by participants than the Global vignetting. One reason could be that it was less noticeable, thus participants were less bothered during the tasks.

The literature notes that during a sensory conflict between visual and vestibular cues, the visual information is predominant on the vestibular and the proprioceptive ones during locomotion. During the task, participants had to compare their perceived virtual rotation with their real rotation. The vignetting restricted information in the peripheral region, generating less visual information than in the baseline condition. Yet, since the rotations asked were constant, the amount of extra-retinal information received by participants remained the same across vignetting conditions (i.e. constant optical flow). Then, we believe that the similar PSEs and DTs across conditions can be explained by three external factors that we could explore in future experiments:

1. **Optic flow** can be used to control heading direction [60] while walking. Research work showed that offsetting the location of the Focus of Expansion (FoE) alters gait behavior, resulting in a walking path that is deviated at in a direction opposite to the FoE [51,60]. Besides, asymmetric optic flow can alter the steering behavior, some studies showed that when there is an inconsistency between the speed of two corridors' walls, the chosen trajectory is the one that reduces the difference between those regions (participants drift towards the slower moving wall) [13,23]. Thus, manipulation of optic flow could alter the perception of rotation gains. It can be interesting to have a look at these manipulations since optic flow is a major component in the perception of self motion. Besides, in our experiment, as only rotation was considered, the optic flow was constant for each pixel. Introducing a translation component could help to determine whether the amount of optical flow could disturb the detection of rotational gains or not.

2. **Saccades (and vestibulo-ocular-reflex)** could contribute to the detection of rotation gains. Saccadic suppression of image has been already used to subtlety reorient participants in the VE. They take advantage of the inability to detect changes in the location of a target when the change occurs

immediately before, during or shortly after the saccade [8]. Bolte and Lappe suggested that participants are more sensitive to scene rotations orthogonal to the saccade than in the same direction of this saccade [7]. Sun et al. implemented a redirected walking controller that rotates up to $0.14°$/frame the virtual camera when a saccade is detected [56]. Moreover, Langbehn et al. assessed the threshold of translation and rotations offset during participants blinks [26]. They reported that it is possible to apply a $+/-$ 5° reorientation in the transverse plane along the line of gaze during saccades >15° (and users tend to fail detecting translations shift from range 4–9 cm). Therefore, it is easier to apply a gain during a saccade than during a fixation. In our experiment, participants had to stare at a sphere at the end of the rotation task. When a gain was applied, the mismatch between the gaze direction and the sphere position in the VE might have been noticeable and therefore have contributed to detect the gain. Recording gaze activity during such experiment would help to determine whether gaze behavior is different according to the gain.

3. **Proprioception** is an important cue while navigating. In our experiment, participants could have relied on computing the amount of rotation done in RE (with their feet orientation) and check if it matches with the final orientation in the VE. Marlinsky showed that blindfolded people tend to overestimate rotations of lower magnitudes and underestimate those of higher magnitudes [31]. Besides, they overestimated passive rotations and this estimation was linearly related to to the magnitude of turn. Research work showed the importance of neck proprioception in the perception of body orientation and motion [40,42]. It may be difficult to assess the impact of proprioception because we cannot isolate this factor. We could, for instance, ask participants the amount of physical rotation they performed at each trial and measure the rotation error with and without gain. We could then see whether the proprioception information was prior to the visual one or not.

6   Limitations and Future Work

In our experiment, we only used gains above 1 because we wanted to assess whether we can increase rotation gains with vignetting. However, this choice could have led to an asymmetry that could have biased our results (and therefore having an overestimation of the PSEs and DTs) since a gain was applied in 80% of the trials (i.e. answering "yes" to the 2AFC question). Besides, participants had to discriminate real and virtual rotations during a single turn. However, some studies showed that PSEs and DTs can differ according to the rotation task (e.g. discrimination between (1) virtual and physical rotation and (2) two successive rotations) [54]. Thus, further experiments are required to assess gains below 1 and varying the rotation task.

The absence of significant differences between the FoV Vignetting Types could be linked to the vignetting model itself. Indeed, its design was based on previous models of the literature, and we respected the maximum of contraction used in most of VR applications. Yet, further work is required to determine how we could improve the vignetting so that it will be adapted to the user and could potentially increase the DTs for redirection techniques in VR.

Finally, other factors might impact the perception of rotation gains in VEs (e.g tangential and angular speeds). For example, Neth et al. investigated the influence of walking speed on the detection of curvature gain [33] and demonstrated that people are significantly less sensitive towards walking on a curved path when walking slower. Further experiment would be needed to assess the perception of rotation gains during virtual translations with different angular speeds.

7   Conclusion

In this paper, we proposed to study the impact of different vignetting implementations on the perception of rotation gains during virtual turns in VE. The results of our experiment showed a difference of the Vignetting Type on the PSEs and DTs, but no effect for the Vignetting Effect nor Rotation. Yet, the average PSEs and DTs remained quite similar across the different conditions, and the results of our experiment might suggest that vignetting could not necessarily alter the perception of rotation gains. It is difficult to conclude that our results encourage the use of vignetting in order to increase the gains used in redirected techniques, since they allow only slight increase of rotation gains while altering users comfort. Nevertheless, we believe that the use of FoV manipulations could be considered as an interesting option for VR applications. Vignetting should therefore be designed with a user-centered approach in order to make it affordable in redirection techniques implementations.

References

1. Adhanom, I.B., Griffin, N.N., MacNeilage, P., Folmer, E.: The effect of a foveated field-of-view restrictor on VR sickness. In: Proceedings of IEEE Conference on Virtual Reality and 3D User Interfaces (VR), pp. 645–652 (2020)
2. Al Zayer, M., Adhanom, I.B., MacNeilage, P., Folmer, E.: The effect of field-of-view restriction on sex bias in VR sickness and spatial navigation performance. In: Proceedings of the ACM CHI Conference on Human Factors in Computing Systems, p. 354 (2019)
3. Bernardin, D., Kadone, H., Bennequin, D., Sugar, T., Zaoui, M., Berthoz, A.: Gaze anticipation during human locomotion. Exp. Brain Res. **223**(1), 65–78 (2012)
4. Bolas, M., Jones, J.A., McDowall, I., Suma, E.: Dynamic field of view throttling as a means of improving user experience in head mounted virtual environments. US Patent 9,645,395, 9 May 2017
5. Bölling, L., Stein, N., Steinicke, F., Lappe, M.: Shrinking circles: adaptation to increased curvature gain in redirected walking. IEEE Trans. Vis. Comput. Graphics **25**(5), 2032–2039 (2019)

6. Bolte, B., Bruder, G., Steinicke, F., Hinrichs, K., Lappe, M.: Augmentation tech-niques for efficient exploration in head-mounted display environments. In: Proceed-ings of the 17th ACM Symposium on Virtual Reality Software and Technology, pp. 11–18 (2010)
7. Bolte, B., Lappe, M.: Subliminal reorientation and repositioning in immersive vir-tual environments using saccadic suppression. IEEE Trans. Vis. Comput. Graphics **21**(4), 545–552 (2015)
8. Bridgeman, B., Hendry, D., Stark, L.: Failure to detect displacement of the visual world during saccadic eye movements. Vision. Res. **15**(6), 719–722 (1975)
9. Bruder, G., Steinicke, F., Wieland, P., Lappe, M.: Tuning self-motion perception in virtual reality with visual illusions. IEEE Trans. Vis. Comput. Graph. **18**(7), 1068–1078 (2012). https://doi.org/10.1109/TVCG.2011.274
10. Bruder, G., Interrante, V., Phillips, L., Steinicke, F.: Redirecting walking and driv-ing for natural navigation in immersive virtual environments. IEEE Trans. Vis. Comput. Graph. **18**(4), 538–545 (2012)
11. Bruder, G., Steinicke, F., Hinrichs, K.H., Lappe, M.: Reorientation during body turns. In: Proceedings of EGVE/ICAT/EuroVR, pp. 145–152 (2009)
12. Budhiraja, P., Miller, M.R., Modi, A.K., Forsyth, D.: Rotation blurring: use of artificial blurring to reduce cybersickness in virtual reality first person shooters. arXiv preprint arXiv:1710.02599 (2017)
13. Chou, Y.H.: Effects of symmetric and asymmetric optic flow speed manipulations on locomotion in younger and older adults. Ph.D. thesis, Boston University (2005)
14. Congdon, B.J., Steed, A.: Sensitivity to rate of change in gains applied by redirected walking. In: Proceedings of the 25th ACM Symposium on Virtual Reality Software and Technology, p. 3 (2019)
15. Fernandes, A.S., Feiner, S.K.: Combating VR sickness through subtle dynamic field-of-view modification. In: Proceedings of IEEE Symposium on 3D User Inter-faces (3DUI), pp. 201–210 (2016)
16. Friston, K., Ashburner, J., Kiebel, S., Nichols, T., Penny, W.: Statistical Parametric Mapping. Academic Press, Cambridge (2007)
17. Hopper, J.E., Finney, H., Jones, J.A.: Field of view and forward motion discrim-ination in virtual reality. In: Proceedings of IEEE Conference on Virtual Reality and 3D User Interfaces (VR), pp. 1663–1666 (2019)
18. Jansen, S.E.M., Toet, A., Delleman, N.J.: Restricting the vertical and horizontal extent of the field-of-view: effects on manoeuvring performance. Ergon. Open J. **3**(1) (2010)
19. Jerald, J., Peck, T., Steinicke, F., Whitton, M.: Sensitivity to scene motion for phases of head yaws. In: Proceedings of the 5th ACM Symposium on Applied Perception in Graphics and Visualization, pp. 155–162 (2008)
20. Jones, J.A., Swan II, J.E., Bolas, M.: Peripheral stimulation and its effect on perceived spatial scale in virtual environments. IEEE Trans. Vis. Comput. Graph. **19**(4), 701–710 (2013)
21. Kennedy, R.S., Lane, N.E., Berbaum, K.S., Lilienthal, M.G.: Simulator sickness questionnaire: an enhanced method for quantifying simulator sickness. Int. J. Aviat. Psychol. **3**(3), 203–220 (1993)
22. Kopper, R., Stinson, C., Bowman, D.: Towards an understanding of the effects of amplified head rotations. In: Proceedings of the 3rd IEEE VR Workshop on Perceptual Illusions in Virtual Environments, vol. 2 (2011)
23. Kountouriotis, G.K., Shire, K.A., Mole, C.D., Gardner, P.H., Merat, N., Wilkie, R.M.: Optic flow asymmetries bias high-speed steering along roads. J. Vis. **13**(10), 23 (2013)

24. Langbehn, E., Raupp, T., Bruder, G., Steinicke, F., Bolte, B., Lappe, M.: Visual blur in immersive virtual environments: does depth of field or motion blur affect distance and speed estimation? In: Proceedings of the 22nd ACM Conference on Virtual Reality Software and Technology, pp. 241–250 (2016)

25. Langbehn, E., Steinicke F.: Redirected walking in virtual reality. In: Lee N. (eds.) Encyclopedia of Computer Graphics and Games. Springer, Cham (2018). https://doi.org/10.1007/978-3-319-08234-9_253-1

26. Langbehn, E., Steinicke, F., Lappe, M., Welch, G.F., Bruder, G.: In the blink of an eye - leveraging blink-induced suppression for imperceptible position and orientation redirection in virtual reality. ACM Trans. Comput. Graph. **37**(4), 1–11 (2018). https://dl.acm.org/doi/10.1145/3197517.3201335. Article No.: 66

27. Lappe, M., Bremmer, F., Van den Berg, A.: Perception of self-motion from visual flow. Trends Cogn. Sci. **3**(9), 329–336 (1999)

28. LaViola, J.J., Kruijff, E., McMahan, R.P., Bowman, D.A., Poupyrev, I.: 3D User Interfaces: Theory and Practice. Addison Wesley Longman Publishing Co., Inc., Boston (2017)

29. Lin, J.J., Duh, H.B.L., Parker, D.E., Abi-Rached, H., Furness, T.A.: Effects of field of view on presence, enjoyment, memory, and simulator sickness in a virtual environment. In: Proceedings of IEEE Virtual Reality Conference, pp. 164–171 (2002)

30. Linares, D., Lopez-Moliner, J.: quickpsy: an r package to fit psychometric functions for multiple groups. R. J. **8**, 122–131 (2016)

31. Marlinsky, V.: Vestibular and vestibulo-proprioceptive perception of motion in the horizontal plane in blindfolded man–II. Estimations of rotations about the earth-vertical axis. Neuroscience **90**(2), 395–401 (1999)

32. Nabiyouni, M., Saktheeswaran, A., Bowman, D.A., Karanth, A.: Comparing the performance of natural, semi-natural, and non-natural locomotion techniques in virtual reality. In: Proceedings of IEEE Symposium on 3D User Interfaces (3DUI), pp. 3–10 (2015)

33. Neth, C.T., Souman, J.L., Engel, D., Kloos, U., Bulthoff, H.H., Mohler, B.J.: Velocity-dependent dynamic curvature gain for redirected walking. IEEE Trans. Vis. Comput. Graph. **18**(7), 1041–1052 (2012)

34. Nguyen, A., Cervellati, F., Kunz, A.: Gain compensation in redirected walking. In: Proceedings of the 23rd ACM Symposium on Virtual Reality Software and Technology, p. 20 (2017)

35. Nilsson, N.C., et al.: 15 years of research on redirected walking in immersive virtual environments. IEEE Comput. Graph. Appl. **38**(2), 44–56 (2018)

36. Nilsson, N.C., Serafin, S., Nordahl, R.: Establishing the range of perceptually natural visual walking speeds for virtual walking-in-place locomotion. IEEE Trans. Vis. Comput. Graph. **20**(4), 569–578 (2014)

37. Nilsson, N.C., Suma, E., Nordahl, R., Bolas, M., Serafin, S.: Estimation of detection thresholds for audiovisual rotation gains. In: Proceedings of IEEE Virtual Reality (VR), pp. 241–242 (2016)

38. Norouzi, N., Bruder, G., Welch, G.: Assessing vignetting as a means to reduce VR sickness during amplified head rotations. In: Proceedings of the 15th ACM Symposium on Applied Perception, p. 19 (2018)

39. Paludan, A., et al.: Disguising rotational gain for redirected walking in virtual reality: effect of visual density. In: Proceedings of IEEE Virtual Reality (VR), pp. 259–260 (2016)

40. Panichi, R., et al.: Self-motion perception and vestibulo-ocular reflex during whole body yaw rotation in standing subjects: the role of head position and neck proprioception. Hum. Mov. Sci. **30**(2), 314–332 (2011)
41. Peck, T.C., Fuchs, H., Whitton, M.C.: Evaluation of reorientation techniques and distractors for walking in large virtual environments. IEEE Trans. Vis. Comput. Graph. **15**(3), 383–394 (2009)
42. Pettorossi, V.E., Schieppati, M.: Neck proprioception shapes body orientation and perception of motion. Front. Hum. Neurosci. **8**, 895 (2014)
43. Ragan, E.D., Scerbo, S., Bacim, F., Bowman, D.A.: Amplified head rotation in virtual reality and the effects on 3D search, training transfer, and spatial orientation. IEEE Trans. Vis. Comput. Graph. **23**(8), 1880–1895 (2016)
44. Razzaque, S., Kohn, Z., Whitton, M.C.: Redirected walking. Technical report, Department of Computer Science, University of North Carolina, Chapel Hill, North Carolina, USA (2001)
45. Rebenitsch, L., Owen, C.: Individual variation in susceptibility to cybersickness. In: Proceedings of the 27th annual ACM Symposium on User Interface Software and Technology, pp. 309–317 (2014)
46. Riecke, B.E., Schulte-Pelkum, J., Avraamides, M.N., von der Heyde, M., Bülthoff, H.H.: Scene consistency and spatial presence increase the sensation of self-motion in virtual reality. In: Proceedings of the 2nd Symposium on Applied Perception in Graphics and Visualization, pp. 111–118 (2005)
47. Riecke, B.E., Schulte-Pelkum, J., Avraamides, M.N., Heyde, M.V.D., Bülthoff, H.H.: Cognitive factors can influence self-motion perception (vection) in virtual reality. ACM Trans. Appl. Percept. (TAP) **3**(3), 194–216 (2006)
48. Ruddle, R.A., Volkova, E., Bülthoff, H.H.: Learning to Walk in Virtual Reality. ACM Trans. Appl. Percept. **10**(2), 11:1–11:17 (2013)
49. Sargunam, S.P., Moghadam, K.R., Suhail, M., Ragan, E.D.: Guided head rotation and amplified head rotation: evaluating semi-natural travel and viewing techniques in virtual reality. In: 2017 IEEE Virtual Reality (VR), pp. 19–28. IEEE (2017)
50. Sargunam, S.P., Ragan, E.D.: Evaluating joystick control for view rotation in virtual reality with continuous turning, discrete turning, and field-of-view reduction. In: Proceedings of the 3rd International Workshop on Interactive and Spatial Computing, pp. 74–79. ACM (2018)
51. Sarre, G., Berard, J., Fung, J., Lamontagne, A.: Steering behaviour can be modulated by different optic flows during walking. Neurosci. Lett. **436**(2), 96–101 (2008)
52. Schmitz, P., Hildebrandt, J., Valdez, A.C., Kobbelt, L., Ziefle, M.: You spin my head right round: threshold of limited immersion for rotation gains in redirected walking. IEEE Trans. Vis. Comput. Graph. **24**(4), 1623–1632 (2018)
53. Serafin, S., Nilsson, N.C., Sikstrom, E., De Goetzen, A., Nordahl, R.: Estimation of detection thresholds for acoustic based redirected walking techniques. In: Proceedings of IEEE Virtual Reality (VR), pp. 161–162 (2013)
54. Steinicke, F., Bruder, G., Jerald, J., Frenz, H., Lappe, M.: Estimation of detection thresholds for redirected walking techniques. IEEE Trans. Vis. Comput. Graph. **16**(1), 17–27 (2010)
55. Strasburger, H., Pöppel, E.: Visual field. In: Encyclopedia of Neuroscience, pp. 2127–2129 (2002)
56. Sun, Q., et al.: Towards virtual reality infinite walking: dynamic saccadic redirection. ACM Trans. Graph. (TOG) **37**(4), 1–13 (2018)

57. Toet, A., van der Hoeven, M., Kahrimanović, M., Delleman, N.J.: Effects of field of view on human locomotion. In: Head-and Helmet-Mounted Displays XIII: Design and Applications, vol. 6955, p. 69550H. International Society for Optics and Photonics (2008)
58. Toet, A., Jansen, S.E., Delleman, N.J.: Effects of field-of-view restrictions on speed and accuracy of manoeuvring. Percept. Motor Skills **105**(3_suppl), 1245–1256 (2007)
59. Usoh, M., et al.: Walking > walking-in-place > flying, in virtual environments. In: Proceedings of the 26th Annual Conference on Computer Graphics and Interactive Techniques, pp. 359–364 (1999)
60. Warren Jr., W.H., Kay, B.A., Zosh, W.D., Duchon, A.P., Sahuc, S.: Optic flow is used to control human walking. Nat. Neurosci. **4**(2), 213 (2001)
61. Williams, N.L., Peck, T.C.: Estimation of rotation gain thresholds considering FOV, gender, and distractors. IEEE Trans. Vis. Comput. Graph. **25**(11), 3158–3168 (2019)
62. Warren, R., Wertheim, A.H.: Field-of-view information for self-motion percepion. In Perception and Control of Self-motion, pp. 125–150. Psychology Press (2014)
63. Zhang, R., Kuhl, S.A.: Human sensitivity to dynamic rotation gains in head-mounted displays. In: Proceedings of the ACM Symposium on Applied Perception, pp. 71–74 (2013)

User Experience in Collaborative Extended Reality: Overview Study

Huyen Nguyen[1,2(✉)] and Tomasz Bednarz[2,3]

[1] Université Paris-Saclay, CNRS, LIMSI, VENISE team, 91400 Orsay, France
`huyen.nguyen@limsi.fr`
[2] EPICentre, University of New South Wales, Sydney, NSW 2021, Australia
`t.bednarz@unsw.edu.au`
[3] CSIRO Data61, Australian Technology Park, Eveleigh, NSW 2015, Australia

Abstract. Recent trends in Extended Reality technologies, including Virtual Reality and Mixed Reality, indicate that the future infrastructure will be distributed and collaborative, where end-users as well as experts meet, communicate, learn, interact with each other, and coordinate their activities using a globally shared network and meditated environments. The integration of new display devices has largely changed how users interact with the system and how those activities, in turn, change their perception and experience. Although a considerable amount of research has already been done in the fields of computer-supported collaborative work, human-computer interaction, extended reality, cognitive psychology, perception, and social sciences, there is still no in-depth review to determine the current state of research on multiple-user-experience-centred design at the intersection of these domains. This paper aims to present an overview of research work on coexperience and analyses important aspects of human factors to be considered to enhance collaboration and user interaction in collaborative extended reality platforms, including: (i) presence-related factors, (ii) group dynamics and collaboration patterns, (iii) avatars and embodied agents, (iv) nonverbal communication, (v) group size, and (vi) awareness of physical and virtual world. Finally, this paper identifies research gaps and suggests key directions for future research considerations in this multidisciplinary research domain.

Keywords: User experience · Coexperience · Virtual Reality · Augmented Reality · Mixed Reality · eXtended Reality · Collaboration · Interaction design

1 Introduction

Advances in eXtended Reality (XR) technologies, which is a term referring to Virtual Reality (VR) and Mixed Reality (MR) (Augmented Reality (AR) and Augmented Virtuality) within the Milgram's reality-virtuality continuum [70],

© Springer Nature Switzerland AG 2020
P. Bourdot et al. (Eds.): EuroVR 2020, LNCS 12499, pp. 41–70, 2020.
https://doi.org/10.1007/978-3-030-62655-6_3

have dramatically changed the human-machine interactions meditated by computers and wearable devices. These technologies give Computer-Supported Collaborative Work (CSCW) the possibility to integrate various elements into a shared world, including heterogeneous user interfaces, data structures, information models, and graphical representations of users themselves. For instance, several overviews on collaboration in MR can be found in [12,61]. The integration of multiple devices and interaction modalities has largely changed how users interact with data and with other users. Using XR systems, the human experience, behaviour, and cognitive performance are an immensely important topic across other domains of Human-Computer Interaction (HCI) design, cognitive psychology, perception and others, particularly to make the most effective use of such systems. Therefore, appropriate standard multi-sensory stimuli interaction design and exchange mechanisms are needed to facilitate the full potential of the interaction between humans, data and artefacts, XR platforms, and the physical world. Furthermore, with recent breakthroughs in AR and great effort in bringing this technology to larger public, there is a need to merge the physical world with the virtual world while preserving the presence, copresence and the sense of collaboration between users using different modalities. In our opinion, it will not be long before the XR will become a platform of choice not only for complex task solving such as scientific data analysis, modelling, simulation, but also for public use such as education, social networking, video games, online custom services, and entertainment. In education, for example, Johnson-Glenberg et al. have argued the importance of collaborative MR environment to learning on the motivation, social cohesion, cognitive development, and cognitive elaboration perspectives [57].

Scientists and developers in HCI, design, and human behaviour research have been working on different factors of User Experience (UX) and how to quantify it, e.g., [112]. As defined in [49], user experience is indeed a complex and dynamic concept which involves a wide range of perspectives from user's internal states (e.g., motivation, emotions, expectations), to system settings (e.g., complexity, usability, functionality, purpose) and interaction context (e.g., environment, organisational/social setting, meaningfulness of activities). On the other hand, Battarbee and Koskinen proposed a taxonomy of existing approaches and considered UX under the three main perspectives: *measuring*, *empathic*, and *pragmatist* approach [11]. They also introduced the *coexperience* concept which explores "how the meanings of individual experiences emerge and change as they become part of social interaction". Sharing the same interest in coexperience, we approach the UX concept from another angle in the collaborative XR context. We focus on the general characteristics and features of multiple-user-experience-centred approach in collaborative XR systems in order to interpret and apply them into the design process. More specifically, we are interested in different factors relating to coexperience and co-interaction, including, but not limited to, presence, copresence, social presence, social effects, group collaboration patterns, embodiment, and so forth. Many existing works on these factors have been done within a short period of trials and experiments thanks to the capacity and flexibility to replicate and control environments that easily fit experimental designs. Immersive projection technology and head-mounted displays (HMDs) are often the most used systems in UX studies and their performance is generally evaluated against existing desktop systems [90]. Therefore, with the recent advances in XR technology, especially in AR, we believe that different aspects of UX in collaborative XR platforms needs to be reviewed and reassessed. In this paper, we provide an overview of research conducted on UX in collaborative XR systems, especially in shared virtual or augmented environments. Our objective is to provide an introduction to researchers to this multidisciplinary domain and present opportunities for future research directions.

2   Context and Scope

In order to situate our study on UX in collaborative XR systems in the current related work, we have conducted a preliminary analysis of the research publications in the multidisciplinary domain of XR, CSCW and UX. Specifically, we used the Citation Network dataset[1] version 12 published on April 9, 2020 for the analysis. This dataset is constructed from DBLP[2], ACM[3], MAG[4], amongst other sources to provide a comprehensive list of research papers in major computer science journals and proceedings. This latest version contains almost five million publications and more than 45 million citation relationships. The sheer amount of data collected in this full dataset begs for some preprocessing steps before we could visualise it in the form of graph. After the data retrieval step, a parser has been used to transform its JSON original format into CSV format with only few fields of interest from each paper, including identification number, title, list of authors, year, and list of field of study (FOS). This dataset was then "standardised" by reformatting each word, removing punctuations and escape sequences, and converting all the characters into lower case. We extracted a smaller subset of this data by using several FOS that reflect the joint domains of interest of XR, CSCW and UX for this study. For instance, 'collaborative virtual environment', 'augmented reality', 'virtual reality', 'augmented virtuality', 'immersive technology', 'user experience design', 'user experience evaluation' and other relevant FOS were selected from the full list of available FOS of the dataset. Any paper that contains at least one of these FOS is picked from the original dataset. As a result, the subset has been reduced to 50,662 papers which are associated with 19,792 FOS. Since each paper is linked to a set of FOS, we proposed to analyse the dataset using seven FOS categories that represent main aspects to be considered in this study. Each category contains many FOS so only few examples are listed as follows:

– Extended reality: 'virtual reality', 'augmented reality', 'mixed reality', '3d interaction', 'immersion (virtual reality)', 'virtual learning environment'

---

[1] https://www.aminer.org/citation.
[2] https://dblp.uni-trier.de/.
[3] https://dl.acm.org/.
[4] https://aka.ms/msracad.

- User experience: 'user experience design', 'user modeling', 'user-centered design', 'quality of experience', 'human factors and ergonomics'
- Communication: 'gesture', 'gesture recognition', 'eye tracking', 'gaze', 'natural interaction', 'facial expression', 'communication skills'
- Collaboration: 'collaborative virtual environment', 'computer-supported collaborative work', 'collaborative learning', 'virtual classroom'
- Emotion: 'uncanny valley', 'anticipation', 'enthusiasm', 'surprise', 'happiness', 'emotional expression', 'confusion', 'pleasure', 'curiosity'
- Psychology: 'social psychology', 'cognitive psychology', 'sociology', 'cognitive science', 'mental health', 'exposure therapy', 'cognitive walkthrough'
- Others: 'situation awareness', 'spatial contextual awareness', 'perception', 'personality', 'sense of presence', 'sensation', 'personal space'

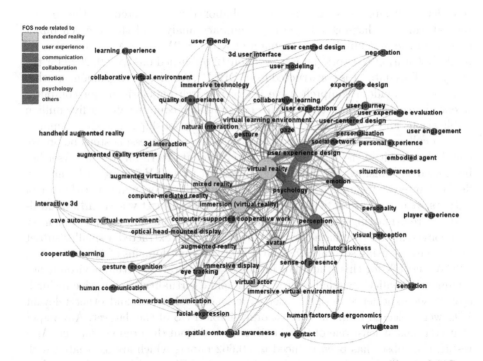

Fig. 1. An undirected graph built from a subset of the citation network dataset which focuses on the multidisciplinary domain of XR, CSCW, and UX. Except the two 'psychology' and 'emotion' nodes, each node represents a FOS of interest. The FOS are categorised in seven groups and represented in distinct colours. The size of each node represents the number of occurrences of its FOS. Each edge connects two FOS nodes when a publication is associated with these two FOS. The number of co-occurrences of two linked FOS is used to weight the width and adapt colour (from orange to green and blue) of each edge. (Color figure online)

Using Gephi[5] software and Force Atlas graph layout algorithm [10], an undirected graph was built representing the number of papers that connect these FOS categories (see Fig. 1). To simplify the graph due to the limited visualisation space, the FOS of the two Psychology and Emotion categories have been generalised to create two 'psychology' and 'emotion' nodes, respectively. Based on this full graph and its subgraphs extracted using Gephi, we have come to some general observations regarding the relationship between XR, CSCW, and UX as follows:

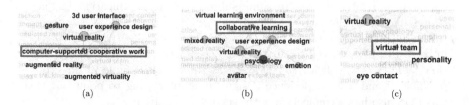

(a)   (b)   (c)

Fig. 2. The connection of the three FOS in Collaboration category: (a) 'computer-supported cooperative work', (b) 'collaborative learning', and (c) 'virtual team' to other FOS. All the FOS present in each figure have a direct connection with the FOS of interest (in red box). The layout of the graph has been slightly adjusted for the readability purpose, which is similarly applied in Fig. 3.

– There are strong connections in research between 'virtual reality', 'user experience design', and 'psychology' as demonstrated in Fig. 1. However, collaboration aspect is only weakly presented in the existing literature in general.
– The 'computer-supported collaborative work' and 'collaborative virtual environment' are only linked to 'user experience design', 'quality of experience', 'gesture' and the FOS of XR field in general (Fig. 2a). However, the 'collaborative learning' shows a more divers correlation with 'avatar', 'emotion', 'psychology', 'user experience design', and 'mixed reality', 'virtual reality' and 'virtual learning environment' (Fig. 2b). In addition, the 'virtual team' is connected solely to 'virtual reality', 'eye contact', and 'personality' (Fig. 2c). These results demonstrate a growing interest in the application of collaborative XR environment in education and training and its effectiveness on learners in terms of psychology and behavioural health care. These observations also lead us to believe that there is a need to study more closely the effect of collaborative XR environment on user experience and perception and vice versa, how to improve users' experience when they work with others in a more general immersive context.
– Avatars have been largely studied relating to many domains of XR, UX, psychology, human emotion, communication, amongst others (Fig. 3a). This confirms the important role of the use of avatar and embodied agents in the context of our study.

---

[5] https://gephi.org/.

- The 'nonverbal communication' and 'natural interaction' are closely linked with XR and UX fields, including 'virtual reality', 'augmented reality', 'user experience design', 'user expectations', and others (Fig. 3b). They are also characterised by 'gesture', 'facial expression', 'gaze', and 'eye tracking'. Surprisingly, from the graph, there is little connection found between the FOS of the Communication category with those of the Collaboration group.
- Similarly, we cannot find the strong connection between the 'sense of presence' and the Collaboration category (Fig. 3c). Besides being linked to XR domain, the presence aspect is often studied in relation to psychology and human emotion, and interestingly, to some subtopics of communication in 'facial expression' and 'negotiation' as well.
- In the same situation, the FOS of the Collaboration category are not present in the list of FOS related to 'spatial contextual awareness' (Fig. 3d). In addition to FOS of XR field, the FOS on awareness also connects directly to psychology and 'user experience design'. It is interesting to point out that this FOS also has a connection with 'gesture recognition'.

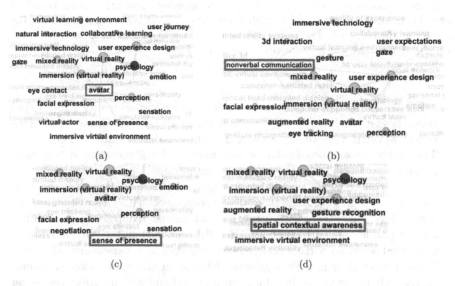

Fig. 3. The connection of (a) 'avatar', (b) 'nonverbal communication', (c) 'sense of presence', and (d) 'spatial contextual awareness' to other FOS.

There are several limits to the above observations that we take into account. Firstly, the graph was built from the Citation Network dataset which contains FOS generated using an automated keyword extraction algorithm with hierarchical topic modelling and natural language processing [93]. It is likely that errors can be accumulated starting from the extraction algorithm to the graph generation, which might limit the accuracy of the result. Secondly, these observations are not intended to be exhaustive. Several topics of the UX such as 'user friendly', 'user expectations', 'user journey', 'experience design' have not been analysed. We consider these observations only as the first guidelines to help us identify important aspects of the related work in this multidisciplinary domain.

In this study, we will focus on the five factors that stand out from the preliminary analysis, including presence-related factors, group dynamics and collaboration patterns with virtual teams, avatars and embodied agents, nonverbal communication, and awareness of physical and virtual world in spatial contextual awareness. We add the group size as another factor to be considered as well. In Sect. 3 we begin by presenting these factors relating to UX in collaborative XR environments, focusing on shared virtual worlds.

3   User Experience in Collaborative Extended Reality Platforms

It has been confirmed that XR technologies applied to collaborative user interfaces help to enhance communication and support seamless functional and cognitive workflows between users [17]. However, the influence of technology on UX and how they behave within XR systems still leave a lot to be explored because most of existing studies have been conducted only in collaborative VR systems. Based on the preliminary study in Sect. 2, we present a deep analysis of the six following aspects considered for coexperience-centred collaborative immersive design. These aspects are seemingly independent and isolated from one another. In contrast, they are the key facets that construct the coexperience concept in collaborative XR systems. Research opportunities arising from this review will be summarised in Sect. 4.

3.1   Presence, Copresence and Social Presence

Presence, also known as physical presence or telepresence, has been one of the most studied research topics in VR and psychology. It is an ultimate goal of all the VR systems to initiate and maintain an individual's sense of "being there" or "being in a virtual place" to make them believe or feel that they exist within the virtual world [50,51,96]. It involves the subconscious and conscious processes of being in and interacting with the virtual world: from automatic reactions to spatial and visual cues and triggers at the low intuitive level of perception, to more complex mental models of virtual spaces to create the illusion of place [19]. IJsselsteijn et al. in [56] emphasised on the importance of high quality mediated environments in terms of fidelity of sensory information, match between sensors and display, contents, and user characteristics to create the sense of "being there". Slater & Wilbur argued that what to be expected when users feel a sense of presence within a virtual world is that their behaviours are consistent with those that would have occurred in the real world in similar situations [96]. Schuemie et al. have produced an overview on how to measure presence using subjective questionnaires and objective measures on behavioural and physiological responses [92]. In this study, we put more focus on social presence and copresence, and how presence influences these two aspects when users interact with each other.

Social presence, as defined by Heeter, is the degree to which users believe that they are with other human beings and interact with them [50]. This definition has been expanded by Biocca & Harms in which social presence is "the moment-to-moment awareness of co-presence of a mediated body and the sense of accessibility of the other being's psychological, emotional, and intentional states" [18]. It is argued that the social presence reflects the actual presence of others, the implied presence of them, or the imagined presence conveyed through sensory information transmission in mediated environments [1]. Therefore, the capacity of XR systems or technology is important in social presence to provide high fidelity of communication cues including proximity and orientation of others, physical appearance, facial expressions, gaze and mutual gaze, postures and gestures, verbal signals. Unfortunately, new technologies in XR have not been able to fully satisfy these requirements yet.

Another similar term which is often mentioned in social psychological research for virtual environments is copresence. Copresence, as summarised by Schroeder in [89], is the sense of "being there together" and acting with other users at the same time. Copresence puts more focus on the individual's feelings of being part of a group and being capable of perceiving others [95]. In other words, a mutual awareness between individuals on the existence of each other is emphasised in copresence measures [24]. Schroeder considered copresence within collaborative virtual environments based on what activities users do together [90]. Compared to social presence, which relies on the quality of the mediated environment and users' perception of it, copresence reflects more psychological interactions between them [89]. Also, studies on copresence need to consider users' experience when they do things together, and not only when they are just immersed together in the virtual world. Schroeder in [89] separated three types of study on users' experience with others: short-term interaction when users collaborate to perform tasks, which requires attention and mutual awareness and is measured mainly on collaborative task performance; long-term interaction for socialising and entertainment via web-based virtual environments, which measures persistence of characters, of groups and of environment, social rules and convention, and effect of virtual world on real life; and the influence of the long-term use of immersive systems on performing short-term tasks.

Considering that many factors can influence UX in collaborative XR environments, the dynamic relationship amongst presence, social presence, and copresence needs to be studied together to understand how presence affects UX in general. Copresence and social presence are often considered as sub mental models of presence. Empirically, it is found that presence and copresence are positively correlated [89, 95, 109], and the same positive correlation occurs between presence and social presence [106]. However, other studies (e.g., [5, 26]) show that the relationship between presence and copresence is not definitively correlated or well defined. Schroeder in [91] proposed the concept of a connected presence cube. It maps presence, copresence and the extent of individual connected presence to three dimensions of a cube representing the end-state of users' experience in shared virtual environments. He argued that the level of presence and copresence will be affected by the medium used to create the virtual world for users to feel a sense of connectedness such as desktop-, projection-, or HMD-based systems. Bulu in [24] suggested that all the three aspects will directly affect the satisfaction of users in immersive environments and they are all closely related in shared virtual environments. What has not been studied yet is how the different device settings of distant users can affect the UX and in particular the individual sense of presence, copresence, and social presence. Especially, XR technology can change the existing social psychology studies in the domain of user interaction and experience in real-and-virtual combined environments.

3.2 Group Dynamics and Collaboration Patterns

In this section, we look into the dynamics of how users work in groups and the collaboration patterns that users explicitly or implicitly employ. In social sciences, group dynamics studies human behaviours within a social group (intragroup) or between social groups (intergroup) [29,105]. However, in collaborative XR systems, especially for remote collaboration, mediated environments change the way research findings in group dynamics are applied. Users working together over such environment are often considered as members of a virtual team. Virtual teams are "teams whose members use technology to varying degrees in working across locational, temporal, and relational boundaries to accomplish an interdependent task" [69]. The task performance of a virtual team is partly decided by how well workload is distributed, managed, and coordinated amongst team's members at group's level and partly by "the extent to which team members use virtual tools to coordinate and execute team processes" [58] at individual's level. It is important, therefore, to study how the collaboration occurs at individuals' level and group dynamics in fully or partly immersive systems.

Considering the processes of how each individual joins in groups or subgroups and how groups are formed over time, four models of change and continuity in group structure have been described [4].

- The first model that depicts stages in which different group structural patterns are formed is called *life cycle*. The Tuckman's four-stage model [111] is its known representative which summarises different stages of group development: *forming* for groups to identify the interpersonal and task behaviours and to establish dependency relationships with leaders, other group members, or predefined standards; *storming* for individuals to resolve interpersonal issues regarding to group influence and task requirements; *norming* to develop new standards for groups and to adopt new roles; and *performing* for groups to finalise interpersonal structure for task activities.
- The second model is *robust equilibrium*, which defines how a group's structure evolves through a short period of fluctuation followed by a stable state [28].
- Another developmental model is *punctuated equilibrium*, which indicates that groups develop through processes of sudden formation, maintenance, and

revision for performance by taking into account timing and mechanisms of change relating to the groups' context [46].

- The last model *adaptive response* describes groups' active changes to adapt to current task [99], technology [55] and environment [83] situations.

In the context of collaborative immersive systems, the Tuckman's four-stage model of groups [111] is often employed in designing communication and navigation mechanisms for users travelling in large-scale virtual world to be aware of other members' activities while performing collaborative tasks [32]. However, in our opinion, all the developmental models described above can be applied and reevaluated more extensively in novel mediated environments, which constitute challenges in creating effective workspace for virtual teams.

While group dynamics study how groups evolve over time under different situational factors, collaboration pattern research, on the other hand, looks into relationships between collaborators within groups and how they can adapt their behaviours to a collaborative task. Several studies in various domains have theorised different patterns and taxonomies of patterns of collaboration. For instance, in a collaboration systems for architectural designers, Caneparo [27] has explored the group coordination mechanism through four cases: *hierarchy order* when a leader of the group establishes the task's outlines and evaluates members' suggestions and performance, *individual initiative* when each member has their own freedom and acts independently, *participation* when members follow a working consensus build from discussion and negotiation, and *collaboration* when the group works on an agreed design solution after comparision and consensus. In the context of collaborative e-learning, Wasson and Mørch [117] have identified collaboration patterns occurring amongst students, teachers, and learning facilitators. The patterns consist of: *adaptation* when students working in groups in order to solve a common problem learn and adapt to others' behaviours, *coordinated desynchronisation* when group members coordinate activities after they have idenfified their common goal, *constructive commenting* when members give comments, and *informal language* when the relationship between group members become more intimate and is measured by the informal language they use.

In addition, another paradigm for collaboration patterns in product designing process was proposed in [65]. It considers four possible scenarios that can occur in group collaboration patterns: *peer-to-peer* when each member of the group contributes equally, *leader-member* when the leader of the group contributes more than other members, *complementary* when subgroups are formed to solve a portion of the task and their contributions are joined at the final stage, and *competitive* when subgroups are formed to compete with other subgroups by approaching the task from different angles.

Amongst all the four patterns defined above, *leader-member* collaboration pattern is one of the most studied topics. From social sciences' perspective, leadership is determined by traits and personality qualities inherent within certain individuals of a group [15]. Leadership skills, therefore, are often gradually developed outside and also within a group setting with or without the involvement of other group members. Competent leaders can help to build solid groups to work productively. However, in many situations, the effectiveness of a group is decided not by the skills of the leader alone but also by the multilaterally shared responsibility in leader-member relationship. Depending on types of collaboration tasks, leader role can be implicitly or explicitly designated. When there is no predefined collaboration structure amongst members of a group, leadership can be regarded and evaluated through the contributions of each member to a shared collaborative task ('division of labor') and/or the act of taking charge by doing most of the talking ('talkativeness'), suggesting ideas, and giving instructions [5].

In real-life face-to-face circumstances, the location of an individual where they sit or stand can create direct assumptions from others about their leadership role [3,52,116]. However, in collaborative XR environments with limited access to non-verbal communication cues, different approaches have been employed by group members to determine or establish the leader-member relationship. Being virtually inhabited in virtual worlds, users are often represented and interact with others through 'avatars' (see Sect. 3.3). Therefore, these avatars can have significant effect on others' perception about social behaviours and can determine collaboration mechanism between members. Yee and Bailenson in [119] studied the effect of height of users' avatars on their negotiation behaviour. This behaviour is a dominant personality trait of people with leadership skills because it is often associated with confidence, high self-esteem and ultimately leadership capability [103]. By isolating other factors which can affect the leadership behaviour in real world, such as age, gender, physical appearance, it shows that the impersonating tall avatar as self-representation of users can significantly increase their confidence in negotiation tasks. Additionally, other study [47] reports that the relative locations of the avatar representation of remote users within collaborative immersive environments should be appropriately chosen to make them appear in virtually equal size to improve their task performance, especially when they follow peer-to-peer collaboration pattern.

In shared virtual environments, users having advantages in computational performance, especially in level of immersion, are likely to emerge as leaders. Several studies [5,94,95,98] report that without even being aware of others' working systems, users who were fully immersed were likely to be perceived as leaders and were rated high on talkativeness scores. In a more recent study, Pan et al. [77] have studied how two users collaborate in four different settings: AR to AR, AR to VR, AR to VR with virtual body, and AR to desktop. The results show that interactions in 3D could facilitate the emergence of leadership pattern, and that the more asymmetry in immersion level between collaborators, the stronger effect of leadership with users using AR interface of high level of immersion and situational awareness. However, if all the users share the same system capacity and are equally immersed, the leader role is often decided by the one who actively takes in the role of task navigator and manager [5].

As it is demonstrated with XR technology and its advantages in psychological therapies, the long-term effect of being confident in immersive environments compared to the sense of confidence and leadership skills in real life still needs to be extensively evaluated. In more general context, leadership skills are mostly determined by personality traits of each individual and can be also attained by training. Therefore, the influence of personality on leadership in immersive systems needs to be studied to verify the correlations between leadership pattern and immersion levels using XR technology. For instance, in the experiment conducted by Slater [94], a questionnaire on Interaction Anxiousness Scale [64] was employed to measure participants' social anxiety, which inversely correlates to the degree of leadership. The results of the experiment have confirmed this special correlation between social anxiety, immersion, and leadership scores.

3.3 Avatars and Embodied Agents

Digital representations of users are an important factor to be considered while designing any collaborative XR platform. They help users to develop a sense of social connection with others, to be aware of others' presence and activities, and to have visual elements to focus on when they communicate with. Those representations can be categorised into: *avatars, embodied agents,* and *hybrid forms* [37]. The main difference between them is the control behind the representation. Avatar is a self-representation of a user who participates in the collaboration session in real time [6,8,37,84]. Embodied agents, on the other hand, are controlled by computer algorithms to appear anthropomorphically and behave similarly like a human being. They are, therefore, defined as 'acting entities', whose behaviours are rendered based on simulation and Artificial Intelligence (AI) [35,84]. An embodied agent has to be incorporated with four main capabilities in an adaptive functionality to be able to interact with humans in real-time: *perception, interpretation, reasoning,* and *autonomous responses* towards predefined goals [9]. Finally, hybrid combination of avatar and intelligent agent [86] is often employed in collaborative XR environments when the real presence and participation of users are not always guaranteed [44,45] or when the use of AI algorithms helps to free user from fine-grained manipulations of avatars. In this section, we explore the usefulness of these virtual representations from two perspectives: how the use of avatars affect perception of users themselves (i.e., self-perception), and how users perceive others, either real-time collaborators or intelligent agents, through their visual representations.

Self-perception via Avatars. Generally, avatars represent people on social media and entertainment platforms such as online chat, video games, networking sites and online virtual worlds (e.g., Second Life[6]). Avatars, in a certain way, can be considered as a projection of users or an external self representation. In the immersive context, users can choose (passively or actively) how to represent themselves within limited options proposed by systems. Their representation can, in turn, influence their performance in executing tasks, communicating, as well as reflecting and perceiving of self independent of how other people perceive them. There are three types of avatar that can be employed: *authentic, modified* or *augmented,* and *non-anthropomorphic* or *novel* representation forms.

---

[6] https://secondlife.com/.

The objective of providing *authentic* avatars is to guarantee high visual fidelity and behavioural authenticity of digital representations [115]. Researchers have tried to incorporate human physical capabilities in expressing nonverbal cues during conversations into digital models, giving avatars more faithful replication and realistic expressions and behaviours. There still are, however, several issues in designing and using avatars, including identity, awareness of current states, availability and degree of presence, gesture and facial expressions [14]. In a collaborative AR system, the self-presentation as an avatar besides the real body can potentially affect body ownership and self-localisation [85].

Modified or *augmented* representations of users are often used in evaluating the self-perception of people through the lens of their avatars. Yee & Bailenson have studied the Proteus effect, a hypothesis on the conformity of people's behaviours to their self-representations [119]. They have discovered that high level of attractiveness of avatar models can make people shorten their interpersonal distance [48]. Users can feel more intimate and open with others, and even the height of avatar can increase their confidence in a negotiation task. These results confirm the self-perception theory proposed by Bem on the dissimilarity in perception between the physical self and the digital modified self-representation [13]. Similarly, positive communication experience for users could be obtained by enhancing the smiling expressions of users through their avatars [76]. Furthermore, the negative effect of over-sexualised representations of women on sexual objectification and rape myth acceptance in virtual platforms has been also studied [38].

Non-anthropomorphic avatar approach represents users in a non-biological human form. This capability in mapping non-linearly the user's body with avatar's can facilitate novel form of interactions and manipulations that are not readily supported in conventional platforms. A concept of homuncular flexibility explores the idea of modifying representations of people to see how they can learn to control new form of avatars with extra limbs [62]. This concept has been further developed in extending avatar with a flexible tail attached to its coccyx [101], and alternating the visuomotor and visuotactile feedback of users' fingers via a six-finger illusion [53]. Verhulst et al. have studied how being embodied in an obese virtual body can help to change people's shopping behaviour [113]. The substitute for physical bodies with virtual ones is often measured by users' senses of ownership (i.e. perception of virtual parts of avatar as their own) and agency (i.e. perception of controlling these new forms). However, the extension of one's virtual body in collaborative context has not been extensively studied yet and it will be an important future research direction.

Perception of Others and Social Influence. Many researchers have studied the aspect of how users perceive others via avatars or visual representations and how that perception will influence social presence. Recent research has explored the potential of AI agents and social actors on the improvement of the social presence and perception of individuals within immersive environments [20]. For instance, the study conducted by Nowak & Biocca finds that people respond socially to human and embodied agents alike in virtual world [75]. High level of copresence and social presence is also recorded when people interact with avatars of low anthropomorphic representations compared to realistic anthropomorphic images of the others, indicating a complex relationship between avatar representations and expectations from users when seeing them.

There are two main theoretical models that explain social influence of avatars and embodied agents on the social behaviour of human interlocutors. The first theoretical model by Nass and Moon in [72] concluded that if there are enough social cues in conversations, people will apply the same rules in real-life social interactions to interactions with agents even though they are aware that the experience is not real. Recently, this model has been revised, evaluated and confirmed [43,84]. Blascovich et al. in [21], on the other hand, predicted that social influence within virtual environments will be decided by two additive factors (behavioural realism and social presence) and two moderating factors (self-relevance and target response system). They also argued that the social influence of a real person behind an avatar will always be higher than an embodied agent, and that the effect of an agent on social influence will depend on its behaviour realism. The hypothesis that avatars are more influential than agents on the social influence scale was confirmed in the research done by Fox et al. [37].

When integrating embodied agents into a collaborative scenario, many requirements are established to satisfy natural interaction with real-time users, which include life-like behaviours in conversations, responsiveness in a dynamic and unscripted environment, plausibility to create a sufficient illusion from users, and interpretable behaviour to allow users to interpret their responses [107]. For conversational agents, several frameworks for conversational interaction between an agent and a human user have been developed. For instance, FMTB (Functions, Modalities, Timing, Behaviours) conversational framework [30] supports conversational behaviours and actions via several modalities of communication such as hand gestures, facial expressions, eye gaze, etc. SmartBody [107] is another framework facilitating creation of animated conversational agents in real-time from hierarchically connected animation controllers. In general, besides the benefits of having automated agents as always-present interactive characters in virtual environments such as video games or online custom services, embodied agents can help to increase the experience of co-presence in shared environments, especially on social networking platforms [16]. Furthermore, it is argued that embodied agents may help people emote freely and reveal more sensitive information compared to conversational situations with real human users. For instance, perceived virtual human can help patients in clinical interviews disclose more sensitive information, hence overcoming the barrier between real and virtual actors behind mediated avatars [68].

Avatars play an important role in reinforcing the perception of others and social influence in collaborative environments. The effect of time and stage of the collaborative task on how users interact with others through avatars has been studied [97]. It is argued that when the collaboration time is short and users work together for the first time, they normally do not inquire about their partners' avatars. The appearance of avatars get more attention when they collaborate for a longer period and the physical appearance of people behind the avatars becomes a topic of interest. Furthermore, the way people treat others' avatar varies from social discomfort and embarrassment when the avatars are in their interpersonal zone or overlapped in a desktop-based shared virtual environment [73,94] to unawareness and disinterest when they go through others' avatar while focusing on performing their task in a immersion projection technology system [97].

In conclusion, the effectiveness of avatar and embodied agents largely depends on their behaviour and appearance realism, and how they are used in different situations. Realism factor is often highly demanded in developing collaborative XR frameworks. However, there is also downside of the realism. Bailenson et al. in [8] found that people emote their feelings more freely when their avatar does not capture and express those emotions. In addition, the Uncanny Valley [71] predicts that negative experience can be evoked in human when robot appears and behaves too close to human-likeness. The same principle can be applied in the case of virtual characters or embodied agents. The study in [108] demonstrates that exaggerated facial expression via magnitude of mouth movements during speech to express different emotions can affect the uncanny for characters.

3.4   Nonverbal Communication

Verbal and nonverbal communication are considered absolutely essential in collaborative systems, whether they are designed for task solving, social networking or entertainment [59]. In problem solving systems, besides the main goal of helping users to convey information and keep in contact with others, communication channels provide means for them to understand the task, negotiate shared workload, form strategies, and be aware of what has been done and what is being done [74]. In general, there are several modalities that are available in 3D shared environments such as auditory channels, embodiment and nonverbal communication, text and 2D/3D annotation, and so forth. Additionally, they can be used explicitly or implicitly by remote users. Cassell et al. in [30] have distinguished between behaviour for propositional purposes and for interaction purposes of conversation. According to the authors, propositional purposes can be obtained through meaningful speech, hand gestures, and intonation to convey, complement, or elaborate upon the information being communicated. On the other hand, interactional functions serve to indicate the current state of the conversation and can include nonverbal cues such as head nods, raising hands, or eye gaze for conversation invitation, speaking turn-taking, feedback, breaking away behaviour in conversations. These two activities often occur simultaneously when speakers and listeners continuously monitor each other's behaviour and hence be able to contribute to the conversation depending on the course of conversation established through information delivered and decoded. In this section, we focus on the nonverbal communication channel for synchronous collaboration, how it has been supported in collaborative XR platforms, and how it can effect the performance of communication amongst users.

Complementing to auditory channels, nonverbal communication, or bodily communication, is defined as another means used by one person to influence others. According to Argyle [2], in face-to-face conversations, many nonverbal communication modalities are subtly employed at the same time including facial expression, gestures, eye gaze, bodily movements and contact, spatial behaviour, and nonverbal vocalisations. Nonverbal signals can be provided intentional or unconscious, and in many cases they can be the mixture of those two. There are mainly five functional types of nonverbal communications including *expressing emotions, communicating interpersonal attitudes, accompanying and supporting speech, self-presenting*, and *rituals*. In other words, nonverbal communication is multidimensional and multifunctional when several modalities (e.g., postures, gestures, eye gazes) can serve different functional types simultaneously [16].

Considering the important roles of nonverbal communication in collaborative XR environments, it is essential to capture nonverbal behaviour of users and replicate it, either faithfully or strategically, to other users. Avatars can be effectively used as a medium to transfer nonverbal cues if the users' body is being tracked partially or completely. If the avatars cannot fully represent the body and/or facial movements of users, they would have to learn to adapt to the missing nonverbal communication channel and convey their activities through verbal explanations [97]. In the case of lack of tracking system, nonverbal communication cues such as gestures or facial expressions can be preprogrammed and triggered via a text chat window during the interaction in a desktop-based virtual environment [110]. Amongst many modalities of nonverbal behaviour that is tracked and rendered in real time, head orientation and eye gaze are considered subtle but critical in providing bidirectional signals for monitoring and synchronising actions. Several studies have been conducted on the impact of eye gaze on communication [41, 42, 100]. The results show that even without eyelid movement and blinking behaviours implemented, representing users' eye gaze on their avatars in real time could improve the interaction between remote users and their collaborative task performance. Compared to static eye or simulated eye gaze integrated on avatars, using tracked eye gaze can help users to indicate and capture accurately focus of current attention, inform and estimate next actions, and effectively communicate. Furthermore, in one-to-many conversations, eye gaze can also be transformed and augmented so that the eye gaze of the speaker is rendered individually to each listener so that they would have an impression that the speaker is gazing at them only [7].

Another nonverbal cues that get attention from researchers are facial expressions, bodily movements, postures and gestures. Thanks to recent advances in real-time facial motion capture technology (e.g., Dynamixyz[7], Faceware[8], Facerig[9]) and 3D modelling, capturing facial expressions of users and rendering them realistically have become largely applicable. In a recent research work, Oh et al. investigated the enhanced smiling expression on communication experience [76].

---

[7] http://www.dynamixyz.com/.

[8] http://facewaretech.com/products/software/.

[9] https://facerig.com/.

The users' smile is recorded and strategically rendered through their avatar. And when the participants' smile is enhanced, it is found that those participants themselves experienced stronger social presence compared to the faithful rendering condition. Another approach has explored three visual transformations for eye contact, joint attention identified by head direction, and grouping based on proxemic behavior to augment social behaviour by extending the physical communication condition into the virtual world [86]. Similarly, many approaches that communicate bodily movements, postures and gestures have been proposed. For instance, there are remote embodiment cues to improved awareness in a desktop-based virtual environment [39], hand movements of remote users via virtual hand shadows [88], remote user's head position, face direction, and hand poses for users using MR platform [80]. Recently, Pan et al. [78] integrated the foot tracking which allows users to see their full body in the shared VR environment, even though its impact on interaction, embodiment and presence is still subtle.

3.5   Does Group Size Matter? Collaboration and Social Interaction in Dyads, Triads, and Large Groups

The impact of different group size on collaboration mechanism, communication, and social interaction between users, especially remote users, in XR environments has not been extensively examined in the literature. Moreover, partially due to the limits of connection bandwidth and the large amount of data that needs to be transferred over the network to ensure a smooth collaboration, face-to-face or dyadic collaboration gets most of the attention from researchers. Since the nature of collaboration techniques in communication and interaction changes according to dyadic, triadic, and large group, we discuss in this section current research trends that have been explored for collaborative XR systems.

Communication patterns and group size have not been a highlighted topic and only limited research has considered the effects of group size on collaboration. In social sciences, it is concluded that increased group size decreases verbally interacting groups [99], individual contribution, perceived responsibility, involvement [63], and ideas generated per person [40]. Burgoon et al. in [25] have determined the limited number of members of a small group participating in a task without affecting interactivity and communication patterns. However, this limit depends on collaboration scenarios (co-located vs. remote) as well as the affordability of technology in supporting interdependent, contingent, participative, and synchronous interaction and communication between users. A theoretical model has been developed depicting the negative influence of group size and positive effect of social presence on the quality of communication within small groups regarding its appropriateness, richness, openness, and accuracy [67]. From the results of the experiment with 3-person and 6-person groups, it is argued that compared to 6-person groups, 3-person groups would obtain better communication in terms of appropriateness, openness, and accuracy.

In regard to dyadic interactions supported in collaborative virtual platforms, many behavioural model and interaction modes have been designed for face-to-face collaboration. Gaze and mutual gaze are the most important factors to be considered in the nonverbal-behaviour-supported platforms. Indeed, Argyle & Cook have analysed closely the relationship between mutual gaze and conversation progress between two interlocutors [3]. Therefore, gaze behaviour has been strongly supported in collaborative virtual systems. For instance, an eye gaze model for dyatic interaction in shared virtual environments has been proposed as part of the support for avatar realism within negotiation scenarios [114]. Avatar realism and nonverbal communication in face-to-face social interactions have also been largely studied, which can be augmented or enhanced to improve user experience in dyadic interaction such as verbal and nonverbal communication, copresence, emotion recognition, and so forth [8,41] (see Sect. 3.3 and 3.4). Furthermore, several social norms such as the gender, degree of intimacy, interpersonal distance, turn-talking in online virtual environments have also been studied [120]. More specifically in the context of cooperative manipulation and task solving, others factors such as concurrency control, collaborative manipulation mechanism need to be taken into consideration. Regarding collaborative manipulation techniques, there are two main categories allowing users to concurrently and synchronously manipulating shared artefacts: splitting the degrees of freedom of the manipulated objects [36], and combining concurrent access to the same artefacts [87]. It is important to note that these two approaches for cooperative manipulation tasks do not limit to only two users but can be extended to multiple collaborators work jointly at the same time. The concurrency control at a higher level has been further investigated for peer-to-peer virtual environments [66]. Through a concurrency control hierarchy, three methods have been proposed to control sudden changes in closely-coupled, object-focuses tasks, which include Change It ('rollback' mechanism for simple shared object property changes without broadcasting updates), Grab It ('transaction-lock' mechanism for exclusive shared object property changes or deletions with broadcasting updates), and Build It ('intention-preservation' mechanism for shared object structure changes in highly dynamic environments).

Collaboration and communication within triad groups and small-size groups bear similar characteristics as in the dyadic groups in terms of cooperative manipulation and concurrency control. However, as there are more members participating in the session, social presence and interaction may change according to the nature of the collaborative and individual tasks as well as each member's roles. For instance, users' behaviour has been studied when they perform a task of puzzle solving in small groups of three people (one HMD and two desktop displays) within a shared virtual environment, and compared to their own behaviour when they continue doing the same task in the real world [95]. During the experiment, the experimenters also asked one member of the group to follow and observe another member without letting them know about it. The results in regard to the silent observation set-up show that shared VR platforms have the capacity to evoke emotional responses such as discomfort and embarrassment, even through simple avatars. Another experiment has been conducted by Steed et al. [98] in which leadership, presence, copresence, social presence, and accord between group members have been investigated within small groups of strangers carrying out collaborative tasks. An overview done by Schroeder [89] lists several factors that need to be considered in order to improve user experience within small groups working together on short-term tasks. Those factors mostly serve synchronous collaboration purposes such as shared focus of attention, mutual awareness, and collaborative task performance.

Finally, regarding collaboration and interaction mechanism within large groups such as social networking or online virtual worlds for entertainment, researchers take a different approach in trying to understand how individuals within these groups form their relationships and adapt to the virtual environment over a long period; how being exposed to virtual worlds can affect their life in the real world; and which social rules are preserved or changed within the worlds of no boundaries [89]. Many parts of these research questions are still left unanswered and require extensive research effort in multiple disciplines. We discuss in this section some early works that have been performed to measure some social responses from an individual viewpoint when a user is interacting with or in front of a big group of others. In social psychology, Zajonc [121] and Taylor et al. [104] have reviewed and analysed the effect of performing a task in the presence of others on the user's performance which depends mostly on the difficulty level of the task and how the user has mastered it in advance. These analyses have been theorised into the concepts of social facilitation and inhibition. To apply and measure these concepts into the collaborative virtual environment, Hoyt et al. [54] have sought to replicate these effects and measure them in a study with participants performed a mastered and a non-mastered task, either alone or in the presence of a virtual human audience which was led to believe that they could be avatars or embodied agents. Their experiment has confirmed the social inhibition theory that performing a novel task in front of avatars can impair users' performance on subordinate responses. Furthermore, the behaviour of members in a big audience (e.g., eye contact, individual facial expressions, gesture, posture, and behavioural pattern between themselves) can also be registered as empirical design basis, which, in turn, can be useful to stimulate the users' experience in a virtual human audience [82].

These aspects relating to social responses mediated by XR technology are summarised in an attempt to identify what features that collaborative immersive systems can provide to make users experience and enjoy their time in immersive world and maximise their potential in using this world for different purposes.

3.6 Physical and Virtual World: How to Increase the Awareness

VR can forge a great sense of immersion in users when their senses (visual, auditory, and others) are replaced by synthesised digital channels. Different to presence experience, immersion is measured by objective technology-related factors such as field of view, field of regard, display resolution, head-based rendering, frame rate, and degree of interactivity [23]. Therefore, the more immersed users are in virtual environment, the more successful the system is in terms of isolating users from their physical world, increasing their perception of self-inclusion and self-movement [118]. However, since users still move in the physical world,

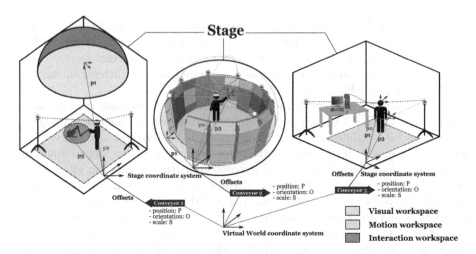

Fig. 4. IIVC model representing an abstraction of users' physical environment including a conveyor, a stage and its workspaces for each user. It was adapted from [33,34] for a collaborative XR platform which includes hemispherical dome (left), 340-degree panoramic projection (middle), and HMD (right) systems [22]

any mismatches between physical and virtual world can break the illusion and even endanger them physically due to collision with physical objects in their surrounding area. In this section, we explore the idea of how to help users to be aware of the physical world while working in the virtual one without losing their immersion, presence and experience, and how to communicate the differences in hardware capabilities to remote collaborators.

The awareness of the physical environment with its constraints and limitations is essential when users are fully immersed. Steed et al. in [97] have pointed out several problems when the physical and virtual world do not align in projection-based systems such as the use of the non-tracked hand or the collision with the wall which to avoid users have to use their hand to feel the wall. Duval et al. in [34] have proposed the model of IIVC (Immersive Interactive Virtual Cabin) to encapsulate an abstraction of users' physical environment and represent it in the virtual world. The IIVC comprises of three main components: workspace (3D space depicting physical area in which the user can move around or limits of physical devices), stage (virtual description of the user' real environment), and conveyor (integration frame of the stage into the virtual world). Figure 4 shows in details the adapted IIVC model for a collaborative XR platform of hemispherical dome, panoramic projection, and HMD system, in which each system has a conveyor carries its stage and its workspaces. This model is useful in helping developers to precisely define the physical world's parameters and integrate them into the virtual world. For instance, in order to enhance the awareness of the user when they work in a CAVE-like system and to prevent them from colliding with its front display screen, a 3D grid which becomes clearer and sharper when the user gets closer to the screen or physical boundaries [74].

By sharing the model or configurations of the user's physical space to others, it helps them to be aware of the working condition of others and can thus predict their possible limits and constraints. Explicit representations of field of view or grasping range are examples of how to communicate users' interaction abilities to others [39]. In asymmetric collaborative virtual environments, there also is a potential desynchronisation problem in coordinating activities between users in real time with different settings and viewpoints, which requires a mutual awareness to be established [31]. Piumsomboon et al. proposed and evaluated the effects of sharing awareness cues (field of view frustum, eye-gaze ray, head-gaze ray) on user performance in a collaborative MR system [81]. And in co-located shared VR environments, a research on mutual awareness has been conducted by Lacoche et al. in [60] for the collaboration between co-located users immersed via HMDs when they share the same physical space but navigate independently in the virtual world. Thus, there is a potential discrepancy in the perception and awareness of the physical and virtual world for co-located users. The authors have proposed and compared three approaches including Extended Grid (a grid cylinder representing physical location of others), Ghost Avatar (an avatar of the HMD model and its two controllers), and Safe Navigation Floor (a rendering of the physical floor with colors marking safe areas and collision zones where the others occupy). It is argued that these representations can also be used for co-located users even when they do not share the same virtual space, or for real static and dynamic objects if their position and occupied space can be tracked in the physical environment.

To conclude, the awareness in collaborative XR environment and of the difference between the physical and virtual environment is always essential to coordinate a group's activities no matter what the nature of the collaborative work is. Awareness of many factors and activities going on in the collaborative session can help to reduce errors and increase efficiency of the group effort. Despite the importance in facilitating a process to obtain the awareness, there are still many factors that have not been fully explored. For instance, Steed et al. have pointed out that when users interact with each other, they expect that others would grasp the context of their interaction and communication via gestures and bodily movements as well as their viewpoints implicitly [97]. Another factor to be considered to increase the presence of users in collaborative virtual environments is the discrepancy between physical moving in the real world and virtual travelling using different metaphors such as 'flying' [79] or 'jumping' [102], which can cause directional disorientation in spatial awareness. Finally, with the emerging technology in AR, the model that represents the physical environment in the virtual world needs to be revised to adapt to new collaborative XR platforms.

4 Research Opportunities

As coexperience in collaborative extended reality is a transdisciplinary research topic at the intersection of human-computer interaction, extended reality, computer-supported collaborative work, cognitive psychology, perception, and social sciences, it is still challenging to fully identify all the pertinent research opportunities. Based on the analysis of several important aspects of human factors outlined in the previous section, we aim to encapsulate main directions in a non-exclusive list in this section for future research projects.

Presence, Copresence, and Social Presence. In the new context of XR platforms, these three factors relating to presence can be re-explored and assessed as XR technology, especially AR, has changed the nature of communication approach for remote collaboration. In the near future, XR technology will be able to provide high fidelity communication cues including virtual proximity and orientation of others, physical appearance, facial expressions, gaze and mutual gaze, postures and gestures, as well as verbal signals. However, there is still a lack of (explicit and implicit) exchange and integration mechanisms of these communication channels and representations of communicational cues in mixed real-virtual environments. Furthermore, dynamic relationship between presence, social presence, copresence and UX needs to be studied further in order to determine decisive factors to be considered when designing user-centred MR systems.

Asynchronous Collaboration. This mode of collaboration will become prevalent once the use of XR in collaborative work expands in the future. Asynchronous collaboration of distant users can affect UX and particularly will influence individual sense of presence and social connection. XR technology will, therefore, change the methodologies of social psychology studies in the domain of user interaction and UX over virtual and augmented environments.

Long-Term Effects of Collaborative Extended Reality on User Experience. From the aspect of using immersive environments in social life, long-term effects of being immersed in such environments and working together with others over a distance on individual personality traits such as social anxiety and leadership skills can become an interesting research undertaking between social scientists, cognitive psychologists, and computer researchers. Moreover, considering collaboration and interaction mechanisms within large group of users when XR platforms are used for social networking, online virtual worlds and entertainment, it is important to understand how individuals within these groups form their relationships and adapt to the mediated environment over a long period, how being exposed to virtual worlds can affect their life in the real world, and which social rules are preserved or changed within the virtual worlds of no boundaries [89]. Many parts of these research questions are still left unanswered and require extensive research effort combined from multiple disciplines.

Group Dynamics and Collaboration Patterns. Task performance of a whole group is partly decided by how well workload is distributed, managed, and coordinated amongst members and partly by how well each member uses tools to coordinate and execute tasks. Therefore, it is an important topic to study how the collaboration occurs at individuals' level and group dynamics in collaborative mixed immersive systems. Moreover, studies can be carried out to measure collaboration performance and competition within a group and between groups.

Virtual Representations of Self and of Others. The use of virtual bodies of users as the representation of self on computer-mediated environments can change their sense of ownership (i.e. perception that extends or modifies virtual parts of avatar as their own) and agency (i.e. perception of controlling these new forms). Accurate representations of users within XR environments extracted from all the tracking systems have the potential to be able to render highly realistic models to facilitate real-time face-to-face interaction and communication between users. The extension of one's virtual body in collaborative context can be extensively studied in the near future for a more complete understanding of how each user perceives and experiences within XR environments. For instance, in a collaborative AR world, a research question can be how the representation of both physical and virtual body can affect the user's self-perception and self-localisation. In addition, another aspect of using virtual representations of avatars and embodied agents with their behavioural realism and appearance realism can be broadly studied on the measures of collaborative tasks performance and UX.

Merging of Physical and Virtual Worlds. The integration of physical world into the virtual world and how the virtual world manifests itself in the physical world need to be revised to adapt to collaborative XR systems within which multiple users have their own hardware capabilities and may not be aware of the differences between them. Since more and more XR devices have been marketed to larger public, it would be necessary to study how mediated environments created by HMD, smart glasses, projection-based or CAVE-like systems can be perceived individually by each user and how these differences in display and interaction devices will affect users' roles in the whole collaboration process.

5   Conclusion

Multiple user experience or coexperience in collaborative extended reality environments is an important topic that requires synergistic research collaboration amongst cognitive psychologists and social scientists, human-computer interaction researchers and designers, extended reality (virtual reality and augmented reality) scientists and developers, data scientists, amongst others. The future outcomes of this research will facilitate greatly the interaction between humans and computer-generated worlds through multi-sensory stimuli interaction design and exchange mechanisms. We present in this paper several main aspects of coexperience in collaborative extended reality environments including presence-related factors, group dynamics and collaboration patterns, avatars and embodied agents, nonverbal communication, group size, awareness of physical and virtual world as the initiative to review the current state of the art of this multi-disciplinary research domain. Many future research opportunities are outlined in the previous section that could be of interest to researchers and scientists in different fields. There are still many unexplored topics in this multi-discipline domain and great research effort, resources, and collaboration need to be initiated to solve these challenges as collaboration between users, especially remotely located users, is technologically challenging in providing seamlessly transferring communication, manipulation and task execution process.

References

1. Allport, G.: The Historical Background of Modern Social Psychology, vol. I, 3rd edn., pp. 1–46. Addison-Wesley, Boston (1985)
2. Argyle, M.: Bodily Communication, 2nd edn. International Universities Press Inc. (1988)
3. Argyle, M., Cook, M.: Gaze and Mutual Gaze. Cambridge University Press, New York (1976)
4. Arrow, H.: Stability, bistability, and instability in small group influence patterns. J. Pers. Soc. Psychol. **72**(1), 75–85 (1997)
5. Axelsson, A.S., Abelin, A., Heldal, I., Schroeder, R., Widestrom, J.: Cubes in the cube: a comparison of a puzzle-solving task in a virtual and a real environment. CyberPsychol. Behav. **4**(2), 279–286 (2001)
6. Bailenson, J.N., Beall, A.C., Loomis, J., Blascovich, J., Turk, M.: Transformed social interaction: decoupling representation from behavior and form in collaborative virtual environments. Presence: Teleoper. Virtual Environ. **13**(4), 428–441 (2004)
7. Bailenson, J.N., Beall, A.C., Loomis, J., Blascovich, J., Turk, M.: Transformed social interaction, augmented gaze, and social influence in immersive virtual environments. Hum. Commun. Res. **31**(4), 511–537 (2005)
8. Bailenson, J.N., Yee, N., Merget, D., Schroeder, R.: The effect of behavioral realism and form realism of real-time avatar faces on verbal disclosure, nonverbal disclosure, emotion recognition, and copresence in dyadic interaction. Presence: Teleoper. Virtual Environ. **15**(4), 359–372 (2006)
9. Balakrishnan, K., Honavar, V.: Evolutionary and Neural Systhesis of Intelligent Agents, pp. 1–26. MIT Press, Cambridge (2001). Book section 1
10. Bastian, M., Heymann, S., Jacomy, M.: Gephi: an open source software for exploring and manipulating networks. In: Proceedings of the 2009 AAI Conference on Weblogsand Social Media, pp. 361–362 (2009)
11. Battarbee, K., Koskinen, I.: Co-experience: user experience as interaction. CoDesign **1**(1), 5–18 (2005)
12. de Belen, R.A.J., Nguyen, H., Filonik, D., Del Favero, D., Bednarz, T.: A systematic review of the current state of collaborative mixed reality technologies: 2013–2018. AIMS Electron. Electr. Eng. **3**, 181 (2019)
13. Bem, D.J.: Self-perception Theory, vol. 6, pp. 1–62. Academic Press, Cambridge (1972)
14. Benford, S., Bowers, J., Fahlen, L.E., Greenhalgh, C., Snowdon, D.: User embodiment in collaborative virtual environments. In: Proceedings of the SIGCHI Conference on Human Factors in Computing Systems, pp. 242–249. ACM Press/Addison-Wesley Publishing Co. (1995). 223935
15. Benne, K.D., Sheats, P.: Functional roles of group members. J. Soc. Issues **4**(2), 41–49 (1948)
16. Bente, G., Rüggenberg, S., Krämer, N.C., Eschenburg, F.: Avatar-mediated networking: increasing social presence and interpersonal trust in net-based collaborations. Hum. Commun. Res. **34**(2), 287–318 (2008)
17. Billinghurst, M., Kato, H.: Collaborative mixed reality. In: Proceedings of the First International Symposium on Mixed Reality (ISMR), pp. 261–284 (1999)
18. Biocca, F., Harms, C.: Defining and measuring social presence: contribution to the networked minds theory and measure. In: Proceedings of the 5th International Workshop on Presence, pp. 7–36 (2002)

19. Biocca, F., Harms, C., Burgoon, J.K.: Toward a more robust theory and measure of social presence: review and suggested criteria. Presence: Teleoper. Virtual Environ. **12**(5), 456–480 (2003)
20. Blascovich, J.: Social influence within immersive virtual environments. In: Schroeder, R. (ed.) The Social Life of Avatars. Computer Supported Cooperative Work, pp. 127–145. Springer, London (2002). https://doi.org/10.1007/978-1-4471-0277-9_8
21. Blascovich, J., Loomis, J., Beall, A.C., Swinth, K.R., Hoyt, C.L., Bailenson, J.N.: Immersive virtual environment technology as a methodological tool for social psychology. Psychol. Inq. **13**(2), 103–124 (2002)
22. Bourke, C., Bednarz, T.: Multi-modal high-end visualization system. In: Proceedings of the 17th International Conference on Virtual-Reality Continuum and Its Applications in Industry, VRCAI 2019, pp. 1–2. Association for Computing Machinery (2019)
23. Bowman, D., McMahan, R.: Virtual reality: how much immersion is enough? Computer **40**(7), 36–43 (2007)
24. Bulu, S.T.: Place presence, social presence, co-presence, and satisfaction in virtual worlds. Comput. Educ. **58**(1), 154–161 (2012)
25. Burgoon, J.K., Bonito, J.A., Ramirez, J.A., Dunbar, N.E., Kam, K., Fischer, J.: Testing the interactivity principle: effects of mediation, propinquity, and verbal and nonverbal modalities in interpersonal interaction. J. Commun. **52**(3), 657–677 (2002)
26. Bystrom, K.E., Barfield, W.: Collaborative task performance for learning using a virtual environment. Presence: Teleoper. Virtual Environ. **8**(4), 435–448 (1999)
27. Caneparo, L.: Coordinative virtual space for architectural design. In: Proceedings of the 6th International Conference on Computer-Aided Architectural Design Futures. CAAD Futures (1995)
28. Carley, K.: A theory of group stability. Am. Sociol. Rev. **56**(3), 331–354 (1991)
29. Cartwright, D., Zander, A.: Group Dynamics, 3rd edn. Harper + Row, Oxford (1968)
30. Cassell, J., Bickmore, T., Campbell, L., Vilhjalmsson, H., Yan, H.: Human conversation as a system framework: designing embodied conversational agents, pp. 29–63. MIT Press (2000)
31. Chenechal, M.L., Chalme, S., Duval, T., Royan, J., Gouranton, V., Arnaldi, B.: Toward an enhanced mutual awareness in asymmetric CVE. In: Proceedings of the 2015 International Conference on Collaboration Technologies and Systems (CTS), pp. 233–240 (2015)
32. Dodds, T.J., Ruddle, R.A.: Mobile group dynamics in large-scale collaborative virtual environments. In: Proceedings of the 2008 IEEE Virtual Reality Conference, pp. 59–66 (2008)
33. Duval, T., Nguyen, H., Fleury, C., Chauffaut, A., Dumont, G., Gouranton, V.: Embedding the features of the users' physical environments to improve the feeling of presence in collaborative virtual environments. In: Proceedings of the IEEE 3rd International Conference on Cognitive Infocommunications, pp. 243–248. CogInfoCom (2012)
34. Duval, T., Nguyen, T.T.H., Fleury, C., Chauffaut, A., Dumont, G., Gouranton, V.: Improving awareness for 3D virtual collaboration by embedding the features of users' physical environments and by augmenting interaction tools with cognitive feedback cues. J. Multimodal User Interfaces **8**(2), 187–197 (2014)
35. Erickson, T.: Designing agents as if people mattered, pp. 79–96. MIT Press (1997)

36. Fleury, C., Duval, T., Gouranton, V., Steed, A.: Evaluation of remote collaborative manipulation for scientific data analysis. In: Proceedings of the 18th ACM Symposium on Virtual Reality Software and Technology, pp. 129–136. ACM (2012). 2407361

37. Fox, J., Ahn, S.J., Janssen, J.H., Yeykelis, L., Segovia, K.Y., Bailenson, J.N.: Avatars versus agents: a meta-analysis quantifying the effect of agency on social influence. Hum. Comput. Interact. **30**(5), 401–432 (2015)

38. Fox, J., Bailenson, J.N., Tricase, L.: The embodiment of sexualized virtual selves: the proteus effect and experiences of self-objectification via avatars. Comput. Hum. Behav. **29**(3), 930–938 (2013)

39. Fraser, M., Benford, S., Hindmarsh, J., Heath, C.: Supporting awareness and interaction through collaborative virtual interfaces. In: Proceedings of the 12th Annual ACM Symposium on User Interface Software and Technology, pp. 27–36. ACM (1999). 322580

40. Gallupe, R.B., et al.: Electronic brainstorming and group size. Acad. Manag. J. **35**(2), 350–369 (1992)

41. Garau, M., Slater, M., V., Brogni, A., Steed, A., Sasse, M.A.: The impact of avatar realism and eye gaze control on perceived quality of communication in a shared immersive virtual environment. In: Proceedings of the SIGCHI Conference on Human Factors in Computing Systems, pp. 529–536. ACM (2003). 642703

42. Garau, M., Slater, M., Bee, S., Sasse, M.A.: The impact of eye gaze on communication using humanoid avatars. In: Proceedings of the SIGCHI Conference on Human Factors in Computing Systems, pp. 309–316. ACM (2001). 365121

43. Garau, M., Slater, M., Pertaub, D.P., Razzaque, S.: The responses of people to virtual humans in an immersive virtual environment. Presence: Teleoper. Virtual Environ. - Spec. Issue: Collabor. Inf. Vis. Environ. **14**(1), 104–116 (2005)

44. Gerhard, M., Moore, D.J., Hobbs, D.J.: Continuous presence in collaborative virtual environments: towards a hybrid avatar-agent model for user representation. In: de Antonio, A., Aylett, R., Ballin, D. (eds.) IVA 2001. LNCS (LNAI), vol. 2190, pp. 137–155. Springer, Heidelberg (2001). https://doi.org/10.1007/3-540-44812-8_12

45. Gerhard, M., Moore, D., Hobbs, D.: Embodiment and copresence in collaborative interfaces. Int. J. Hum. Comput. Stud. **61**(4), 453–480 (2004)

46. Gersick, C.J.G.: Time and transition in work teams: toward a new model of group development. Acad. Manag. J. **31**(1), 9–41 (1988)

47. Goebbels, G., Lalioti, V.: Co-presence and co-working in distributed collaborative virtual environments. In: Proceedings of the 1st International Conference on Computer Graphics, Virtual Reality and Visualisation, pp. 109–114. ACM (2001). 513891

48. Hall, E.T.: The Hidden Dimension. Doubleday, Garden City (1966)

49. Hassenzahl, M., Tractinsky, N.: User experience - a research agenda. Behav. Inf. Technol. **25**(2), 91–97 (2006)

50. Heeter, C.: Being there: the subjective experience of presence. Presence: Teleoper. Virtual Environ. **1**(2), 262–271 (1992)

51. Held, R.M., Durlach, N.I.: Telepresence. Presence: Teleoper. Virtual Environ. **1**(1), 109–112 (1992)

52. Howells, L.T., Becker, S.W.: Seating arrangement and leadership emergence. J. Abnorm. Soc. Psychol. **64**(2), 148–150 (1962)

53. Hoyet, L., Argelaguet, F., Nicole, C., Lécuyer, A.: "Wow! I have six fingers!": would you accept structural changes of your hand in VR? Front. Robot. AI **3**(27), 1–12 (2016)

54. Hoyt, C.L., Blascovich, J., Swinth, K.R.: Social inhibition in immersive virtual environments. Presence: Teleoper. Virtual Environ. **12**(2), 183–195 (2003)
55. Hulin, C.L., Roznowski, M.: Organizational technologies: effects on organizations' characteristics and individuals' responses. Res. Organ. Behav. **7**, 39–85 (1985)
56. IJsselsteijn, W.A., Ridder, H.d., Freeman, J., Avons, S.E.: Presence: concept, determinants, and measurement. In: Proceedings of the Electronic Imaging conference, vol. 3959, p. 10. SPIE (2000)
57. Johnson-Glenberg, M.C., Birchfield, D.A., Tolentino, L., Koziupa, T.: Collaborative embodied learning in mixed reality motion-capture environments: two science studies. J. Educ. Psychol. **106**(1), 86–104 (2014)
58. Kirkman, B.L., Mathieu, J.E.: The dimensions and antecedents of team virtuality. J. Manag. **31**(5), 700–718 (2005)
59. Knapp, M.L., Hall, J.A., Horgan, T.G.: Nonverbal Communication in Human Interaction, 8th edn. Wadsworth CENGAGE Learning (2013)
60. Lacoche, J., Pallamin, N., Boggini, T., Royan, J.: Collaborators awareness for user cohabitation in co-located collaborative virtual environments. In: Proceedings of the 23rd ACM Symposium on Virtual Reality Software and Technology, pp. 1–9. ACM (2017). 3139142
61. Ladwig, P., Geiger, C.: A literature review on collaboration in mixed reality. In: Auer, M.E., Langmann, R. (eds.) REV 2018. LNNS, vol. 47, pp. 591–600. Springer, Cham (2019). https://doi.org/10.1007/978-3-319-95678-7_65
62. Lanier, J.: Homuncular flexibility (2006)
63. Latane, B., Wolf, S.: The social impact of majorities and minorities. Psychol. Rev. **88**(5), 438–453 (1981)
64. Leary, M.R.: Social anxiousness: the construct and its measurement. J. Pers. Assess. **47**(1), 66–75 (1983)
65. Linebarger, J.M., Janneck, C.D., Kessler, G.D.: Leaving the world behind: supporting group collaboration patterns in a shared virtual environment for product design. Presence: Teleoper. Virtual Environ. **14**(6), 697–719 (2005)
66. Linebarger, J.M., Kessler, G.D.: Concurrency control mechanisms for closely coupled collaboration in multithreaded peer-to-peer virtual environments. Presence: Teleoper. Virtual Environ. **13**(3), 296–314 (2004)
67. Lowry, P.B., Roberts, T.L., Romano, N.C., Cheney, P.D., Hightower, R.T.: The impact of group size and social presence on small-group communication: does computer-mediated communication make a difference? Small Group Res. **37**(6), 631–661 (2006)
68. Lucas, G.M., Gratch, J., King, A., Morency, L.P.: It's only a computer: virtual humans increase willingness to disclose. Comput. Hum. Behav. **37**, 94–100 (2014)
69. Martins, L.L., Gilson, L.L., Maynard, M.T.: Virtual teams: what do we know and where do we go from here? J. Manag. **30**(6), 805–835 (2004)
70. Milgram, P., Takemura, H., Utsumi, A., Kishino, F.: Augmented reality: a class of displays on the reality-virtuality continuum. In: Photonics for Industrial Applications, vol. 2351, pp. 282–292. SPIE (1995)
71. Mori, M.: Bukimi no tani (the uncanny valley). Energy **7**, 33–35 (1970)
72. Nass, C., Moon, Y.: Machines and mindlessness: social responses to computers. J. Soc. Issues **56**(1), 81–103 (2000)
73. Nassiri, N., Powell, N., Moore, D.: Avatar gender and personal space invasion anxiety level in desktop collaborative virtual environments. Virtual Reality **8**(2), 107–117 (2004)

74. Nguyen, T.T.H., Duval, T.: A survey of communication and awareness in collaborative virtual environments. In: Proceedings of the 2014 International Workshop on Collaborative Virtual Environments, pp. 1–8. 3DCVE (2014)

75. Nowak, K.L., Biocca, F.: The effect of the agency and anthropomorphism on users' sense of telepresence, copresence, and social presence in virtual environments. Presence: Teleoper. Virtual Environ. **12**(5), 481–494 (2003)

76. Oh, S.Y., Bailenson, J., Krämer, N., Li, B.: Let the avatar brighten your smile: effects of enhancing facial expressions in virtual environments. PLOS One **11**(9), e0161794 (2016)

77. Pan, Y., Sinclair, D., Mitchell, K.: Empowerment and embodiment for collaborative mixed reality systems. Comput. Animat. Virtual Worlds **29**(3–4), 1–11 (2018)

78. Pan, Y., Steed, A.: How foot tracking matters: the impact of an animated self-avatar on interaction, embodiment and presence in shared virtual environments. Front. Robot. AI **6**, 1–13 (2019)

79. Pausch, R., Burnette, T., Brockway, D., Weiblen, M.E.: Navigation and locomotion in virtual worlds via flight into hand-held miniatures. In: Proceedings of the 22nd Annual Conference on Computer Fraphics and Interactive Techniques, pp. 399–400. ACM (1995). 218495

80. Piumsomboon, T., Day, A., Ens, B., Lee, Y., Lee, G., Billinghurst, M.: Exploring enhancements for remote mixed reality collaboration. In: Proceedings of the SIGGRAPH Asia 2017 Mobile Graphics & Interactive Applications, pp. 1–5. ACM. (2017). 3139200

81. Piumsomboon, T., Dey, A., Ens, B., Lee, G., Billinghurst, M.: The effects of sharing awareness cues in collaborative mixed reality. Front. Robot. AI **6**, 1–18 (2019)

82. Poeschl, S., Doering, N.: Designing virtual audiences for fear of public speaking training - an observation study on realistic nonverbal behavior. Stud. Health Technol. Inf. **181**, 218–222 (2012)

83. Poole, M.S., Roth, J.: Decision development in small groups V test of a contingency model. Hum. Commun. Res. **15**(4), 549–589 (1989)

84. von der Putten, A.M., Kramer, N.C., Gratch, J., Kang, S.H.: "it doesn't matter what you are!" explaining social effects of agents and avatars. Comput. Hum. Behav. **26**(6), 1641–1650 (2010)

85. Rosa, N.: Player/avatar body relations in multimodal augmented reality games. In: Proceedings of the 18th ACM International Conference on Multimodal Interaction, ICMI 2016, pp. 550–553 (2016)

86. Roth, D., Klelnbeck, C., Feigl, T., Mutschler, C., Latoschik, M.E.: Beyond replication: augmenting social behaviors in multi-user virtual realities. In: Proceedings of the 2018 IEEE Conference on Virtual Reality and 3D User Interfaces (VR), pp. 215–222 (2018)

87. Ruddle, R.A., Savage, J.C.D., Jones, D.M.: Symmetric and asymmetric action integration during cooperative object manipulation in virtual environments. J. ACM Trans. Comput.-Hum. Interact. (TOCHI) **9**(4), 285–308 (2002)

88. Sakong, K., Nam, T.J.: Supporting telepresence by visual and physical cues in distributed 3D collaborative design environments. In: Proceedings of CHI 2006 Extended Abstracts on Human Factors in Computing Systems, CHI EA 2006, pp. 1283–1288 (2006)

89. Schroeder, R.: Copresence and interaction in virtual environments: an overview of the range of issues. In: Proceedings of the 5th International Workshop on Presence, pp. 274–295 (2002)

90. Schroeder, R.: social interaction in virtual environments: key issues, common themes, and a framework for research. In: Schroeder, R. (ed.) The Social Life of Avatars. Computer Supported Cooperative Work, pp. 1–18. Springer, London (2002). https://doi.org/10.1007/978-1-4471-0277-9_1

91. Schroeder, R.: Being there together and the future of connected presence. Presence: Teleoper. Virtual Environ. **15**(4), 438–454 (2006)

92. Schuemie, M.J., van der Straaten, P., Krijn, M., van der Mast, C.A.: Research on presence in virtual reality: a survey. CyberPsychol. Behav. **4**(2), 183–201 (2001)

93. Shen, Z., Ma, H., Wang, K.: A web-scale system for scientific knowledge exploration. In: Proceedings of the 2018 Meeting of the Association for Computational Linguistics, pp. 87–92 (2018)

94. Slater, M.: Real people meeting virtually real people – a review of some experiments in shared virtual environments. BT Technol. J. **17**(1), 120–127 (1999)

95. Slater, M., Sadagic, A., Usoh, M., Schroeder, R.: Small-group behavior in a virtual and real environment: a comparative study. Presence: Teleoper. Virtual Environ. **9**(1), 37–51 (2000)

96. Slater, M., Wilbur, S.: A framework for immersive virtual environments (five): speculations on the role of presence in virtual environments. Presence: Teleoper. Virtual Environ. **6**(6), 603–616 (1997)

97. Steed, A., Roberts, D., Schroeder, R., Heldal, I.: Interaction between users of immersion projection technology systems. In: Proceedings of the 11th International Conference on Human Computer Interaction (HCI), pp. 1–10 (2005)

98. Steed, A., Slater, M., Sadagic, A., Bullock, A., Tromp, J.: Leadership and collaboration in shared virtual environments. In: Proceedings of the IEEE Virtual Reality, pp. 112–115 (1999)

99. Steiner, I.D.: Group Process and Productivity (Social Psychological Monograph). Academic Press, New York (1972)

100. Steptoe, W., et al.: Eye tracking for avatar eye gaze control during object-focused multiparty interaction in immersive collaborative virtual environments. In: Proceedings of the 2009 IEEE Virtual Reality Conference, pp. 83–90 (2009)

101. Steptoe, W., Steed, A., Slater, M.: Human tails: ownership and control of extended humanoid avatars. IEEE Trans. Vis. Comput. Graph. (TVCG) **19**(4), 583–590 (2013)

102. Stoakley, R., Conway, M.J., Pausch, R.: Virtual reality on a WIM: interactive worlds in miniature. In: Proceedings of the SIGCHI Conference on Human Factors in Computing Systems, pp. 265–272. ACM Press/Addison-Wesley Publishing Co. (1995). 223938

103. Stogdill, R.M.: Personal factors associated with leadership: a survey of the literature. J. Psychol. **25**(1), 35–71 (1948)

104. Taylor, S.E., Peplau, L.A., Sears, D.O.: Social Psychology, 12th edn. Pearson, London (2005)

105. Thibaut, J.W., Kelley, H.H.: The Social Psychology of Groups, 1st edn. Routledge, New York (1959)

106. Thie, S., Wijk, J.V.: A general theory on presence: experimental evaluation of social virtual presence in a decision making task. In: Proceedings of the Presence in Shared Virtual Environments Workshop, pp. 53–63 (1998)

107. Thiebaux, M., Marsella, S., Marshall, A.N., Kallmann, M.: SmartBody: behavior realization for embodied conversational agents. In: Proceedings of the 7th International Joint Conference on Autonomous Agents and Multiagent Systems, vol. 1. pp. 151–158. International Foundation for Autonomous Agents and Multiagent Systems (2008). 1402409

108. Tinwell, A., Grimshaw, M., Abdel-Nabi, D.: Effect of emotion and articulation of speech on the uncanny valley in virtual characters. In: D'Mello, S., Graesser, A., Schuller, B., Martin, J.-C. (eds.) ACII 2011. LNCS, vol. 6975, pp. 557–566. Springer, Heidelberg (2011). https://doi.org/10.1007/978-3-642-24571-8_69

109. Tromp, J., Bullock, A., Steed, A., Sadagic, A., Slater, M., Frecon, E.: Small group behaviour experiments in the coven project. IEEE Comput. Graph. Appl. **18**(6), 53–63 (1998)

110. Tsiatsos, T., Terzidou, T.: Supporting collaborative learning processes in CVEs by augmenting student avatars, with nonverbal communication features. In: Proceedings of the 10th IEEE International Conference on Advanced Learning Technologies, pp. 578–580 (2010)

111. Tuckman, B.W.: Developmental sequence in small groups. Psychol. Bull. **63**(6), 384–399 (1965)

112. Tullis, T., Albert, B.: Measuring the User Experience: Collecting, Analyzing, and Presenting Usability Metrics, 2nd edn. Elsevier Inc., Amsterdam (2013)

113. Verhulst, A., Normand, J.M., Lombart, C., Sugimoto, M., Moreau, G.: Influence of being embodied in an obese virtual body on shopping behavior and products perception in VR. Front. Robot. AI **5**, 1–20 (2018)

114. Vinayagamoorthy, V., Garau, M., Steed, A., Slater, M.: An eye gaze model for dyadic interaction in an immersive virtual environment: practice and experience. Comput. Graph. Forum **23**(1), 1–11 (2004)

115. Vinayagamoorthy, V., Steed, A., Slater, M.: Building characters: lessons drawn from virtual environments. In: Proceedings of the Toward Social Mechanisms of Android Science: A CogSci 2005 Workshop, pp. 119–126 (2005)

116. Ward, C.D.: Seating arrangement and leadership emergence in small discussion groups. J. Soc. Psychol. **74**(1), 83–90 (1968)

117. Wasson, B., Mørch, A.I.: Identifying collaboration patterns in collaborative tele-learning scenarios. J. Educ. Technol. Soc. **3**(3), 237–248 (2000)

118. Witmer, B.G., Singer, M.J.: Measuring presence in virtual environments: a presence questionnaire. Presence: Teleoper. Virtual Environ. **7**(3), 225–240 (1998)

119. Yee, N., Bailenson, J.: The proteus effect: the effect of transformed self-representation on behavior. Hum. Commun. Res. **33**(3), 271–290 (2007)

120. Yee, N., Bailenson, J.N., Urbanek, M., Chang, F., Merget, D.: The unbearable likeness of being digital: the persistence of nonverbal social norms in online virtual environments. CyberPsychol. Behav. **10**(1), 115–121 (2007)

121. Zajonc, R.B.: Social facilitation. Science **149**(3681), 269–274 (1965)

Shopping with Virtual Hands

Aline Simonetti$^{(\boxtimes)}$, Enrique Bigné, and Shobhit Kakaria

University of Valencia, 46022 Valencia, Spain
{aline.simonetti,enrique.bigne,shobhit.kakaria}@uv.es

Abstract. Retailers can use virtual reality as a new touchpoint for their customers: within an existent channel or as a new sales channel. Thus, it is crucial to understand the differences and similarities between the physical and the virtual shopping environment. Shopping simulations make it possible to test, observe, and collect data in a controlled, low-cost, and fast way compared to field experiments. However, past studies might have provided biased results due to the characteristics of the sample used. This study analyzes how consumers behave in two virtual shopping tasks. The exploratory, experimental research uses an immersive VR shopping environment and a sample of participants balanced across demographic characteristics and previous experience with VR. Moreover, it uses both self-reported and implicit metrics gathered through eye- and hand-tracking system. The findings demonstrate the value of having those two sources of metrics to better understand consumer shopping behavior in a virtual reality setting.

Keywords: Virtual reality · Shopping behavior · Consumer behavior

1 Introduction

The perspective in retailing is changing from "what" to sell to "how" to sell [1]. Physical stores are superior in generating multisensory perceptions; however, digital technology can enhance customer experience by recreating many of those sensory experiences also in digital environments (e.g., e-commerce website) [2]. An important characteristic of virtual experiences is the possibility of user-medium interaction [3]. It has been recently suggested to adopt VR as a distribution channel [4–6]. Thus, retailers can use new technologies, such as virtual reality (VR) and augmented reality (AR), as a new touchpoint for their customers, aiming to improve customer experience by helping them accomplish a shopping goal, providing convenience, changing shopping habits [7]. As noted by Cowan and Ketron (p. 1603), "The world is becoming more virtual in all aspects of life, and more purchases are likely to occur virtually" [8], probably due to the convenience VR brings, in which it is possible to access a virtual store regardless the consumer physical location [5, 9]. With this new perspective in mind, this study intent to explore how consumers behave in virtual shopping tasks.

In the context of shopping, the extra possibilities provided by immersive virtual environments compared to traditional online shopping can raise the consumer's interest in using this tool [10]. What the impact of VR in physical stores is and whether it is a feasible tool for retailers are essential questions [9]. For example, the use of VR in the

© Springer Nature Switzerland AG 2020
P. Bourdot et al. (Eds.): EuroVR 2020, LNCS 12499, pp. 71–82, 2020.
https://doi.org/10.1007/978-3-030-62655-6_4

shopping process may differ depending on the customer journey stage. It is expected that VR stores are preferred over physical stores in the initial stages of the journey, while physical stores may be more relevant in the purchase step, where consumers seek to face the physical product [9]. As stated by Grewal et al. (p. 5), "the worlds of online and offline are converging. Knowing what is different and what is similar in these two worlds, as well as how new technologies are going to impact both, is key for the future of retailing" [11]. Furthermore, contrary to regular e-commerce websites, VR can produce situations not able to be experienced in real life, overcoming the limitations of VR experiences over physical shops (e.g., touching or tasting a product) [5]. As Farah et al. (p. 136) advise, "the prominence of VR in the world of retail and its impact on the demise of physical stores can no longer be overlooked nor placed at the back end of priorities" [9]. Supporting this view, a recent review about VR related to consumer research conducted by Wedel and colleagues emphasizes two central areas for retailing: VR used within an existent channel and VR as a new sales channel [12]. Based on it, research is needed to understand how consumers behave at the point of sale.

Considering that VR stores are being currently used to simulate real environments to derive conclusions of consumer behavior for applications in physical shops, and the potential they have in becoming a new sales channel, it is central that studies provide unbiased results. For example, many studies (i) evaluate only one product or only one product category and (ii) use participants that have never used VR before, (iii) with most of the samples formed by students; thus, a question that arises is whether the findings can be generalized across different products and populations. Attempting to provide some useful responses to this issue, this study aims to contribute to investigate the consumers' shopping behavior at the point of sale of a virtual reality supermarket. To address this issue, we conducted an exploratory, experimental study using an immersive VR shopping environment. We recruited a sample that is balanced across demographic characteristics and previous experience with VR, and investigated explicit and implicit metrics of consumer shopping behavior.

2 Background

Virtual reality is a valuable tool for academic research. By recreating realistic shopping simulations, it is possible to test, observe, and collect data in a controlled, low-cost, and fast way compared to experiments conducted in the field [6]. However, only recently that academic journals are the main mean of publications in VR and AR [13], showing how the area is still in their infancy in academia. The use of virtual environments in retailing research can give insights into in-store design and decision processes, and to the retail environment itself [3]. Review papers show that the application of VR in marketing research is mainly focused on gathering knowledge about consumer behavior [5] and, in the context of retailing, in assessing the impact of the technology within the existent channels [12]. Through a text-mining analysis of 150 articles in VR related to marketing, Loureiro et al. delineated four topic groups with more papers: (i) Experiential Marketing; (ii) Manufacturing and New Product Development; (iii) Virtual Setting; (iv) Interaction. Within the third topic, the main focus is on the store elements, such as music, lighting, layout, information cues, social presence [14].

In VR experiences, the concepts of sense of presence and immersion are crucial and positively highly correlated; however, their difference relies on that the former is the subjective perception of the user during the VR experience, while the latter is what the technology can deliver [14]. A VR environment that gives the feeling that the user is part of it is an immersive VR [14]. Immersive VR stores can replicate elements of physical sores, such as displays, the store layout, promotions, product assortment, prices [10], creating more valid assumptions of generalization of the findings to real-world consumption contexts [8]. Interactive features are able to create more enjoyable environments [15–20]. Besides, when virtual products can be manipulated, it increases perceived informativeness and playfulness of the shopping interface [17].

The impact of new technologies such as VR on the shopping process is still uncertain, which raises the need to investigate how and where those technologies are and will change the retailing field [11]. The marketing research in VR is scant, and immersive VR experiences are more favorable for future research due to the possibility of recreating real-world environments, hence, improving ecological validity [8]. Furthermore, the majority of the existing marketing academic research on VR relies on self-reported and explicit measures; yet, implicit responses are gaining the attention of the researchers [5]. Cowan and Ketron point out the use of eye-tracking with immersive VR tools as future potential research [8]. And the integration of eye-tracking into the VR system "offers a unique research opportunity" [3] (p. 445). However, scarce research has been developed using eye-tracking and navigation metrics as implicit measures of behavior response in a VR store.

Immersive devices can be combined with motion and orientation sensors and also eye-tracking systems [13]. There are low-cost body-motion tracking systems that permit to capture the natural behavioral responses of the users to the VR environment, and integrated eye-tracking tools that capture the gaze of the user, allowing inferences about the cognitive process employed during the experience [5]. Eye-tracking integrated with VR can help to understand in-store decision processes, assess the impact of the store elements to enhance store layout, and help consumers achieving better purchase decisions [3]. Moreover, as pointed by Wedel et al. [12], one relevant topic to understand consumer information processing in VR environments is how attention (bottom-up or top-down) is allocated in the virtual context.

Although VR with gaze tracking can bring valuable insights about a VR store environment and its elements, only a few studies are related to gaze tracking and service configuration [14]. Open questions are how immersive VR can bring knowledge to services and retailing by examining consumer shopping patterns using eye-tracking, touching interactions, and body position, and how virtual stores should be designed to be effective for retailers [8]. The inspection of how consumers interact with the shelves of a VR store can provide answers to not yet solved questions [3]. Additionally, moderators (e.g., socio-demographic, personality variables) are neglected in most of the VR studies related to marketing [14]. Also, "past experience with VR technologies should not be neglected as a moderator since the number of times VR is used could change the emotions and the sensation of novelty toward the technology" [14] (p. 526).

3 Method

3.1 Virtual Environment

A virtual supermarket with dimensions 6 m × 6 m was developed using the Unity3D development platform (Unity Technologies, San Francisco, USA) by the European Immersive Neurotechnology's Laboratory (LabLENI). The environment recreated two small sectors for the shelves of the products of interest: one for snacks and one for sneakers (Fig. 1). To recreate a more realistic scenario, the rest of the environment showed shelves with other grocery products (Fig. 2). Each shelf of the environment had three shelf levels: "up" (145 cm; eyes level), "middle" (90 cm; hands level), and "down" (25 cm; floor level). For the selves of interest, within each level, three products were displayed (left, center, and right), with a total of nine different products per shelf (Fig. 2). When a product was purchased, it vanished from the shelf, and participants could not see it anymore. The environment was divided into three zones of interest (ZOI; Fig. 1), namely: far, near, and adjacent, based on the proximity of the shelf of interest.

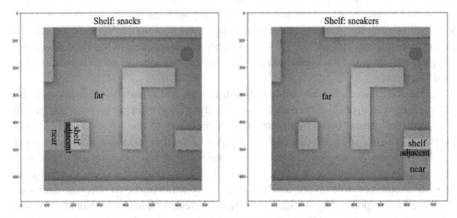

Fig. 1. The layout of the virtual supermarket and the definitions of the zones of interest (ZOI) for each task. Left: location of the snacks shelf and ZOI for Task 2. Right: location of the sneakers shelf and ZOI for Task 3. The blue circle represents the starting point for the tasks.

The products were chosen to represent a fast-moving consumer good (snacks) and a durable good (sneakers). The prices of the snacks ranged from 1.25 to 3.00 € (Fig. 2), and the sneakers from 115.00 to 180.00 €. The products and their prices were displayed in the same order and combination for all participants.

3.2 Design

A 3 – task (free navigation task, forced task snacks, forced task sneakers) – within-subjects design was implemented. For this study, we considered only the forced tasks. The variables under analysis are the explicit and implicit behavioral metrics detailed in Sect. 3.5.

Fig. 2. Representation of part of the virtual supermarket, shelf levels (up, middle, down), and distribution of the products and their prices. The shelf on the front: snacks shelf (Task 2).

3.3 Procedure and Tasks

The experiment was conducted at the LabLENI and approved by the local ethics committee. Participants arrived at the laboratory, signed an informed consent form, and answered a short questionnaire on pleasure and arousal (PA; short form of the PAD scale) in a laptop. After it, they wore the VIVE Pro headset (HTC Corporation, Taiwan) VR tool. This VR device is considered an immersive type of VR since the VR environment fully surrounds the person. After receiving the instructions about the equipment (device, controllers), the participants performed a familiarization and training task in a neutral environment to learn how to use the VIVE controllers to grab and purchase objects. Then they were virtually placed in the VR scenario at the start point (blue circle on Fig. 1). At this moment, calibration of the eye-tracking system was performed, followed by the instructions for the first task. The tasks were conducted in the same order for all participants, and they returned to the start point after each task to answer two questionnaires (PA and Hedonic and Utilitarian Shopping Values) and receive the instructions for the next task. The three tasks were as follows: (i) Task 1: Free Navigation Task. To familiarize with the VR environment [6], participants had up to four minutes to freely navigate and interact with the scenario; (ii) Task 2: Forced Task Snacks. Participants were informed they had a budget of 5 € and were instructed to find the snacks shelf and buy snacks; (iii) Task 3: Forced Task Sneakers. The same as Task 2, but with a limited budget of 180 € and having sneakers as the target product. The budget of Task 2 allowed the purchase of more than one snack pack, whereas in Task 3, only one sneaker could be bought. At the end of the experiment, participants answered a questionnaire on a laptop.

3.4 Participants

Sixty participants living in Spain (50% female; $M_{age} = 25.83$, $SD_{age} = 5.01$, age range: 20–36; 43% with no previous experience in VR); 45% workers, 45% students, 10% unemployed (following the advice of Loureiro et al. [14] to a recruit mixed sample). The age range was chosen to represent the group of potential users of the technology.

Participants were recruited via an external agency and monetarily compensated. The data were collected between October and November 2019.

3.5 Measures and Analysis

Here we define the measures provided by the questionnaire as "explicit" measures; and the measures obtained by the eye-tracking and body posture tracking system, as well as the measures of interaction with the VR scenario and navigation as "implicit" measures. The scales were adopted from the literature and slightly adapted for the current study and translated into Spanish. This experiment was part of a larger study, and not all data collected were used for this research.

We selected the following metrics: (i) explicit metrics: the rational and experiential dimensions of the Situation-Specific Thinking Styles (STSS) scale [21]; the pleasure dimension of the pleasure-arousal-dominance (PAD short form) scale [22]; the hedonic dimension of the Hedonic and Utilitarian Shopping Values (HUSV) scale [23]; the state dimension of the State-Trait Anxiety Inventory (STAI short form) scale [24]; the open-mindedness dimension of the Big Five Inventory (BFI-2 short form) [25]; cybersickness scale [26]; the sense of physical space and engagement dimensions of the Sense of Presence Inventory (ITC-SOPI) [27] (the "sense of physical presence" dimension was used as an indicator of the sense of presence in general). (ii) Implicit metrics: the number of objects picked and dropped (interaction metric; INT); the total time to complete the task (navigation metric; NAV); the time spent in each zone of interest (ZOI; NAV); the number of visits of the hand per shelf level (position metric; POS); the total time of the hands per shelf level (POS); the total distance (displacement) of the hands per shelf level (POS); the number of visits (eyes fixation) per shelf level (eye-tracking metric; ET); the total time looking at each shelf level (ET); the total distance (displacement) of the eyes per shelf level (ET).

The data were analyzed using SPSS 26.0 statistical software and Microsoft Excel 2016.

4 Results and Discussion

For the analysis of the explicit metrics, we averaged the questions within the same dimension of each scale. For the analysis of the implicit metrics, we combined and averaged the data of Task 2 and Task 3 into a single data point for each metric, as well as for the pleasure and hedonic shopping value scale (that were measured after each task).

Data of three participants were excluded due to technical recording errors of the eye-tracking system; hence, the final dataset comprised of 57 participants. Additionally, data of two other participants were partially excluded due to controller device failure.

4.1 Explicit Metrics

The reliability (Cronbach's alpha) and average scores of each scale or scale dimension are as follows: (i) the rational and experiential dimensions of the STSS scale: $\alpha_{rational}=$ .84 (10 five-point Likert items), $M_{rational}= 3.86, SD = 0.57$; $\alpha_{experiential}= .88$ (10 five-point Likert items), $M_{experiential}= 3.89, SD = 0.60$; the means above three indicate participants employed both a rational and experiential style while shopping. (ii) The pleasure dimension of the PAD scale: $\alpha = .96$ (four nine-point items), $M = 7.84, SD = 0.96$; the mean (above the middle-point 5) indicates participants felt a high level of pleasure after finishing the tasks. (iii) The hedonic dimension of the HUSV scale: $\alpha = .83$ (11 five-point Likert items), $M = 3.88, SD = 0.47$; the mean above three indicates the shopping task was perceived as a hedonic experience. (iv) The state dimension of the STAI: $\alpha = .69$ (four four-point Likert items), $M = 14.30, SD = 9.29$; the mean below 20 indicates participants felt no or little anxious after completing the tasks. (v) The open-mindedness dimension of the BFI-2: $\alpha = .71$ (six five-point Likert items), $M = 75.55, SD = 13.02$; the mean much above 50 indicates participants scored high in this dimension, showing they are open to new experiences. (vi) The cybersickness scale: $\alpha = .80$ (16 four-point items), $M = 1.21, SD = 0.21$; the mean below two indicates participants felt only a mild level of sickness after the experiment. The cybersickness measure was included following the advice given by Alcañiz et al. [5]. (vii) The sense of physical space and engagement dimensions of the SOPI: $\alpha_{SPS}= .89$ (10 five-point Likert items), $M_{SPS}= 3.92, SD = 0.46$; $\alpha_{eng}= .80$ (13 five-point Likert items), $M_{eng}= 4.20$, $SD = 0.39$; the means much above three indicate participants felt the VR environment as a physical space and felt highly engaged, pleasantly and enjoyably, with the VR experience.

The relationship between the variables under study was analyzed through a bivariate Pearson's correlation. Surprisingly, there was a moderate positive correlation between the rational and the experiential dimensions of the STSS scale $(r(55) = .48, p < .000)$. This is particularly interesting since it is expected that the metrics go in different directions, as they reflect oppose thinking styles. One possible explanation might be due to the VR environment and VR tool itself, which could have evoked high affective states, whereas the goal-oriented task might have induced a rational state. An indication for this is the significant relationship between engagement and the experiential dimension of the STSS $(r(55) = .34, p = .009)$, while no significant relationship was found for the rational dimension $(r(55) = .18, p = .169)$. Moreover, pleasure and hedonic shopping value were positively correlated $(r(55) = .40, p = .002)$, and both were correlated with engagement $(r(55) = .34, p = .009$ and $r(55) = .32, p = .014$, respectively).

The correlation between the engagement metric and the open-mindedness personality domain was not significant $(r(55) = -.15, p < .260)$. It could be expected that as higher the score for open-mindedness, higher would be the engagement with the VR experience, due to the definition of that domain. However, this was not the case. It seems that engagement is independent of how open a person is for new experiences. However, the sense of physical space was highly correlated with engagement $(r(55) = .75, p < .000)$, medium correlated with pleasure $(r(55) = .39, p < .002)$ and hedonic shopping $(r(55) = .32, p < .015)$, and negatively correlated with anxiety feelings (STAI-state) $(r(55) = -.28, p < .38)$. This latter find is thought-provoking. Although from this analysis it is not possible to claim a causal relationship, and the strength of the relationship is weak, it is relevant for future VR studies to investigate whether the perception of being in a physical environment while in a VR shopping environment decreases anxiety levels, or whether anxiety feelings decrease the perceived physicality of the shopping environment. Furthermore, the anxiety level was highly correlated with the cybersickness measurement ($r(55) = .71, p < .000$). This is also pertinent for VR applications since anxiety could provoke cybersickness feelings and/or the opposite could happen. Besides, cybersickness was negatively correlated with pleasure ($r(55) = -.50, p < .000$).

4.2 Implicit Metrics

A bivariate Pearson's correlation was conducted to analyze the relationship between the variables of interest. The variables represent the mean of the metrics of the two tasks combined (i.e., snacks and sneakers forced purchase). The correlation between the number of objects picked and dropped from a shelf is highly correlated with the time spent in the ZOI near ($r(53) = .72, p < .000$), but not with the ZOI far ($r(53) = . 15, p = .282$). Moreover, the metrics of "number of visits", "total time", and "total distance (displacement)" of the three shelf levels for both the hand and the eyes were medium to highly positively correlated to the number of objects picked and dropped (all $r > .40; p < .001$); and the highest correlations were found for the "shelf middle". All the metrics for the looking behavior (eyes) and the action behavior (hands) were medium to highly positively correlated among them within a shelf level (all $r > .40; p < .001$). This indicates that motor action is intrinsically related to visual behavior. We cannot state the direction of the relationship from the analysis; however, considering the nature of the actions, the most plausible explanation is that people tended to drive a motor action towards the place where the eyes were attending to. Furthermore, those metrics were significantly and positively correlated among the three shelf levels (all $p < .05$). This means that participants considered the entire shelf space while shopping in the VR environment, and the actions (driven by the eyes or hand) performed in one of the shelf levels positively impacted on the number of actions taken for the other levels.

The results of the differences in viewing and motor behavior across the shelf levels are summarized in Fig. 3. The analysis revealed that the middle shelf captured more visual attention (total fixation time), and the hands stayed there for longer (total hand time). Besides, participants moved their eyes (eyes total distance) and hands (hand total distance) more in the middle level compared to the other levels. This supports the common knowledge that central locations, in general, attract the most attention. Interestingly, the bottom shelf attracted equal levels of attention as the upper shelf. Considering that the upper shelf was at the eyes level, this finding is intriguing. It might be that in virtual environments, people tend to explore more the entire shelf. However, it seems this is valid for visual exploration and not physical exploration. The relative difference in the number of eyes and hands visits in the shelf down provides evidence that participants found it easier to direct their gaze to the bottom part of the shelf than their hands.

A further step was to correlate the explicit metrics (engagement with the VR environment and the use of experiential thinking style) with the implicit metrics (total time spent in the VR environment and number of objects picked and dropped). There was no

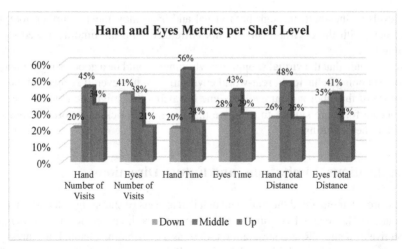

Fig. 3. Metrics for the hands and eye behavior per shelf level. The percentages represent the contribution of each shelf level per metric. Error bars were omitted for better visualization.

significant correlation between these explicit and implicit metrics. This is in line with the results found by Beatty and Elizabeth Ferrell, in which there was no support for the relationship between enjoyment and in-store browsing behavior [28].

5   Conclusions

The present study addressed the question of how consumers behave in the shopping experience in a VR supermarket. We analyzed implicit and explicit metrics of shopping behavior by combining the data of two forced purchase tasks: one involving a fast-moving consumer good (snacks) and the other a durable good (sneakers). The participants were given a budget and free time to complete each task, resembling real-life shopping circumstances.

The findings of this study showed that the immersive VR shopping environment of our experiment generated high levels of sense of physical space and engagement with the task while led to only a low level of cybersickness sensation. Moreover, we found that the sense of physical space of the VR environment is positively correlated with the level of engagement and pleasure with the VR experience and hedonic shopping. Furthermore, unexpectedly, participants reported both a rational and an experiential thinking style during the tasks. Noteworthy, our VR environment had a rather simple design compared to a real supermarket, and, even though, participants derived high levels of pleasure with the shopping experience and felt the ambient like a physical space.

Regarding the behavior measured thought the implicit metrics, the findings showed that the level of interaction with the products had a strong positive relationship with the time spent close to the shelf. Besides, the visual system and the motor system were closely related. More time spent looking to a product seemed to have induced more physical action towards the product. The findings also demonstrated the tendency of focusing attention on the central level of a shelf. Nevertheless, participants attended to all levels of the shelf, through both visual and hand movements. Furthermore, the engagement with the environment was not correlated with the time dedicated to the shopping task.

We conclude that the virtual shopping environment could be a good proxy for understanding shopping behavior in real-world environments; however, it seems that the virtual nature of the environment evokes some behaviors that might be context-specific. We advocate for more studies to compare this issue with brick and mortar settings or pure e-commerce settings.

6   Implications, Limitations, and Future Directions

This research demonstrated the main and detailed aspects of shopping behavior in a VR supermarket. The results have direct implications for both companies and academics. Irrespective of using VR as a simulation tool or as a distribution channel, we stress the importance of considering both explicit and implicit metrics, their intra- and inter-play relationship on consumers' shopping behavior. VR environments should produce sensations of real-life experience (i.e., high sense of physical space) with low adverse effects (i.e., cybersickness feelings) since both are correlated with high levels of engagement, pleasure, and hedonic shopping. Besides, we show that the time spent in the environment, specifically when a person is close to a shelf, is related to how much interaction that person will have with the products exposed. Thus, managers must promote strategies that lead consumers to stay longer in the store. Further analysis could investigate the relationship between the total time spent in the environment with a thorough examination of how consumers interact with the products. Moreover, since the results showed a tendency towards attention to central locations, we reinforce the importance of creating choice architecture actions that increase attraction to all the parts of a shelf to overcome the central bias tendency.

However, this study has limitations that could be addressed in future research. First, our VR supermarket had a simple design and did not replicate many aspects of real supermarkets, such as the level of product assortment, the use of branded products, the placement of communication and advertisement signs, the presence of other consumers, the presence of sounds. As stated by Burke (p. 78), "for the simulation to produce a valid measure of consumer behavior, it must accurately recreate these cues in the virtual store" [6]. Therefore, future research that aims to use VR as a simulation tool for real environments should incorporate those elements for studying shopping behavior in a more realistic setting. Second, we analyzed browsing behavior for each shelf-level; however, the lack of randomization of the products and prices might have influenced on the metrics, since some products can be more salient than others, capturing more attention. Future studies can overcome this problem by randomizing the products and price labels across the shelf levels. Another further avenue is to inspect if there are differences in shopping behavior depending on the type of the products, demographic and personality characteristics, and previous experience with VR.

Even if participants had low levels of cybersickness and low levels of anxiety on average in this study, it is relevant for future VR applications to investigate the direction of such relationship. Also, whether the perception of being in a physical space while in a VR shopping environment decreases anxiety levels, or whether anxiety feelings decrease the perceived physicality of the shopping environment. An exciting future direction that could shed light on those and other unexplored questions is to gather neurophysiological reactions, such as galvanic-skin-responses, heart-rate variability, and brain signals through electroencephalography while shopping.

Acknowledgments. The authors gratefully acknowledge the financial support of Rhumbo (European Union's Horizon 2020 research and innovation program under the Marie Skłodowska-Curie Grant Agreement No 813234).

References

1. Sachdeva, I., Goel, S.: Retail store environment and customer experience: a paradigm. J. Fash. Mark. Manag. **19**, 290–298 (2015)
2. Blázquez, M.: Fashion shopping in multichannel retail: the role of technology in enhancing the customer experience. Int. J. Electron. Commer. **18**, 97–116 (2014)
3. Meißner, M., Pfeiffer, J., Pfeiffer, T., Oppewal, H.: Combining virtual reality and mobile eye tracking to provide a naturalistic experimental environment for shopper research. J. Bus. Res. **100**, 445–458 (2019)
4. Martínez-Navarro, J., Bigné, E., Guixeres, J., Alcañiz, M., Torrecilla, C.: The influence of virtual reality in e-commerce. J. Bus. Res. **100**, 475–482 (2019)
5. Alcañiz, M., Bigné, E., Guixeres, J.: Virtual reality in marketing: a framework, review, and research agenda. Front. Psychol. **10**, 1530 (2019)
6. Burke, R.R.: Virtual reality for marketing research. In: Moutinho, L., Sokele, M. (eds.) Innovative Research Methodologies in Management, pp. 63–82. Springer, Cham (2018). https://doi.org/10.1007/978-3-319-64400-4_3
7. Grewal, D., Noble, S.M., Roggeveen, A.L., Nordfalt, J.: The future of in-store technology. J. Acad. Mark. Sci. **48**(1), 96–113 (2019). https://doi.org/10.1007/s11747-019-00697-z
8. Cowan, K., Ketron, S.: Prioritizing marketing research in virtual reality: development of an immersion/fantasy typology. Eur. J. Mark. **53**, 1585–1611 (2019)
9. Farah, M.F., Ramadan, Z.B., Harb, D.H.: The examination of virtual reality at the intersection of consumer experience, shopping journey and physical retailing. J. Retail. Consum. Serv. **48**, 136–143 (2019)
10. Lombart, C., et al.: Effects of physical, non-immersive virtual, and immersive virtual store environments on consumers' perceptions and purchase behavior. Comput. Hum. Behav. **110**, 106374 (2020)
11. Grewal, D., Roggeveen, A.L., Nordfält, J.: The future of retailing. J. Retail. **93**, 1–6 (2017)
12. Wedel, M., Bigné, E., Zhang, J.: Virtual and augmented reality: advancing research in consumer marketing. Int. J. Res. Mark. (2020). https://doi.org/10.1016/j.ijresmar.2020.04.004
13. Cipresso, P., Giglioli, I.A.C., Raya, M.A., Riva, G.: The past, present, and future of virtual and augmented reality research: a network and cluster analysis of the literature. Front. Psychol. **9**, 2086 (2018)
14. Loureiro, S.M.C., Guerreiro, J., Eloy, S., Langaro, D., Panchapakesan, P.: Understanding the use of virtual reality in marketing: a text mining-based review. J. Bus. Res. **100**, 514–530 (2019)
15. Childers, T.L., Carr, C.L., Peck, J., Carson, S.: Hedonic and utilitarian motivations for online retail shopping behavior. J. Retail. **77**, 511–535 (2001)

16. Cyr, D., Head, M., Ivanov, A.: Perceived interactivity leading to e-loyalty: development of a model for cognitive-affective user responses. Int. J. Hum. Comput. Stud. **67**, 850–869 (2009)
17. Kang, H.J., Shin, J., Ponto, K.: How 3D virtual reality stores can shape consumer purchase decisions: the roles of informativeness and playfulness. J. Interact. Mark. **49**, 70–85 (2020)
18. Kim, J., Fiore, A.M., Lee, H.-H.: Influences of online store perception, shopping enjoyment, and shopping involvement on consumer patronage behavior towards an online retailer. J. Retail. Consum. Serv. **14**, 95–107 (2007)
19. Lee, H.-H., Kim, J., Fiore, A.M.: Affective and cognitive online shopping experience. Cloth. Text. Res. J. **28**, 140–154 (2010)
20. Yim, M.Y.-C., Chu, S.-C., Sauer, P.L.: Is augmented reality technology an effective tool for E-commerce? An interactivity and vividness perspective. J. Interact. Mark. **39**, 89–103 (2017)
21. Novak, T.P., Hoffman, D.L.: The fit of thinking style and situation: new measures of situation-specific experiential and rational cognition. J. Consum. Res. **36**, 56–72 (2009)
22. Mehrabian, A., Russell, J.A.: An Approach to Environmental Psychology. MIT Press, Cambridge (1974)
23. Babin, B.J., Darden, W.R., Griffin, M.: Work and/or fun: measuring hedonic and utilitarian shopping value. J. Consum. Res. **20**, 644 (1994)
24. Buela-Casal, G., Guillén-Riquelme, A.: Short form of the spanish adaptation of the state-trait anxiety inventory. Int. J. Clin. Heal. Psychol. **17**, 261–268 (2017)
25. Soto, C.J., John, O.P.: Short and extra-short forms of the Big Five Inventory–2: The BFI-2-S and BFI-2-XS. J. Res. Pers. **68**, 69–81 (2017)
26. Lawson, B.: Motion sickness scaling. In: Hale, K.S., Stanney, K.M. (eds.) Handbook of Virtual Environments: Design, Implementation, and Applications, pp. 601–626. CRC Press (2014). https://doi.org/10.1201/b17360-30
27. Lessiter, J., Freeman, J., Keogh, E., Davidoff, J.: A cross-media presence questionnaire: the ITC-sense of presence inventory. Presence Teleoperators Virtual Environ. **10**, 282–297 (2001)
28. Beatty, S.E., Ferrell, M.E.: Impulse buying: modeling its precursors. J. Retail. **74**, 161–167 (1998)

Psychophysical Effects of Experiencing Burning Hands in Augmented Reality

Daniel Eckhoff[1]([envelope]) [iD], Alvaro Cassinelli[1] [iD], Tuo Liu[2] [iD],
and Christian Sandor[1] [iD]

[1] City University of Hong Kong, Kowloon, Hong Kong
daniel.eckhoff@gmail.com
[2] University of Oldenburg, Oldenburg, Germany

Abstract. Can interactive Augmented Reality (AR) experiences induce involuntary sensations through additional modalities? In this paper we report on our AR experience that enables users to see and hear their own hands burning while looking through a Video See-Through Head-Mounted Display (VST-HMD). In an exploratory study (n = 12, within-subject design), we investigated whether this will lead to an involuntary heat sensation based on visual and auditory stimuli. A think-aloud protocol and an AR presence questionnaire indicated that six out of twelve participants experienced an involuntary heat sensation on their hands. Despite no significant change of perceived anxiety, we found a significant increase in skin conductance during the experiment for all participants; participants who reported an involuntary heat sensation had higher skin conductance responses than participants who did not report a heat sensation. Our results support our initial hypothesis as we found evidence of cross-modal audiovisual-to-thermal transfers. This is an example of virtual synaesthesia, a sensation occurring when single-modal (or multi-modal) stimulus sets off the simultaneous sensation over other senses—involuntarily and automatically. We believe that our results contribute to the scientific understanding of AR induced synaesthesia as well as inform practical applications.

1 Introduction

Augmented Reality (AR) systems supplement the real world with virtual objects that appear to coexist in the same space as the real world [1]. The character Morpheus in the movie The Matrix (1999) posed the following questions: *"What is real? How do you define real?"*. These are simple yet profound questions. Recent technological advances have enabled content developers to create photorealistic graphics, making these questions increasingly important. In the near future, virtual objects in AR experiences may become barely distinguishable from real ones [35]. Already, AR experiences can induce significant feelings of presence, making people respond as they would in relation to real stimuli [38].

We hypothesize that AR experiences have the potential to fool various senses. Inspired by BurnAR by Weir et al. [42]; we set out to explore more deeply how

© Springer Nature Switzerland AG 2020
P. Bourdot et al. (Eds.): EuroVR 2020, LNCS 12499, pp. 83–95, 2020.
https://doi.org/10.1007/978-3-030-62655-6_5

AR experiences create involuntary sensations in alternate pathways. This is a form of synaesthesia—an individual sensation, occurring when a stimulus creates a simultaneous sensation on other sensory modalities [31]. The experiment described in this paper is creating virtual synaesthesia, which is induced by experiencing realistically burning hands in AR.

Our contribution is to show the physiological and psychological stress response of user's experiencing their own hands burning in AR. We are reporting about an exploratory user study that supports our initial hypothesis as we found some evidence of cross-modal audiovisual-to-thermal illusion. In spite of no significant change of perceived anxiety, we found a significant increase in skin conductance during the experiment. Moreover, participants who experienced involuntary heat sensations had a higher skin conductance response.

Insights from our experiment may be of significance in a neuroscientific or clinical context, as we were able to demonstrate a cross-modal audiovisual-to-thermal transfer using AR technology. This allows insights into the perceptual and cognitive effects of AR experiences. Significant work in this area has been previously done in the framework of VR, using avatars to provide a virtual proxy representation of the user's body. Our experiment departs from that research in that the AR setup integrates the real body into the experience.

2   Related Work

In this section, we summarize existing works that report on the induction of sensations (e.g., temperature, touch, smell, taste, sound) as a result of stimulation of the visual and auditory senses.

Cytowic [7] defined synaesthesia as an involuntary joining of the senses in which the real information of one sense is accompanied by a (virtual) perception in another sense. In addition to being involuntary, this additional perception is regarded by the synaesthete (a person experiencing synaesthesia) as real, often outside the body, instead of imagined in the mind's eye.

There has been several works reporting the occurrence of synaesthesia, sometimes called cross-modal illusions in virtual environments: Visual-to-haptic illusions in VR have been observed in psychological experiments [2,24]. An AR system called Hand-displacEMent-based Pseudo-haptics (HEMP) induces haptic sensations from purely visual input, using a VST-HMD to displace the visual representation of the user's hand dynamically [30]. Similar results from other research into cross-modal sensory illusions involve the visual, olfactory, and gustatory senses [27,28].

A more related approach is to present objects or effects which humans associate with ambient temperatures or thermal sensations: In a variation of the classic Rubber Hand Illusion, the rubber hand was hit with a strong light beam, resulting in thermal sensations of the participant's real hand [11]. Hoffman et al. [17] placed patients in a virtual environment depicting snow and ice and gave them the task of throwing snowballs when undergoing usually painful treatment for burn injuries. They could prove that this strategy significantly reduces pain-related brain activity.

This paper is a spiritual successor to BurnAR from Weir et al. [42]. In their demonstration the user can experience the illusion of seeing their own hands burning by looking through a VST-HMD. In a questionnaire-based user study, some of the participants reported an involuntary heat sensation in their hands. Several studies have used VR experiences to treat anxiety disorders in the form of VR Exposure Therapy (VRET) [23]. The immersive nature of the VR and AR [22] experiences can induce measurable stress responses. The main differences of our current paper are a more sophisticated experimental platform, as well as additional measurements of physiological effects (skin conductance) and psychological effects (perceived anxiety).

Several studies indicate that participants react to virtual stressors as if they were real [12]. Martens et al. [26] found that exposure to a realistic stressful situation in a VR elevator could increase physiological and subjective stress responses. Yeh et al. compared the VR and AR on induced anxiety using heart rate and skin conductance as indicators of anxiety. They found a significant increase in skin conductance and heart rate, but not in subjective anxiety [44].

The majority of publications investigates the sense of presence and immersion with VR systems [5,34,36,45]. Very few investigations have been done on AR systems, and even fewer on AR systems using VST-HMDs. Slater [38] proposed two orthogonal components that contribute to realistic responses in immersive VR systems: (1) "Being there", often called "presence", the quality of having a sensation of being in a real place. We call this place illusion (PI). (2) Plausibility illusion (PSI) refers to the illusion that the scenario being depicted is actually occurring. Place illusion/presence is an illusion that the user is located inside the rendered virtual environment. In the literature, this illusion has been referred to as the "sense of being there" in a virtual environment [34]. PSI is determined by the extent to which the system can produce events that directly relate to the participant, the overall credibility of the scenario being depicted in comparison with expectations. In the context of Slater's definition of presence, place illusion (PI), initially defined for VR systems, is not an illusion in AR. Thus, what remains to be satisfied for presence is the plausibility illusion to achieve presence. Previous work has demonstrated that the degree of presence is increased by using audio to enhance visual perception [8], and hence adding to the feeling of presence. Gandy et al. [14] investigated whether the findings from VR presence studies can be transferred to AR, as Slater's definitions of presence (PI, PSI) are initially defined for VR systems. They discuss a crucial difference between AR systems and VR systems: the ability of the participant to observe their own body and its movement in real-time, which is not available in VR. This results in a much stronger sense of "being there". Their work highlighted the differences in AR systems that need to be considered, from the use of physiological measures to the design of questionnaires to assess the participant's level of presence. Our work builds on the previous experiment by Weir et al. and demonstrates that increased realism alone can significantly heighten the synaesthetic experience, providing much more insight into the cross-modal illusions induced by AR experiences [43].

3   Experiment

We performed an exploratory study, that addresses the following three research questions: **RQ1:** Can the observation of virtual flames result in an involuntary heat sensation? **RQ2:** Do participants exhibit stress responses during the observation of virtual flames using subjective self-report and different physiological measures (skin conductance or heart rate)? **RQ3:** Do participants who report an involuntary heat sensation experience a higher level of presence and stress responses compared to participants who do not report it?

System Design. Our AR system will alter the perception of the user's body. Therefore, it needs to be capable of precise body tracking and recreating its volumetric representations in real-time. For this experiment, we only need to create volumetric representations of the user's hand, which we achieved with the Leap Motion sensor together with its SDK. The sensor was mounted on the headset (See Fig. 1 a)). The volumetric representation of the hand will be fed into our fire simulation software based on nVidia GameWorks nvflow, a voxel-based fluid simulation capable of creating a realistic interactive fire and smoke simulation. The nvflow-SDK was integrated into a custom-built version of the Unreal Engine. This simulation was later fine-tuned to provide a system response time of 11.1 ms (equals one frame in a 90fps system). The AR experience provides multiple sensory stimuli. To play auditory cues, we used the spatial audio system of the Unreal Engine for playing fire sound effects.

We use an HTC Vive Pro as a VST-HMD. The display has a resolution of 1440×1600 pixels, a refresh rate 90 Hz, and a field of view of $110°$. The dual front-facing cameras of the Vive Pro have a resolution of 480p at 90fps [18]. The Valve Lighthouse tracking system was used to track the headset. To achieve a video see-through mode, we used the HTC Vive SRWorks SDK.

Participants. We recruited twelve participants (six female, six male) from the staff and student population of the City University of Hong Kong. All participants were in the range of 20–32 years, with a mean age of 28.25 ± 3.7. The experiment had the approval of the ethics committee at our university.

Measures. We gathered stress responses of participants, both subjective (self-report) and objective (physiological measurements).

The state version of the State-Trait Anxiety Inventory (S-STAI) was used to measure perceived anxiety. This questionnaire consists of 20 items using a 4-point Likert scale [37]. A higher score represents a higher level of perceived anxiety. We deployed the questionnaire before and after the AR experience to assess a change of perceived anxiety.

Regarding the physiological level, the central part is the interaction between the sympathetic and parasympathetic branches in the autonomic nervous system. The most immediate stress response is related to the activation of the sympathetic branch and inhibition of the parasympathetic branch, which represents the 'fight or flight' mechanism obtained from human evolution [29]. The skin conductance level (SCL) is a good indicator of sympathetic activity [20]. It has been also shown, that it increases in response to psychological stress [20].

We used the BitAlino to measure physiological data[16]. We connected the BitAlino through electrodes to the participant. The device was mounted on an armband attached to the participant's left arm (See Fig. 1). We started logging three minutes before the experiment and stopped logging five minutes after the end of the experiment.

Questionnaires. To measure the level of presence and immersion, we have employed a customized questionnaire based on the AR presence questionnaire from Gandy et al. [14]. The presence questionnaire consists of 7 questions (e.g., "How natural did the fire appear on your left hand?") on a 7-point Likert scale (See Table 1). We added one question, where we asked the participant how strong they felt a heat sensation. For this questionnaire, the internal consistency was satisfactory, Cronbach's $\alpha = 0.78$, McDonald's $\omega = 0.78$. After the experiment, we collected basic demographic data, including gender and age.

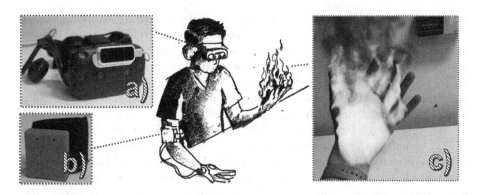

Fig. 1. Experimental platform. **a)** HTC Vive Pro, a VST-HMD, with attached Leap Motion. **b)** BitAlino, measuring various bio-markers, worn by the participant on an armband. The device measures biomarkers through electrodes placed on the participant's hand. **c)** The fire as a visual stimuli appearing in the participants hand.

Procedures. Before the experiment began, all participants were provided with information sheets and consent forms, containing basic information about the experiment. However, we never mentioned that they would see a virtual fire on their left hand, as we did not want to influence the outcome.

The data collection for the questionnaires was divided into two parts, i.e, before and after the AR experience. Physiological data (HR and GSR) was recorded continuously. We recorded for an additional three minutes after the participants put on their headset to take a baseline, as putting up a headset might result in techno-stress [32].

These self-report questionnaires are needed to determine the influence of the burning hand experiment on the participant's subjective anxiety level. Before the start of the experiment, the first set of questionnaires was given to the participant (demographic, S-STAI). After the participant gave consent and filled all questionnaires, the experimenter set up all devices for collecting the physiological measurements. During the experiment, the participants were seated at a table, which would allow them to rest their arm. The experimenter helped the participant to put on the HMD. The participants were asked to sit still, but were allowed to move their left hand as long as it stayed in the field of view of the HMD. A camera started recording after correct placement of the headset. After three minutes of baseline recording the virtual fire appeared on the participant's left hand. The fire stopped five minutes later, and the experience ended. The headset was removed, and all connected devices detached. After that, participants filled out a second S-STAI and the AR presence questionnaire.

4   Results

We observed that six out of 12 participants reported a strong involuntary heat sensation on their left hand in the self-report questionnaire. We counted a value higher than five as a positive heat sensation. We divided the participants into two groups based on their responses using the method of median split [19]: **Group A**, in which participants have felt an involuntary heat-sensation on their left hand during the AR experience; **Group B** in which participants did not feel a heat sensation on their left hand.

We processed electrodermal activity (EDA) and the electrocardiogram (ECG) signals using NeuroKit [25]. Due to noisy measurements, we decided to rely solely on SCL signals for our analysis and conclusions. EDA signals contain two components: a tonic component, the SCL, which varies slowly in time, and a shorter phasic component, called the skin conductance response (SCR), which changes quickly over time [9]. According to Braithwaite [3], averaging across the whole signal will over-estimate the SCL. One solution is subtracting the amplitudes of SCRs from the tonic signal and then establishing a true score of SCL. Hence, we used the cvxEDA algorithm proposed by Greco et al. [15] to decompose the signal to the tonic (SCLl) and phasic (SCR) components.

The following time windows were considered: the baseline time (30s after setting up the headset and before the virtual fire appeared); three intervals during the AR experience: the first third of the total time (early stage), the second third of the total time (middle stage), and the third of the total time (late stage). We normalized the score using a log transformation and then averaged only the SCL scores within each time window.

In the following we present both descriptive and inferential statistical analysis based on our research questions. As this is an exploratory study, we did not conduct a priori power analysis to analyze the sample size. Both statistic tests were carried out using the open source statistics software JASP [21].

Table 1. Results of our AR Presence questionnaire.

Questions	Group A Mean	Group B Mean	All participants Mean	Min	Max
1. In the application, did you feel like an observer or a participant?	5.83 ± 0.98	5.83 ± 0.98	5.83 ± 0.94	4	7
2. How natural did the fire appear on your left hand?	5.33 ± 0.52	5.17 ± 1.33	5.25 ± 0.97	3	7
3. How aware were you of events occurring in the real world around you?	4.00 ± 1.41	4.50 ± 2.17	4.25 ± 1.76	1	7
4. How comfortable did you feel interacting with the fire?	5.67 ± 1.21	6.00 ± 0.89	5.83 ± 1.03	4	7
5. How much did the visual display quality interfere or distract you from interacting with the fire?	3.33 ± 1.86	3.83 ± 2.48	3.58 ± 2.11	1	7
6. How much delay did you experience between your actions and expected outcomes?	3.33 ± 0.82	2.50 ± 1.87	2.92 ± 1.44	1	6
7. Was the information provided through sight consistent with your other senses?	5.50 ± 0.55	5.17 ± 1.72	5.33 ± 1.23	2	7

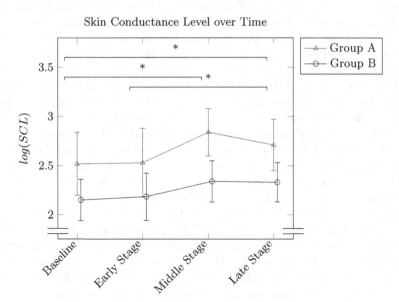

Fig. 2. Log transformed SCL of Group A (reported a heat sensation) and Group B (no heat sensation) over time. Error bars denote the standard error. Connected bars represent significant differences ($p < 0.001$).

4.1 Analysis

Skin Conductance Level. We processed the EDA signals using the NeuroKit package in Python [25]. We used the cvxEDA algorithm proposed by Greco et al. [15] to decompose the signal to the tonic (SCL) and phasic (skin conductance response SCR) components.

We examined the SCL at baseline, early stage, middle stage, and late-stage using a repeated-measures analysis of variance (RM-ANOVA) with time as a within-subject factor. For the frequentist RM-ANOVA, the Greenhouse-Geisser correction was used due to the violation of sphericity ($\chi 2(5) = 18.46, p = .003$). The result showed a significant within-subject effect of time, ($F(1.35, 15.56) = 9.11, p = .005, \eta 2p = 0.45$). A high Bayes factor ($BF10 = 145.55$) also decisively supports this outcome using Bayesian RM-ANOVA. This results shows a changing of SCL between different time points.

In post hoc tests with an applied Bonferroni correction, we found significant differences between the baseline and the middle stage, ($t(11) = 4.36, p < .001$), between the baseline and late stage, ($t(11) = 3.21, p = .018$) and between the early stage and middle stage, ($t(11) = 3.98, p < .002$). The Bayes factor showed strongly ($BF10 = 30.96$) substantial ($BF10 = 8.06$ and $BF10 = 5.39$) support, respectively. In general, these results showed an increase of the SCL from baseline to the middle stage. Notably, the difference between early stage and late stage is just significant, ($t(11) = 2.83, p = .047$), while the Bayes factor only indicates an small evidence to support, ($BF10 = 1.63$). In contrast, despite the lack of statistical significance ($t(11) = -1.15, p = .275$), the Bayes Factor nearly substantial supported a decrease of the SCL from the middle stage to late stage, ($BF01 = 2.38$). This results suggest a descending trend back to the early stage of the SCL over time when participants became used to the exposure.

A mixed-ANOVA test with the within-subjects factor time and the between-subjects factor heat sensation was conducted (see Fig. 2). We used the Greenhouse-Geisser correction to adjust the biased result because of the violation of sphericity ($\chi^2(5) = 19.93, p = .001$). We found the main effect of within-subjects factor time was also significant, ($F(1.35, 13.51) = 8.88, p = .007, \eta 2p = 0.30$) and a decisive evidence-based the Bayesian statistics, ($BF10 = 145.55$). In contrast to the result in descriptive statistic, the interaction effect between the within-subjects factor time and the between-subjects factor heat sensation was non-significant, ($F(1.35, 13.51) = 0.71, p = .45$). However, the Bayes factor based on the model comparison just showed slightly over substantial evidence to the null hypothesis (without this interaction), ($BF10 = 0.25, BF01 = 4.08$). Furthermore, we compared the SCL in the middle stage using an independent t-test. The results show a non-significant higher score in Group A, ($t(10) = 1.55, p = .15, BF10 = 0.96, BF01 = 1.04$). No significant differences were found for age and gender.

Presence. In order to test if there was a significant difference between the two groups in terms of presence, we used an independent t-test that contrasted the summed score of presence and immersion between Group A and B. The questions and results are shown in Table 1. Because of the violation of equality of variance,

$(F(1,2) = 11.92, p = .006)$, the result was reported using Welch's correction: We found a non-significant difference between the two groups, $(t(6.14) = 0.18, p = .864)$. However, the Bayes factor gave an anecdotal support to no difference, $(BF10 = 0.47, BF01 = 2.12)$.

Subjective Level of Stress Response. Overall, a paired t-test revealed no significant differences $(p = 0.08)$ in self-reported anxiety through the S-STAI questionnaire before and after the experiment.

5 Discussion

Our exploratory study has produced three key findings: **1)** Half of the participants report a cross-modal heat illusion: they experienced heat on their left hand, induced through purely visual and acoustic stimuli from our AR experience in the absence of a real heat source. **2)** In spite of no significant change of perceived anxiety at subjective level, we discovered a significant increase in skin conductance when the participants observed their left hand burning in our AR experience. **3)** Participants who reported experiencing this illusion had a higher skin conductance response compared to the participants who did not report experiencing it. The following three paragraphs discuss our hypothesis in light of these results.

RQ1: Can the observation of virtual flames result in an involuntary heat sensation? We observed that six out of twelve participants reported an involuntary heat sensation in the form of cross-modal audiovisual-to-thermal transfers. However, it is still unknown which variables are responsible for inducing cross-modal illusions in Augmented Reality. One of the external factors could have been the high plausibility, as we designed the fire simulation to make it look, behave and sound as realistic as possible. But we are unsure how much that contributed to the cross-modal illusion. Would an unrealistic fire also induce heat sensations? Other external factors might involve the technical aspects of the AR system, for example, it might be harder to induce cross-modal illusions if the headset would feature a high latency or low resolution. Other than the AR system and the plausibility of the simulation, we hypothesize that various internal factors of the participant's personality play an important role. Personality traits already have been shown to have a significant impact on presence and immersion [33,41] and sense of embodiment [10].

RQ2: Do participants exhibit stress responses during the observation of virtual flames using subjective self-report and different physiological measures (skin conductance or heart rate)? We found a significant increase in participant's skin conductance observing their hands burning in our AR experience. The systematical change of skin conductance shows evidence of a real stress response induced by our experiment. In other words, this result shows that participant's reaction elicit physiological mechanisms similar to those engaged when exposed to real world stressors. However, we did not find a significant change of perceived anxiety or stress at the subjective level. This result matches the study by Yeh et al. [44], but not the results of [12,26]. One possible explanation is that stress response is not regarded as a unitary construct in the field of psychophysiology; instead, it includes multiple interacting components [40]—subjective, physiological, and behavioral effects of threat and challenge appraisal [39]. So a dissociation between the subjective emotional component and physiological component is possible, thus making these results not directly comparable.

RQ3: Do participants who report an involuntary heat sensation experience a higher level of presence and stress responses compared to participants who do not report it? Overall, based on our AR presence questionnaire (See Table 1), the level of presence did not correlate to the intensity of the observed cross-modal illusion. Since we observed a high level of presence through all participants, we believe that our AR system, especially our tracking and fire simulation, leads to an illusion experienced as highly plausible. Some participants noted the high realism and fidelity of our fire simulation. Moreover, participants who experienced an involuntary heat sensation had a higher skin conductance response. One possible reason is the small sample size in our study, making it difficult to find significant results due to the lack of statistical power [13].

6   Conclusions and Future Work

This paper describes the design, implementation, and evaluation of an AR experience that enables users to see their own hands burning. We showed in an exploratory user study that it is possible to use AR to induce an involuntary cross-modal sensation in some individuals, without direct sensory stimulation. We also discovered that participants that experienced an involuntary cross-modal sensation in our AR experience, had a higher skin conductance response than participants who did not.

We suggest that in a future user study, the plausibility of the AR experience could be made an independent, controlled variable. This could be the control of the level of realism of the fire (e.g., color, level of interaction) or external factors of the AR system (e.g., system latency, display refresh rate, resolution ..). As audio can enhance the immersion in VR or plausibility in AR [8], we will look into ways to integrate real-time fire-like sound synthesis (such as [4]) into our system. Our experimental setup did not allow the participants a huge degree of freedom due to the reliance of electrodes. We recommend that in future studies, more non-invasive ways to measure biometric data to be used. For example, Collins et al. used a wristband to measure SCL and ECG data, allowing participants to move freely [6]. We chose to use AR for this experiment, as there already have been a big number of experiments conducted using VR to examine presence, embodiment and cross-modal illusions. However, it is still not clear, whether this experiment would lead to the same results in VR. This could be examined in a future study. To further answer the question of why only some participants experience a thermal sensation from the audiovisual input provided by our system, we want to additionally explore how important personality traits are in explaining the emergence and strength of these AR-based cross-modal illusions.

References

1. Azuma, R., Baillot, Y., Behringer, R., Feiner, S., Julier, S., MacIntyre, B.: Recent advances in augmented reality. IEEE Comput. Graph. Appl. **21**(6) (2001). https://doi.org/10.1109/38.963459
2. Biocca, F., Jin, K., Choi, Y.: Visual touch in virtual environments: an exploratory study of presence, multimodal interfaces, and cross-modal sensory illusions. Presence: Teleoperators Virtual Environ. **10**(3), 247–265 (2001). https://doi.org/10.1162/105474601300343595
3. Braithwaite, J., Watson, D., Robert, J., Mickey, R.: A guide for analysing electrodermal activity (EDA) & skin conductance responses (SCRs) for psychological experiments. Psychophysiology **49**, 1017–1034 (2013).
4. Chadwick, J.N., James, D.L.: Animating fire with sound. ACM Trans. Graph. (TOG) **30**(4), 1–8 (2011)
5. Coelho, C., Tichon, J., Hine, T.J., Wallis, G., Riva, G.: Media presence and inner presence: the sense of presence in virtual reality technologies. Emerging Communication: Studies in New Technologies and Practices in Communication, vol. 9, pp. 25–45 (2012)
6. Collins, J., Regenbrecht, H., Langlotz, T., Can, Y.S., Ersoy, C., Butson, R.: Measuring cognitive load and insight: a methodology exemplified in a virtual reality learning context. In: Proceedings - 2019 IEEE International Symposium on Mixed and Augmented Reality, ISMAR 2019, Beijing, China, pp. 351–362. IEEE (2019). https://doi.org/10.1109/ISMAR.2019.00033
7. Cytowic, R.E.: Synesthesia: A Union of the Senses. MIT Press, London (2002)
8. Davis, E.T., Scott, K., Pair, J., Hodges, L.F., Oliverio, J.: Can audio enhance visual perception and performance in a virtual environment? In: Proceedings of the Human Factors and Ergonomics Society Annual Meeting, vol. 43, no. 22, pp. 1197–1201 (1999). https://doi.org/10.1177/154193129904302206
9. Dawson, M.E., Schell, A.M., Filion, D.L.: The electrodermal system. In: Handbook of Psychophysiology, Fourth Edition, pp. 217–243. Cambridge University Press, New York (2017). https://doi.org/10.1017/9781107415782.010
10. Dewez, D., et al.: Influence of personality traits and body awareness on the sense of embodiment in virtual reality. In: Proceedings - 2019 IEEE International Symposium on Mixed and Augmented Reality, ISMAR 2019, Beijing, China, pp. 123–134. IEEE (2019). https://doi.org/10.1109/ISMAR.2019.00-12
11. Durgin, F.H., Evans, L., Dunphy, N., Klostermann, S., Simmons, K.: Rubber hands feel the touch of light. Psychol. Sci. **18**(2), 152–157 (2007). https://doi.org/10.1111/j.1467-9280.2007.01865.x
12. Felnhofer, A., Kothgassner, O.D., Hetterle, T., Beutl, L., Hlavacs, H., Kryspin-Exner, I.: Afraid to be there? Evaluating the relation between presence, self-reported anxiety, and heart rate in a virtual public speaking task. Cyberpsychol. Behav. Soc. Netw. **17**(5), 310–316 (2014). https://doi.org/10.1089/cyber.2013.0472
13. Gallagher, E.J.: No proof of a difference is not equivalent to proof of no difference. J. Emerg. Med. **12**(4), 525–527 (1994)

14. Gandy, M., et al.: Experiences with an AR evaluation test bed: presence, performance, and physiological measurement. In: 9th IEEE International Symposium on Mixed and Augmented Reality 2010: Science and Technology, ISMAR 2010 - Proceedings, Seoul, Korea, pp. 127–136. IEEE (2010). https://doi.org/10.1109/ISMAR.2010.5643560

15. Greco, A., Valenza, G., Lanata, A., Scilingo, E.P., Citi, L.: CvxEDA: a convex optimization approach to electrodermal activity processing. IEEE Trans. Biomed. Eng. **63**(4), 797–804 (2016). https://doi.org/10.1109/TBME.2015.2474131

16. Guerreiro, J., Martins, R., da Silva, H., Lourenco, A., Fred, A.: BITalino: a multimodal platform for physiological computing. In: ICINCO 2013 - Proceedings of the 10th International Conference on Informatics in Control, Automation and Robotics, Reykjavík, Iceland, vol. 1, pp. 500–506. INSTICC (2013)

17. Hoffman, H.G., et al.: Modulation of thermal pain-related brain activity with virtual reality: evidence from fMRI. NeuroReport **15**(8), 1245–1248 (2004). https://doi.org/10.1097/01.wnr.0000127826.73576.91

18. HTC: HTC Vive pro (2020). https://www.vive.com/hk/product/vive-pro/

19. Iacobucci, D., Posavac, S.S., Kardes, F.R., Schneider, M.J., Popovich, D.L.: Toward a more nuanced understanding of the statistical properties of a median split. J. Consum. Psychol. **25**(4), 652–665 (2015). https://doi.org/10.1016/j.jcps.2014.12.002

20. Jacobs, S.C., et al.: Use of skin conductance changes during mental stress testing as an index of autonomic arousal in cardiovascular research. Am. Heart J. **128**(6 Part 1), 1170–1177 (1994). https://doi.org/10.1016/0002-8703(94)90748-X

21. JASP Team: JASP (Version 0.12.2). https://jasp-stats.org/

22. Juan, M.C., Alcañiz, M., Monserrat, C., Botella, C., Baños, R.M., Guerrero, B.: Using augmented reality to treat phobias. IEEE Comput. Graphics Appl. **25**(6), 31–37 (2005). https://doi.org/10.1109/MCG.2005.143

23. Krijn, M., Emmelkamp, P.M., Olafsson, R.P., Biemond, R.: Virtual reality exposure therapy of anxiety disorders: a review (2004). https://doi.org/10.1016/j.cpr.2004.04.001

24. Lecuyer, A., Coquillart, S., Kheddar, A., Richard, P., Coiffet, P.: Pseudo-haptic feedback: can isometric input devices simulate force feedback? In: Proceedings - Virtual Reality Annual International Symposium, New Brunswick, NJ, US, pp. 83–90. IEEE (2000). https://doi.org/10.1109/vr.2000.840369

25. Makowski, D.: NeuroKit: A Python Toolbox for Statistics and Neurophysiological Signal Processing (EEG, EDA, ECG, EMG...) (2016)

26. Martens, M.A., Antley, A., Freeman, D., Slater, M., Harrison, P.J., Tunbridge, E.M.: It feels real: physiological responses to a stressful virtual reality environment and its impact on working memory. J. Psychopharmacol. **33**(10), 1264–1273 (2019). https://doi.org/10.1177/0269881119860156

27. Nambu, A., Narumi, T., Nishimura, K., Tanikawa, T., Hirose, M.: Visual-olfactory display using olfactory sensory map. In: Proceedings - IEEE Virtual Reality, Waltham, Massachusetts, USA, pp. 39–42. IEEE (2010). https://doi.org/10.1109/VR.2010.5444817

28. Narumi, T., Nishizaka, S., Kajinami, T., Tanikawa, T., Hirose, M.: Augmented reality flavors: gustatory display based on Edible Marker and cross-modal interaction. In: Conference on Human Factors in Computing Systems - Proceedings, Vancouver, Canada, pp. 93–102. ACM SIGCHI (2011). https://doi.org/10.1145/1978942.1978957

29. Pinel, J.P.J.: Biopsychology of Emotion. Stress and Health (2011)

30. Pusch, A., Martin, O., Coquillart, S.: HEMP-hand-displacement-based pseudo-haptics: a study of a force field application and a behavioural analysis. Int. J. Hum. Comput. Stud. **67**(3), 256–268 (2009). https://doi.org/10.1016/j.ijhcs.2008.09.015

31. Rogowska, A.: Categorization of synaesthesia. Rev. General Psychol. **15**(3), 213–227 (2011). https://doi.org/10.1037/a0024078

32. Saha, D.P., Knapp, R.B., Martin, T.L.: Affective feedback in a virtual reality based intelligent supermarket. In: UbiComp/ISWC 2017 - Adjunct Proceedings of the 2017 ACM International Joint Conference on Pervasive and Ubiquitous Computing and Proceedings of the 2017 ACM International Symposium on Wearable Computers, Maui, Hawai'i, USA, pp. 646–653. ACM (2017). https://doi.org/10.1145/3123024.3124426

33. Samana, R., Wallach, H.S., Safir, M.P.: The impact of personality traits on the experience of presence. In: 2009 Virtual Rehabilitation International Conference, VR 2009, Haifa, Israel, pp. 1–7. IEEE (2009). https://doi.org/10.1109/ICVR.2009.5174197

34. Sanchez-Vives, M.V., Slater, M.: From presence to consciousness through virtual reality (2005). https://doi.org/10.1038/nrn1651

35. Sandor, C., et al.: Breaking the barriers to true augmented reality. CoRR abs/1512.05471 (2015). http://arxiv.org/abs/1512.05471

36. Slater, M., Steed, A.: A virtual presence counter. Presence: Teleoperators Virtual Environ. **9**(5), 413–434 (2000). https://doi.org/10.1162/105474600566925

37. Spielberger, C.D.: State-Trait Anxiety Inventory (2010). https://doi.org/10.1002/9780470479216.corpsy0943

38. Steptoe, W., Steed, A., Slater, M.: Human tails: ownership and control of extended humanoid avatars. IEEE Trans. Vis. Comput. Graph. **19**(4), 583–590 (2013). https://doi.org/10.1109/TVCG.2013.32. https://doi.org/10.2312/egve.20151320

39. Tomaka, J., Blascovich, J., Kelsey, R.M., Leitten, C.L.: Subjective, physiological, and behavioral effects of threat and challenge appraisal. J. Pers. Soc. Psychol. **65**(2), 248–260 (1993). https://doi.org/10.1037/0022-3514.65.2.248

40. Tomaka, J., Palacios, R., Schneider, K.T., Colotla, M., Concha, J.B., Herrald, M.M.: Assertiveness predicts threat and challenge reactions to potential stress among women. J. Pers. Soc. Psychol. **76**(6), 1008–1021 (1999). https://doi.org/10.1037/0022-3514.76.6.1008

41. Weibel, D., Wissmath, B., Mast, F.W.: Immersion in mediated environments: the role of personality traits. Cyberpsychol. Behav. Soc. Netwo. **13**(3), 251–256 (2010). https://doi.org/10.1089/cyber.2009.0171

42. Weir, P., et al.: Burnar: involuntary heat sensations in augmented reality. In: Proceedings - IEEE Virtual Reality, Orlando, Florida, pp. 43–46. IEEE (2013). https://doi.org/10.1109/VR.2013.6549357

43. Weir, P.C.: Effects of Augmented Reality on Bodily Perception, October 2013

44. Yeh, S.C., Li, Y.Y., Zhou, C., Chiu, P.H., Chen, J.W.: Effects of virtual reality and augmented reality on induced anxiety. IEEE Trans. Neural Syst. Rehabil. Eng. **26**(7), 1345–1352 (2018)

45. Youngblut, C.: What a decade of experiments reveals about factors that influence the sense of presence. Technical report, Institute for Defense Analyses Alexandria VA (2006)

Training, Teaching and Learning

Integrating Virtual Reality in a Lab Based Learning Environment

Nils Höhner[1][(✉)], Mark Oliver Mints[1], Julien Rodewald[1], Anke Pfeiffer[2],
Kevin Kutzner[2], Martin Burghardt[1], David Schepkowski[1],
and Peter Ferdinand[1]

[1] Knowledge Media Institute, University of Koblenz-Landau, Koblenz, Germany
nhoehner@uni-koblenz.de
[2] University of Applied Sciences Stuttgart, Stuttgart, Germany
anke.pfeiffer@hft-stuttgart.de

Abstract. In engineering education, practical laboratory experience is essential and typically universities own expensive laboratory facilities that are deeply embedded in their curricula. Based on a comprehensive requirements analysis in a design based research approach, we have created a virtual clone of an existing RFID (radio-frequency identification) laboratory with the aim of integrating it into an existing teaching and learning scenario. The resulting application prepares students for real experiments by guiding them through the process assisted by an avatar. We have had our application tested in a qualitative evaluation by students as well as experts and we assess which design decisions have a positive impact on the learning experience. Our results suggest that the appearance of the environment, the avatar and the interactions of our virtual reality application have a strong motivational character but a closer content-wise link of the virtual and real experiments is crucial for students to perceive the application as part of the learning environment.

1 Introduction

In engineering education practical laboratory experience has always been of great importance as essential preparation for professional careers of prospective engineers [12,27] and as a requirement for the education on IoT and I4.0 [2]. Already in the 90s and before, much attention was paid to the research and development of virtual reality applications. Especially in the industrial sector they were particularly well received, but could not establish themselves in the practical workaday world [7]. However, the technology matured in recent years resulting in many useful applications in aforementioned areas [6]. It is therefore not surprising that the number of virtual training and education scenarios is increasing since providing practical learning scenarios results in high costs due to expensive laboratory equipment and the requirement of specialised supervisors to monitor trainees. Additionally laboratories are not constantly open and most of the equipment is left unused [28]. In contrast virtual reality hardware is relatively cheap and

P. Bourdot et al. (Eds.): EuroVR 2020, LNCS 12499, pp. 99–114, 2020.
https://doi.org/10.1007/978-3-030-62655-6_6

Fig. 1. Overview of the virtual RFID laboratory. One can see the transponders and the avatar (*left*). In addition, the actual measuring chamber (*background*) and the PC including the input hologram can be seen (*right*).

allows multiple students to experience experiments from home to any given time while being reusable throughout different applications as they are not tied to specific scenarios.

Many universities own specialized laboratories and equipment that is deeply integrated into the existing curricula. Typically the learning scenarios include hands-on experiments and offer situated learning experiences which are hard to replace with computer simulations. Virtual reality, however, offers a immersive and more realistic way to interact with digital clones and allows for similar didactical methods [1,16]. Due to haptic aspects and typically occurring noise of real life experimenting it is not desired to replace whole lectures or laboratory exercises with virtual reality. Therefore we want to explore the possibilities of supplementing an existing laboratory learning environment in the sense of Bell et al. [3] and to benefit from reported potential of VR-Technology in education [19]. This means not only creating an independently usable, thematically fitting scenario, but also integrating the application into the existing didactical context while keeping the overall learning objectives in mind. For this purpose we conducted a requirements analysis of an existing laboratory learning scenario at the University of Applied Sciences Stuttgart. Based on that we decided to create a true to size digital clone of a RFID laboratory including a RFID measuring chamber, which serves as a preliminary exercise for the visit to the real laboratory (see Fig. 1). In the application, students are guided through the process by a robot themed avatar and learn the basics necessary to perform experiments by themselves. This includes theoretical basics as well as typical lab procedures, the use of different control elements and the handling of the measurement software. It is of particular interest to see the potential of the virtual lab in relation to its real counterpart. In this context, we want to find out whether students and teachers are able to establish a connection between both and whether their learning benefits from this connection. This includes spatial and optical recognition, motivating aspects as well as the transfer of what has been learned. We want to find out which factors promote this connection and where things can be improved, both in terms of content and technology. Thus we evaluated our application qualitatively with four experts, two on RFID and two on didactics and tested it with two bachelor students.

Training Scenarios and Education in Virtual Reality

The potential of virtual reality (VR) in the teaching and training of engineering subjects was recognized early on. Research works by Bell et al. [4,5] in the mid-90s show first successful experiments with a virtual 3D environment of a chemical laboratory. The aim of this was to create an opportunity for undergraduate students to deal with the subject matter of teaching in a practical, though limited way, without having to spend time in a laboratory. Furthermore, it was investigated which properties of VR as a learning tool are particularly effective for teaching. As a result, a ten-point guideline based on the findings of evaluations of previous work was drawn up, which describes how the development of teaching in VR should be implemented [3].

In the last years many specific training and education scenarios emerged in areas like construction [23], aviation [11], geology [26], architecture [21] and medicine [25], which indicates the potential and versatility of virtual reality training. Especially in engineering education application-oriented as well as safety-relevant topics are relevant. Carruth [10] for example created an industrial workspace in which two training scenarios are provided. One is concerned with learning the operation of tools in an industrial environment while the other focuses on safety training. The aim is to give low-skilled or novice workers fundamental knowledge about the use and dangers of available tools. In the work of Winther et al. [24] a virtual reality assembly scenario was presented in which the user had to assemble a pump system. They offer haptic as well as visual feedback to guide users through the assembly task. Their application was compared to video and pairwise hands-on training. Whilst the VR trainees successfully learned how to assemble the pump, both the hands-on and video trained users showed better results.

In contrast to the specific training scenarios, the virtual laboratories offer less step-by-step instructions and more freedom. Wang et al. [22] propose a microfabrication laboratory training system where users are able to learn self-regulated with an automatic hint system how to use different machines.

2   Creating a Virtual Laboratory

We want to learn about the potential of the virtual clone in terms of replacing or complementing the practical learning experience in engineering education. To draw meaningful conclusions, the real-life learning experience as a whole should be recreated as close as possible.

The creation of the virtual RFID laboratory followed a design based research approach, so we improved it in several iterations. First, a requirements analysis was carried out in which a basic scenario description was given and expert interviews were conducted [8]. As a second step we created a working prototype and evaluated it with two logistics experts using the valence method [9]. Afterwards we derived the structure and the requirements of the virtual scenario from all results. In the following section we describe the result of the requirements analysis, followed by the major results of the expert interviews and the valence method. Based on this we derive our design decisions.

Scenario Description. The measuring chamber is a real industry-related application and functions as a test environment to check the read range or the 360° reading profile of UHF transponders (ultra high frequency - 800–1000 MHz). Based on an realistic application scenario students have to check different transponders fixed on the same substrate or just one transponder fixed on different substrates. They will check the needed power for activation in a specific frequency range in order to compare the transponders with each other. Based on the detected power they are able to calculate theoretical read ranges to prove several scenario theories in a profound way afterwards. In the end the students have to take up position for the chosen test setting and evaluate the gained data in terms of charts and diagrams. The effectiveness analysis of different transponders enable the students for expert consultations, so they are able to assess the ideal use a give recommendations for their practical usage in industry. The scenario depicts a realistic case and requires students' actions in a certain sequence:

1. Students are given a competence-oriented (case-based) task: they can choose between two options:
   (a) The examination of three identical transponders on different substrates
   (b) The investigation of three different transponders on the same substrate
2. Students receive an introduction to the use of the measuring chamber in the laboratory by the teacher or an assistant
3. The students place the transponders, which are attached to plates, by hand into the foam device of the RFID measuring chamber
4. The students open the software on the computer, select the *Threshold measurement* method and measure the transmitted energy in dBm
5. Students shall store the results of the first three measurements of the energy to be applied
6. Students evaluate the theoretical reading range of their transponders by selecting the appropriate function of the program and answering some related questions from the test report
7. The students start another measurement of the orientation sensitivity of their transponders and answer a corresponding question from the test report

Expert Interviews. A total of eight logistics experts were asked a wide range of questions on various topics about engineering education. The most relevant ones for the creation of the virtual reality application are briefly summarized as follows. All experts agreed that hands-on experience must have a high priority in engineering education as evidenced by statements such as *"The learning objective in this environment is to gain practical experience"*. However, the experts agreed that traditional computer simulations are lacking typical noise and could not replace the experience of the real laboratory: *"Virtual simulations are limited somewhere - in practice cross effects can still occur"* or *"It is a virtual toy that lacks the connection to practice"*.

Valence Method. Following the requirements analysis, a first prototype of the virtual learning environment was created within the design-based research approach. This included the laboratory with the measuring chamber, a transponder and a virtual button to start the measurement. This first prototype was evaluated with two of the experts using the valence method [9]. Both experts were filmed while performing the experiment and were able to set a time stamp by pressing a button on the controller. They should do this whenever they had a negative or positive emotion. Afterwards we watched the video at the time stamps together and discussed the remarks the experts had in an open discussion. The following additional suggestions for improvement resulted from observation and discussion:

1. The virtual chamber only supports one measuring method, but it should support two as the real chamber does
2. It is essential that the chamber has to be opened with both hands to avoid damage
3. The virtual buttons lack realism. The students need to learn how the software works
4. In the real laboratory there is always an assistant on site to answer questions and instruct the students

Derived Requirements. Based on the scenario description (SD), the expert interviews (EI) and the valence method (VM) evaluation we derived the following requirements for the improved version of the virtual reality laboratory:

1. The students should be guided through an experiment (VM)
2. The VR environment should be a sandbox to experiment (SD)
   (a) All experiments from the scenario description should work
   (b) The sequence and settings should be freely selectable
3. The real world should be reproduced as accurately as possible, as the VR chamber is used as preparation for the real laboratory (EI, VM). This includes:
   (a) Size, arrangement and colour of all objects/control elements
   (b) Operating software should have recognition value in relation to the real laboratory (VM)

    (c) The chamber may only be opened with two hands at the same time to avoid damage. This must also be the case in the virtual version (VM)

4. The results should not be a perfect simulation (EI)

In order to meet the derivation of the requirements the design of the virtual measuring chamber follows the design-oriented media didactics according to Kerres [14]. This offers the developers a pragmatic framework model as an open planning scaffold. That means for example, concepts such as case- or problem-based learning are not preferred from the outset. Rather, methodical-didactic solutions are aligned with the concrete requirements situation, which includes a first line learning goals, course contents, target groups, and general conditions. The selection of appropriate methods and the didactical decisions must correspond to these. Furthermore, it must be taken into account that errors in the planning of digital learning offers are more difficult to compensate, since the learning situation in this case will be largely self-directed. An evaluation of the virtual chamber, as described in Sect. 3 in advance is therefore essential (ibid.). Based on the requirement analyses we identified the following relevant aspects to get a better representation of the real scenario: *Environment, Interactions, Sequence* and *Feedback & Guidance*.

2.1   Environment

The virtual 3D environment aims to closely recreate the actual physical laboratory, including the relevant equipment found within. To this end an extensive survey was performed on location using a variety of tools to document relevant aspects of the laboratory, including measurements of size and orientation and image data. The relevant elements of the environment include the RFID measuring chamber itself, directly attached peripherals and a PC used to control the chamber, all of which are placed on tables. An additional working bench is used to deposit RFID chips mounted on different substrates that are placed inside the chamber for measurements. The surrounding room contains a lot more equipment, however the reconstruction focuses on the corner of the room containing the chamber and only its immediate surroundings. Notable architectural features in the area of interest include a pillar, a radiator, and an outside window.

    To get an accurate reconstruction the physical environment was surveyed using photographs and measurements. It was intended to use photogrammetry to gather additional data, so a separate set of photographs was recorded specifically for that purpose, using a ultra-wide angle lens with strong overlap between consecutive images while varying the perspective. Additional photographs were taken to serve as texture maps of different materials found in the scene. To process the ultra-wide angle photographs into a photogrammetry a correction of the strong barrel distortion caused by the lens was necessary and performed using the analysis of a photographed pattern with a regular grid of dots [20].

(a)   (b)

Fig. 2. (a) Reference photo shown in viewport; (b) Wireframe overlay on reference photography.

The quality of the resulting mesh was, however, deemed insufficient to serve as a reference for the modeling of the final asset. Instead, an alternate workflow for modeling was derived from the reconstructed data. The reconstructed scene was exported to Blender 3D[1], including the calculated camera positions for each image. This allows for viewing the scene from the perspective of the original camera at the moment of the image capture. By setting up the corresponding image to be the image background for the camera view, the content of the 3D scene can be viewed as a wireframe overlay over the actual object being reconstructed (Fig. 2). To aid modeling, the orientation of the whole scene was corrected so that the edges of the room are parallel to the coordinate axis in each direction. This method allows for accurate 3D placement of polygons, since edges and vertices will align with the corresponding image features in multiple views that can be viewed simultaneously.

2.2 Sequence

The scenario is divided into three stations, which are marked as green spheres in Fig. 3. The stations consist of: The workbench on which the RFID transponders are located (Station 1), the desk from which the PC for controlling the chamber is operated (Station 2) and the RFID measuring chamber itself (Station 3). The experiment sequence starts at station 1, where the avatar greets the user and asks him to look around the lab first. Then the user is prompted to touch the avatar with his hand to proceed to the next section. When the user does this, the avatar moves to Station 2 and explains that the large stainless steel chamber is the RFID measuring chamber. It is also mentioned that it can be controlled via the PC. The user is asked to touch the magnifying glass whereupon the control panel is enlarged as a hologram (Fig. 5a). The avatar continues to clarify technical details and the settings of the software. The user is told to open the chamber and to keep in mind that the opening mechanism needs to be operated

---

[1] https://www.blender.org/.

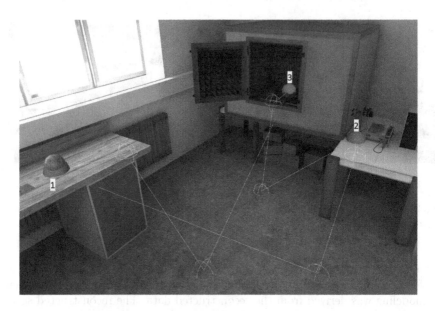

Fig. 3. Movement path and waypoints (white) as well as stations (green markers) of the robot avatar. (Color figure online)

with both hands. After the chamber is fully opened, the avatar moves to the 3rd station. Inside the chamber the avatar explains to the user what the components are called and what their functions are. Then the avatar moves to the first station again and asks the user to place the transponder in the chamber. The user does this with the controller, whereupon the chip snaps into a predetermined position. Now the avatar returns back to the PC, prompts the user to close the chamber again and describes how a measurement can be started with the hologram. The necessary buttons are activated one after another guiding the user through the process. During the measurement, the result gradually appears on the screen while technical details are explained. After completing the first measurement, the user has to change the scan mode to perform a second measurement following the same procedure. After the second measurement is completed successfully, the user is asked to remove the RFID chip from the chamber. Finally, the avatar congratulates the user on the successful completion of the exercise and switches the chamber into the experiment mode. This involves additional transponders appearing on the table and the activation of all control elements. The user is now able to carry out any desired measurements by himself.

2.3   Guidance and Feedback

To lead students through the virtual experiment different guidance techniques were applied. On the one hand, we integrated an avatar with voice output that is supposed to convey knowledge about RFID technology and gives a step by step tour through the experiment. Special attention was paid to a nonchalant tone of voice to potentially increase motivation. To give an example, the avatar tells the student about the measuring chamber in the following way: *"Let's go! You have probably already discovered the large steel box in the corner. This is the RFID measuring chamber. But before we can measure anything, we need to power it up"*.

On the other hand the voice output is supplemented with a number of visual attention guidance techniques. An overview of which is given in Fig. 4. While the avatar is able to perform a pointing animation to roughly direct the user in one direction (Fig. 4c), 3-dimensional arrows can be additionally displayed in context of the spoken word to draw attention to details. In Fig. 4b, for example, it is pointed out that the chip in the measuring chamber is difficult to read from the rear side.

As one of the goals is to teach students how to open the chamber in the real world, animated and colored highlights were used to illustrate where and how the mechanisms in the chamber can be used. For example, the animated hands disappear when the controllers are in the right place. Similarly, the color of the handles changes from red to green when both are operated simultaneously. In addition, green colors and audio feedback signal when the chamber has been opened successfully.

2.4   Interaction

Based on the requirements analysis, the RFID chips, the RFID chamber and the operating software were identified as three essential components with which the user must interact. The operating concept in virtual reality should correspond to that of the real world as much as possible or make use of clear metaphors. First of all, it is important that the door opening mechanism of the chamber can only be operated with two hands simultaneously to avoid damage. This was visualized by hand animations and by colored highlights that switch from red to green as soon as the user puts both hands on the handles (Fig. 5b). After fully opening the handles, he or she receives haptic feedback in the form of controller vibrations and an acoustic signal.

The relevant aspects of the operating software have been enlarged and can be displayed in the form of a hologram by touching a magnifying glass (Fig. 5a). In this way, the software can be conveniently controlled in virtual reality without losing touch with the real software.

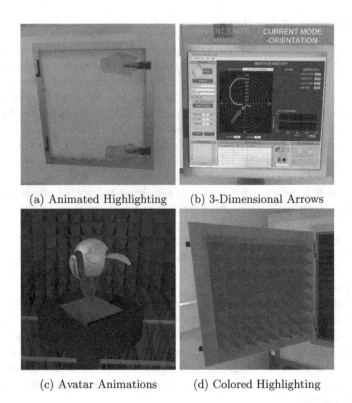

(a) Animated Highlighting   (b) 3-Dimensional Arrows

(c) Avatar Animations   (d) Colored Highlighting

Fig. 4. Overview of the implemented guidance techniques.

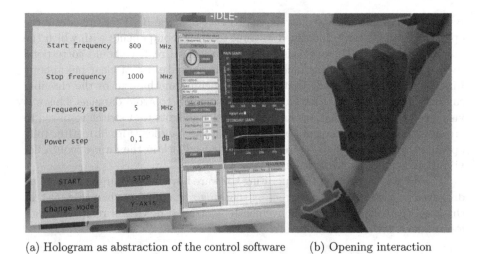

(a) Hologram as abstraction of the control software   (b) Opening interaction

Fig. 5. Overview of the implemented interaction elements.

3   Evaluation

A total of four experts were interviewed. Two from the field of logistics, who use corresponding laboratories in teaching and two from the area of pedagogics. Additionally two bachelor students of information logistics completed the virtual scenario. All participants had none to very little experience with virtual reality applications. The evaluation process was split in two parts. First the participants went through the virtual scenario described in Sect. 2.2 using a HTC Vive Pro Headset[2]. While doing the experiment they were encouraged to verbalize their thoughts (thinking aloud method [17]). Afterwards they were interviewed about their experience and filled out a questionnaire. Since the interviews were conducted in the mother tongue of the respective respondent, the statements are paraphrased in English.

3.1   Thinking Aloud and Semi Structured Interview

Both, experts and students gave a lot of positive feedback, criticized similar things and made interesting and valuable suggestions for improvement. In the following we have summarized the results of our observations and interviews in different categories:

Motivation: All participants were enthusiastic about the experience of virtual reality and attributed a high motivational character to this fact alone. In particular, the avatar's voice and animation were seen as motivating accompaniments during the experiment. Two of the experts, however, had some negative associations concerning the shape of the avatar which was compared to a football or an insect while one of the students was enjoying that the avatar moved on the ground. Additionally it was difficult to follow its path on the floor despite having spatial sound. This was attributed to the weight of the VR-headset which was seen as a hindrance while looking down.

Immersion and Transferability to the Real World. Both the orientation and the recognition value of the lab were praised, which is reflected in statements such as *"I really felt myself transferred to that lab, that was pretty cool"*. Furthermore, all experts who knew the real lab said that they were satisfied or surprised with the realistic presentation of the RFID laboratory (*"I loved the modeling of the measuring chamber"*). This was confirmed by interviewing the students after the real experiment was completed, as X of them stated that the preparation in the virtual chamber helped them to orientate themselves in the previously unknown lab. However, some critical remarks were made about the door opening mechanism. Especially the need to grip the door handles with both controllers at the same time while performing the realistic opening movement was difficult for all testers, as they lacked the sensation of grip in the virtual world (*"I slip away with my hand, as I cannot hold on to something real"*).

---

[2] https://www.vive.com/.

It was noted that instead of synthetic, realistic sound effects can help to provide feedback for successful opening and closing of the measuring chamber.

Acceptance: Experts as well as students were asked whether they could imagine using VR technology in their own teaching or during their studies respectively. Both groups agreed that they see added value in the use of VR and would like to integrate such applications into teaching. However, they criticized the logistical effort involved in providing hardware, so that they considered it a prerequisite that students must possess their own VR equipment and have to be able to use it appropriately. The pedagogical experts, in particular, pointed out that the VR application has a rather playful, non-binding character at times. It would be desirable to continue working with findings or results of the virtual experiment in the real world experiment afterwards.

3.2   Usability Questionnaire

In order to assess the general usability of the VR application and to classify areas in need of improvement, the well-known Usability Questionnaire [15] was used. It also provides a benchmark to compare the application with 452 studies (as of July 2020) [18]. A total of eight testers (6 experts and 2 students) completed the questionnaire directly after the VR scenario. Although there were only a few test persons due to the COVID-19 pandemic, we decided to include the test results because the standard deviation, as well as the confidence interval is relatively small, especially in the areas of attractiveness (Mean: 2.06 SD: 0.38), stimulation (Mean: 1.87 SD: 0.58) and novelty (Mean: 1.68 SD:0.49) (Figs. 6 and 7).

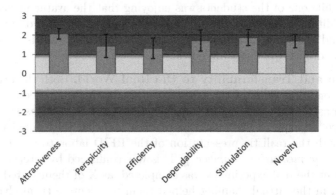

Fig. 6. The User Experience Questionnaire for both students and experts. The scale ranges from −3 (very bad) to +3 (very good).

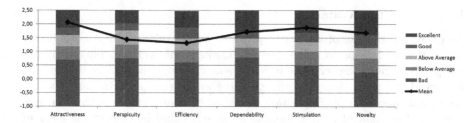

Fig. 7. The benchmark of the User Experience Questionnaire.

4 Discussion

The results of the evaluation give us a good insights into which aspects of our application work and in which areas there is potential for improvement. These are now explained in the following sections:

Transferability of the Virtual Laboratory to the Real One

As the interviews and observations clearly showed, the test persons found it very easy to find their way around the virtual environment. Both students and experts stated that they found the visualization of the lab realistic and recognized the real lab. It was also clear that the realistic or metaphorically simulated interactions could be easily transferred to the real environment. This leads to the conclusion that a replica as described in Sect. 2.1 offers an added value despite the effort involved, especially since it allows for both a realistic visualization and interactions through manually created models. The latter is more difficult to realize with pure photogrammetry. Ideally, one offers a mixture of automatically created scenery and manually created interactive models.

It was also shown that the reproduction of the control software by using a hologram gave the participants more security when using the real software. There are several reasons for this. Firstly, only the relevant elements of the software are highlighted and can be operated intuitively by touch. On the other hand, the interactive elements of the software are displayed piece by piece in a scaffolding approach, so that the sequence of actions is initially presented. This example illustrates that a good metaphor (hologram) does not have to differ completely from the original control element. On the contrary, a similar operating method makes the transfer to the real world more natural.

This finding should also be applied to the chamber's door opening mechanism, as this caused problems for almost all participants which is also shown in the *Perspicuity* and *Efficiency* rating of the usability questionnaire. It is necessary to find a good compromise between realistic appearance and operation as well as usability in virtual reality.

Influence of the Avatar

As expected, the use of an avatar provides added value, as it is both highly motivating and helps to guide the user through the scenario. Interesting are the partly negative associations in movement type and appearance that should be considered when designing and selecting an avatar. In particular, it seems important that the avatar's position should be clear at all times so that the user does not lose sight of it. A promising approach would be to combine ideas of attention guidance approaches with the movement model of the avatar.

Integration in the Existing Learning Environment

The VR scenario was designed as a preparation course covering the basics of an RFID measurement chamber and preparing the user for further experiments in the real world. According to the students, it fulfilled this purpose and was well received. Nevertheless, there were statements that suggest that the VR course was perceived as an add-on or game environment. This is related to the fact that there was no direct obligation between the virtual and real experiments. It would be desirable, for example, to have a content dependency so that students need their virtual results in the real experiment later on or a technical connection in which, for example, a real laboratory can be remotely controlled from within the virtual laboratory [13].

5 Conclusion

We were able to create a working virtual clone of an RFID laboratory that students can use as preparation for a real laboratory visit. As was shown by the interviews, observations and the usability questionnaire, the test subjects perceived the scenario to be very beneficial. Both experts and students saw an added value in the use of the application and were able to orientate themselves better in the real experiment, had less difficulties in using the software and felt overall more confident during the laboratory visit. In the future the tie between the virtual environment and the real laboratory, both in terms of content and technology will be strengthened in order to achieve even better learning outcomes.

Acknowledgement. Funded by the German Federal Ministry of Education and Research (BMBF), grants no. 16DHB2115 "DigiLab4U".

References

1. Abulrub, A.G., Attridge, A.N., Williams, M.A.: Virtual reality in engineering education: the future of creative learning. In: 2011 IEEE Global Engineering Education Conference (EDUCON), pp. 751–757 (2011)
2. Acatech: Kompetenzentwicklungsstudie Industrie 4.0: Erste Ergebnisse und Schlussfolgerungen. München (2016)

3. Bell, J.T., Fogler, H.S.: Ten steps to developing virtual reality applications for engineering education. In: ASEE Annual Conference Proceedings, pp. 1–8 (1997)
4. Bell, J.T., Fogler, H.S., Arbor, A.: The investigation and application of virtual reality as an educational tool. In: Proceedings of the American Society for Engineering Education, vol. 2513, pp. 1–11 (1995)
5. Bell, J.T., Scott Fogler, H.: Vicher: a virtual reality based educational module for chemical reaction engineering. Comput. Appl. Eng. Educ. 4(4), 285–296 (1996)
6. Berg, L.P., Vance, J.M.: Industry use of virtual reality in product design and manufacturing: a survey. Virtual Reality 21(1), 1–17 (2016). https://doi.org/10.1007/s10055-016-0293-9
7. Brooks, F.P.: What's real about virtual reality? IEEE Comput. Graphics Appl. 19(6), 16–27 (1999)
8. Burghardt, M., Ferdinand, P., Pfeiffer, A., Reverberi, D., Romagnoli, G.: Integration of new technologies and alternative methods in laboratory-based scenarios. In: Auer, M.E., May, D. (eds.) REV 2020. AISC, vol. 1231, pp. 488–507. Springer, Cham (2021). https://doi.org/10.1007/978-3-030-52575-0_40
9. Burmester, M., Mast, M., Jäger, K., Homans, H.: Valence method for formative evaluation of user experience. In: Proceedings of the 8th ACM Conference on Designing Interactive Systems, DIS 2010, pp. 364–367. Association for Computing Machinery, New York (2010)
10. Carruth, D.W.: Virtual reality for education and workforce training. In: ICETA 2017–15th IEEE International Conference on Emerging eLearning Technologies and Applications, Proceedings (2017)
11. Chittaro, L., Buttussi, F.: Assessing knowledge retention of an immersive serious game vs. a traditional education method in aviation safety. IEEE Trans. Vis. Comput. Graph. 21(4), 529–538 (2015)
12. Feisel, L.D., Rosa, A.J.: The role of the laboratory in undergraduate engineering education. J. Eng. Educ. 94, 121–130 (2005)
13. Höhner, N., Rodewald, J., Mints, M.O., Kammerlohr, V.: The next step of digital laboratories: connecting real and virtual world. In: The 17th International Conference on Virtual-Reality Continuum and Its Applications in Industry, VRCAI 2019. Association for Computing Machinery, New York (2019)
14. Kerres, M.V. (ed.): Mediendidaktik: Konzeption und Entwicklung mediengestützter Lernangebote. Oldenbourg, München, 4, überarb. und aktualisierte aufl. edn. (2013), für Studenten der Informatik und Pädagogik sowie Entwickler von Bildungsmedien. - Literaturverz. S. [515] - 537
15. Laugwitz, B., Held, T., Schrepp, M.: Construction and evaluation of a user experience questionnaire. In: Holzinger, A. (ed.) USAB 2008. LNCS, vol. 5298, pp. 63–76. Springer, Heidelberg (2008). https://doi.org/10.1007/978-3-540-89350-9_6
16. Psotka, J.: Immersive training systems: virtual reality and education and training. Instr. Sci. 23(1), 404–431 (1995)
17. Schnell, C.: lautes denken als qualitative methode zur untersuchung der validität von testitems - erkenntnisse einer studie zur diagnose des ökonomischen fachwissens von schülerinnen und schülern der sekundarstufe i. ZföB Zeitschrift für ökonomische Bildung Heft 5, Jahrgang 2016, pp. 26–49 (2016)
18. Schrepp, M., Hinderks, A., Thomaschewski, J.: Construction of a benchmark for the user experience questionnaire (UEQ). Int. J. Interact. Multimedia Artif. Intell. 4, 40–44 (2017)
19. Tang, Y.M., Au, K.M., Lau, H.C.W., Ho, G.T.S., Wu, C.H.: Evaluating the effectiveness of learning design with mixed reality (MR) in higher education. Virtual Reality (2020). https://doi.org/10.1007/s10055-020-00427-9

20. Tsai, R.: A versatile camera calibration technique for high-accuracy 3D machine vision metrology using off-the-shelf TV cameras and lenses. IEEE J. Robot. Autom. **3**(4), 323–344 (1987)

21. Villagrasa, S., Fonseca, D., Durán, J.: Teaching case: applying gamification techniques and virtual reality for learning building engineering 3D arts. In: ACM International Conference Proceeding Series, pp. 171–177 (2014)

22. Wang, F., Xu, X., Feng, W., Vesga, J.B., Liang, Z., Murrell, S.: Towards an immersive guided virtual reality microfabrication laboratory training system. In: 2020 IEEE Conference on Virtual Reality and 3D User Interfaces Abstracts and Workshops (VRW), pp. 796–797 (2020)

23. Wang, P., Wu, P., Wang, J., Chi, H.L., Wang, X.: A critical review of the use of virtual reality in construction engineering education and training. Int. J. Environ. Res. Public Health **15**, 1204 (2018)

24. Winther, F., Ravindran, L., Svendsen, K.P., Feuchtner, T.: Design and evaluation of a VR training simulation for pump maintenance. In: Extended Abstracts of the 2020 CHI Conference on Human Factors in Computing Systems Extended Abstracts, CHI 2020, pp. 1–8. Association for Computing Machinery, New York (2020)

25. Xiao, X., Zhao, S., Meng, Y., Soghier, L., Zhang, X., Hahn, J.: A physics-based virtual reality simulation framework for neonatal endotracheal intubation. In: 2020 IEEE Conference on Virtual Reality and 3D User Interfaces (VR), pp. 557–565 (2020)

26. Zhao, J., LaFemina, P., Carr, J., Sajjadi, P., Wallgrün, J.O., Klippel, A.: Learning in the field: comparison of desktop, immersive virtual reality, and actual field trips for place-based stem education. In: 2020 IEEE Conference on Virtual Reality and 3D User Interfaces (VR), pp. 893–902 (2020)

27. Zubía, J.G., Alves, G.: Using remote labs in education: two little ducks in remote experimentation (2011)

28. Zvacek, S.: Preface: University of Kansas, (USA). In: Zubía, J.G., Alves, G. (eds.) Using Remote Labs in Education: Two Little Ducks in Remote Experimentation (2011)

A Virtual Reality Surgical Training System for Office Hysteroscopy with Haptic Feedback: A Feasibility Study

Vladimir Poliakov[1,2]([✉]), Kenan Niu[1], Bart Paul De Vree[3,4],
Dzmitry Tsetserukou[2], and Emmanuel Vander Poorten[1]

[1] Robot-Assisted Surgery Group, The Mechanical Department,
KU Leuven, Leuven, Belgium
`vladimir.poliakov@kuleuven.be`
[2] Space Center, Skolkovo Institute of Science and Technology, Moscow, Russia
[3] Department of Obstetrics and Gynaecology, Ziekenhuis Netwerk Antwerpen,
Campus Middelheim, Antwerp, Belgium
[4] Department of Obstetrics and Gynaecology, Universitair Ziekenhuis Antwerpen,
Edegem, Belgium

Abstract. Hysteroscopy is a widely used gynaecological procedure to evaluate and treat cervical and intra-uterine pathology. In the last few decades, technical refinements in the optics technology, surgical accessories and the reduction of the outer diameter of the instrument have made it possible to perform many hysteroscopic procedures, including some operative procedures, in the office setting and without any anesthesia. Mini-hysteroscopic procedures in the office setting are associated with less pain, lower complication rate and faster recovery compared hysteroscopic procedures in day surgery under general anesthesia.

The main challenge for the clinician in performing office hysteroscopy is to pass the narrow cervical canal. Inaccurate motion or excessively applied force can lead to a cervical or uterine perforation. This study introduces a novel VR training platform for office hysteroscopy. The presented system was tested in the laboratory setting to prove the feasibility of using VR simulation for office hysteroscopy training. Conducted experiments demonstrated the potential of the system to transfer the essential skills and confirmed the set of proposed metrics for effective assessment.

Keywords: Virtual reality · Surgical training · Hysteroscopy · Gynecology · Haptics

1 Introduction

Hysteroscopy is a widely used gynaecological procedure to evaluate and treat cervical and intra-uterine pathology (Fig. 1). Today, hysteroscopy includes a whole series of diagnostic and operative procedures, including polypectomy, myomectomy, adhesiolysis, treatment of cervical stenosis, treatment of uterine anomalies

© Springer Nature Switzerland AG 2020
P. Bourdot et al. (Eds.): EuroVR 2020, LNCS 12499, pp. 115–127, 2020.
https://doi.org/10.1007/978-3-030-62655-6_7

and many more. Technical refinements, especially in the optics technology and the reduction of the outer diameter of the instrument, have made it possible to perform many hysteroscopic procedures, including some operative procedures, in the office setting and without anesthesia. This approach is referred to as office hysteroscopy. Office hysteroscopy is performed with a hysteroscope, which is a long, small-diameter endoscope connected to a light source. A camera is attached to the proximal end of the hysteroscope to transmit the image onto a monitor. The procedure starts in the vagina. In the case of vaginoscopic approach, no speculum is used [1]. The cervix is visualized and the hysteroscope is introduced into the cervical canal without dilatation. Then, under direct visualization, the instrument is advanced step by step into the uterine cavity. Passing the cervical canal without prior dilatation is a thorough procedure requiring a high level of dexterity. In the presence of risk factors, such as anatomical variation, stenotic cervix, postmenopause, previous cesarean section or conisation, passage of the cervical canal can be even more difficult and attention has to be paid to avoid perforation [2].

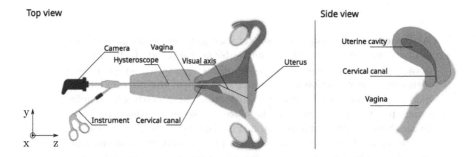

Fig. 1. The schematic diagram of hysteroscopy (top and side views). The hysteroscope is inserted through the vaginal canal and the endocervix to perform treatment in the uterine cavity.

In order to acquire the necessary skills in office hysteroscopy, both theoretical knowledge and practical surgical training are essential. The options for surgical training in hysteroscopy mostly include artificial platforms: physical simulators, also known as box trainers, and virtual reality (VR) simulators. Compared to physical simulators, VR training can potentially provide a higher level of immersion [3]. VR enables rendering of various clinical scenarios in the digital scene with minimal setup time, whereas physical simulators would require considerable workloads to mimic complex pathological conditions. Yet, to the best of our knowledge, no research has been done in VR training for hysteroscopic passage of the endocervix with an office setup. Consequently, surgical treatment performed inside the cervical canal, including biopsy, polyp removal, and surgical treatment of a stenotic cervix, has been left out in the current VR training systems.

The hypothesis of this study is that VR training is capable of transferring the essential skills needed to perform an outpatient hysteroscopic intervention.

To prove this hypothesis, the first steps towards the development of a VR surgical simulation system designed specifically for office hysteroscopy training are described. The proposed system integrates the real-time physics simulation framework SOFA [4] with Filament [5], a real-time physics-based rendering (PBR) engine. This resulted in a high fidelity VR simulation environment that is close to the actual clinical environment. The developed system was tested and evaluated by experiments in a laboratory setting, which indicates that the proposed training system has a great potential to fill the research gap and to be applied in clinical practice in the mid-term future.

2   Related Works

A broad body of research has been dedicated to VR surgical training in various domains. Most types of endoscopic procedures share a common set of the basic required skills. Hence, similar assessment methods and metrics can be encountered in such fields as laparoscopy, arthroscopy, ureteroscopy and hysteroscopy training. These metrics typically belong to one of the three following categories: time-based metrics, position-based metrics, and force-based metrics. Time-based metrics are one of the most common metrics. Generally, the total time of performing a certain task or an entire experiment is measured, such as total execution time [6,7] or phase execution time [8].

Position-based metrics involve a user's performance attributes related to the absolute or relative position of instruments in the simulation. Position-based metrics can indicate task completion rate, for instance, the proximity of the deployed intra-uterine device (IUD) to fallopian tubes ostium in the case of an IUD insertion exercise; or the level of dexterity in motion, as in the simulator presented by Bajka et al. [6] Other studies, such as [9,10], also employ this type of metric in the training process.

Force-based metrics aim to evaluate a user's performance based on forces that are generated by physical or virtual interaction between instruments and operated tissues. Force-based metrics are part of assessment frameworks presented in [11,12]. Evaluating force in the simulation imposes additional requirements, namely precise physics modeling methods and realistic haptic feedback. The latter requirement implies that the system should be capable of giving the user kinaesthetic sensations that are close to the real feeling and providing him/her with information about the applied pressure.

Research on VR surgical training for hysteroscopy revolves mainly around works that describe validation experiments on either of two commercial simulators: GynoS^{TM}(Virtamed, Switzerland) and HystMentor^{TM}(3D Systems, U.S.) [8,13,14]. The training program of these platforms includes exercises on diagnostic and operative hysteroscopy: polypectomy, myoma resection, septoplasty. Both hysteroscopy training systems focus on surgical training in the OR setup, assuming that prior dilation of the cervix has been performed before the procedure, thus bypassing the endocervix passage phase in the exercises. However, the endocervix passage phase plays an important role in the entire procedure.

Clinicians require a considerable amount of practice to become proficient in performing this operation and to be able to avoid all potential complications.

Savran et al. presented a study on ensuring the basic hysteroscopic competency using the HystMentor^{TM} simulation system. Participants were given a pass/fail score based on a multimodal assessment system. Reported results showed that false positive and false negative scores were 6.7% and 27.3%, respectively [13]. Thus, the established metrics still can be improved for more precise assessment. Panel et al. conducted a comparative analysis of overall and subset scores for novice and expert users when performing four types of hysteroscopic intervention in HystMentor^{TM}: polypectomy, myomectomy, rollerball endometrial ablation and septum resection [8]. The overall multi-metric scores were statistically different between the mentioned groups for three out of four exercises. Panel et al. considered that experienced users obtained low scores for the septum resection exercise due to the incorrect choice of recommended treatment type in the assessment system. Subset scores also demonstrated certain ambiguity. Whilst fluid handling score and economy score demonstrated significant difference between novices and experts, other scores failed to distinguish between the two groups. This ambiguity has also been highlighted by Neis et al. [15] and Elessawy et al. [16], where other subset scores demonstrated no statistical difference.

Apart from objective assessment, another important feature required for effective VR hysteroscopy training is haptic feedback. This particular topic has not been widely addressed in the literature. Bajka et al. presented the HystSim simulation system for diagnostic and operative hysteroscopy [17]. The HystSim platform is augmented with active haptic feedback, allowing its users to perceive forces generated by the interaction between the instrument and objects in the scene. This feature, however, was reported to be in the early stage of development, and thus, according to Bajka et al., might not provide a sufficient level of realism. Moreover, the developed haptic interface allows motions in four degrees of freedoms (DOFs), constraining translation in two directions around the pivot point. However, four DOFs are no sufficient in the case of an office procedure, as the instrument should be capable of unconstrained motion in six DOFs when passing through the cervical canal.

To summarize, there are several gaps in the current methods of VR training for hysteroscopy. First, the training methods for office hysteroscopy fully exclude the passage of the cervical canal and treatment of endocervical pathologies from the training process. Second, presented systems do not provide an active haptic interface suitable for simulating outpatient hysteroscopic interventions.

Based on the mentioned points, in this paper, we aim to design a simulation platform for office hysteroscopy to achieve a high level of haptic and graphical realism. The goal is to design a system that allows clinicians to exercise manipulation of a hysteroscope when passing through the cervical canal and treatment of endocervical and intrauterine pathologies with the office setup. Eventually, the developed VR surgical training system can be used to improve surgical skills in outpatient hysteroscopic intervention.

3   Materials and Methods

In this study, a simulation platform was designed, which features a spatial navigation and instrument manipulation task. The presented VR simulation system mimics an office hysteroscopic procedure, starting from locating the external os of the cervix, then passing through the cervical canal and operating inside the uterine cavity. With this exercise, the authors aimed to design an approach for medical students to learn how to safely introduce a hysteroscope inside the uterine cavity and perform simple surgical procedures, such as biopsy or polyp removal inside the cavity and the cervical canal.

Participants should pass through the cervical canal and perform tasks inside the uterine cavity. In this context, several spherical objects located on the surface of the endocervix and inside the uterine cavity were regarded as checkpoints, on which participants had to perform a grasping manipulation.

3.1   Purpose of the Exercise

The aim of the exercise is to enter the uterine cavity and collect ten checkpoints while maintaining a minimal level of applied force. In the VR training scene, checkpoints are rendered as one millimeter green spheres, which are evenly distributed along the surface of the cervical canal and the uterine cavity. The starting position of the checkpoints is always the same, so the minimal path length does not change. A user can collect checkpoints by grasping them with a hysteroscopic forceps: once a checkpoint is collected, it disappears. When all checkpoints are collected, the exercise is terminated.

3.2   Hardware Setup

Figure 2 depicts the hardware layout of the system. A user operates the Touch^{TM} haptic interface (3D Systems Inc., U.S.) to manipulate the hysteroscope in the VR environment in six DOFs and the keyboard to control the forceps in two DOFs, including one translation along the hysteroscope and one joint at the distal part of the forceps to control grasping motion. The Touch^{TM} interface controls the position of the virtual hysteroscope and provides haptic feedback to the user. Up and down arrows on the keyboard are mapped to deploying and retracting motion of the forceps, respectively. Left and right arrows control the grasping motion. A PC (Intel Core I7-9850H, NVIDIA Quadro T1000 w/4 GB GDDR6, 8 GB RAM) runs the simulation and renders 3D visual representation on a screen from the perspective of a virtual camera attached to the tip of the hysteroscope. The virtual camera is rotated 12° around the x axis of the hysteroscope (Fig. 1), which corresponds to the typical optical angle of a hysteroscope [18].

3.3   Scene Generation

The Visible Human cryosection dataset was used to acquire the geometrical models of the uterus [19]. The visual mesh was obtained using manual segmentation in ImageJ [20] and subsequently optimised using quadric collapse edge

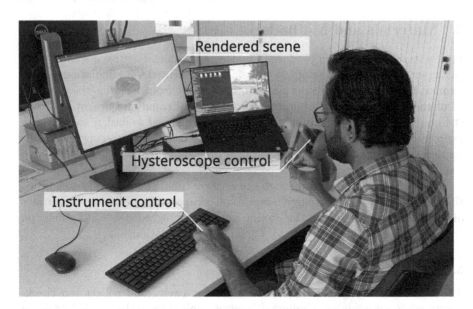

Fig. 2. The illustration of the VR simulation system for office hysteroscopy training.

decimation method in Meshlab [21] in order to reduce the number of vertices, resulting in 22893 elements. Three models depicted in Fig. 3 were used to simulate different aspects of body behaviour: (1) the visual model, responsible for visual appearance of the uterus; (2) the structural model, used to simulate deformations; and (3) the collision model, detecting intersections with other objects in the simulation. The structural mesh of the uterus was created from the visual mesh using CGAL software [22], which generated an object containing 1310 elements in total. Mechanical deformation of the uterus was modeled in SOFA with the finite element method (FEM) using the structural mesh. In order to optimize the collision pipeline, a simplified version of the visual mesh was used for collision detection containing 900 polygons.

Mechanical properties of the uterus were obtained from quasi in-vivo measurements performed by Omari et al. [23]. The Young's modulus of the organ was set to 12 kPa. The mass was assumed to be uniformly distributed between the structural elements in the body. To preserve the position of the body in the scene, the uterus is rigidly fixed in space at left and right ostia.

The hysteroscope is simulated as a cylinder, four millimeters in diameter and 130 mm in length, with a virtual camera attached to the tip and angled at 12°. In order to improve stability of the simulation and haptic feedback, the haptic interface controls the position of the hysteroscope via the proxy model. The proxy model does not have a collision or a visual representation in the simulation, but rather copies the position of the haptic interface and attracts the hysteroscope to it via a generic six DOF spring. This method ensures that no discrete change of the position occurs in the simulation. The forceps are simulated as an articulated

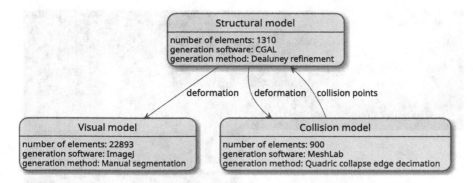

Fig. 3. The multi-model representation diagram. Links denote the relations between the models. Nodes specify the number of elements in the model, the generation software and the generation method.

rigid body, one millimeter in diameter, with two DOF and the base attached to the hysteroscope.

Checkpoints were represented as one-millimeter green spheres. The total number of the checkpoints was ten, with five checkpoints located in the cervical canal and five checkpoints located in the uterine cavity. The initial position of all checkpoints was the same for each experiment. However, as the geometry of the uterus can change due to tissue deformation, checkpoint positions should be also updated with each simulation step. To solve this problem, each checkpoint is mapped to a subset of uterus vertices around it, thus preserving the relative position with respect to the uterus during the simulation. The barycentric mapping was used to update the checkpoints position [24].

3.4   Software Architecture

The software architecture of the simulator consists of three main components: the physics engine, the visual renderer and the haptic loop. All mentioned components run in separate threads as all of them have different timing requirements.

The SOFA framework [4] is used as the physics engine of the system. It runs at the update rate of approximately 150 frames per second (FPS) and performs collision detection, structural deformation simulation, and mapping between models. The mechanical model is represented by a tetrahedral mesh, which is mapped to the collision model and the visual model polygon meshes. The geometry of the models is synchronised using the barycentric mapping.

The Filament renderer [5] is used for 3D graphical representation. Figure 4 depicts an example of a rendered scene in the simulation. The visual server runs at 50 FPS and is fully decoupled from the physics simulation. The physics engine passes the geometry of each object to the visual server at the initialisation phase. During simulation, the visual server queries updates of the objects geometry at the start of each iteration using a mediator class, which ensures decoupling between these components.

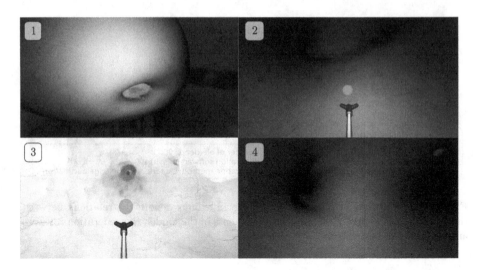

Fig. 4. The examples of the rendered scene: (1) external os, (2) uterine cavity, (3) cervical canal, (4) fundus and left ostium.

Finally, the haptic loop is implemented using the OpenHaptics [25] libraries. In order to provide realistic haptic feedback, the haptic loop should run at the update rate of 1 kHz, meaning that it should be detached from the physics simulation. The physics loop is connected to the haptic loop using the LCP-ForceFeedback component, which utilizes constraints generated by the contact points between the instrument and the uterus to calculate force feedback at the required update rate.

3.5   Experiments and Assessment Metrics

Ten subjects, eight male and two female, with no prior experience in hysteroscopy participated in the study to evaluate the proposed concept. The subjects had no to moderate gaming and virtual reality experience. Assessment of a subject's performance was based on following metrics: total number of grasping attempts (n_a), total execution time (t_e), cervical canal passage time (t_c), total trajectory length (l_t), effective jerk (mean jerk excluding idle states) (j_e), effective force (mean force excluding idle states) (f_e), cumulative force (integrated force value) (f_c), and force fast Fourier transform (FFT) (f_{FFT}). The latter metric is the cumulative sum of the real component of applied force in the frequency domain.

Each participant performed five repetitive trials of the exercise to investigate the potential of transferring the essential skills for office hysteroscopy in the proposed system. Each participant was asked to take the required time to rest between trials. To check statistical significance, the obtained results were tested using the Mann-Whitney U-test. A metric was considered to be significant when the significance level was less than or equal to 0.05.

4   Results

Table 1 shows the measured metrics across all participants for each trial. Mean and standard deviation were calculated for each metric. The p-values that were calculated between the first and the last trial are listed in the last column and denoted with an asterisk symbol (∗) if a metric has statistical significance ($p \leq 0.05$). Among nine metrics, five demonstrated statistical significance: total execution time t_e, cervical canal passage time t_c, total trajectory length l_t, cumulative force f_c, and total number of grasping attempts n_a. Force FFT f_{FFT} also showed a high level of significance, although the p-value did not reach the required level. These metrics are depicted in Fig. 5.

Table 1. Mean and standard deviation of the experiments across all participants for each trial. The p-values were calculated between the first and the last trial.

Metric	Trial number					p-value
	1	2	3	4	5	
n_a	44.67 ± 10.37	42.44 ± 18.37	37.11 ± 7.49	32.44 ± 5.72	36.00 ± 9.93	0.037∗
t_e [s]	248.7 ± 78.9	205.1 ± 62.7	179.9 ± 60.9	155.5 ± 37.7	143.2 ± 46.6	0.002∗
t_c [s]	168.2 ± 76.6	119.3 ± 35.0	105.0 ± 43.8	93.7 ± 30.5	88.1 ± 43.1	0.006∗
l_t [cm]	41.36 ± 22.32	36.34 ± 16.65	34.55 ± 15.75	34.37 ± 23.31	33.43 ± 28.99	0.046∗
j_e [km/s^3]	10.76 ± 0.81	11.09 ± 0.77	11.36 ± 1.35	12.24 ± 3.21	11.94 ± 1.92	0.961
f_e [N]	0.62 ± 0.08	0.62 ± 0.06	0.65 ± 0.09	0.63 ± 0.09	0.67 ± 0.11	0.760
f_c [$N \cdot s$]	133.1 ± 48.4	108.2 ± 32.8	105.6 ± 38.8	85.2 ± 31.0	87.2 ± 52.8	0.021∗
f_{FFT}	10.18 ± 3.40	9.49 ± 2.58	9.26 ± 2.79	9.02 ± 2.78	8.85 ± 3.99	0.092

Three participants reported to experience fatigue during the experiments, which was confirmed by the recorded drop in performance. However, the cause-effect relationship between fatigue and performance is out of the scope of the presented study.

5   Discussion

Overall, the proposed system demonstrated skill acquisition capabilities. Time-based metrics (total execution time and cervical canal passage time) showed the biggest change, gradually decreasing both in mean and standard deviation. These findings correlate with previous studies in other domains of hysterscopic training, in which total procedure time demonstrated significant difference between novices and expert clinicians [8]. The results also indicated another important metric to effectively assess a subject's performance: cumulative force. Both mean and standard deviation of this metric significantly improved with each trial, although the progress was somewhat slower compared to pure time-based metrics (Fig. 5). Being both a time- and a force-based metric, this value can better

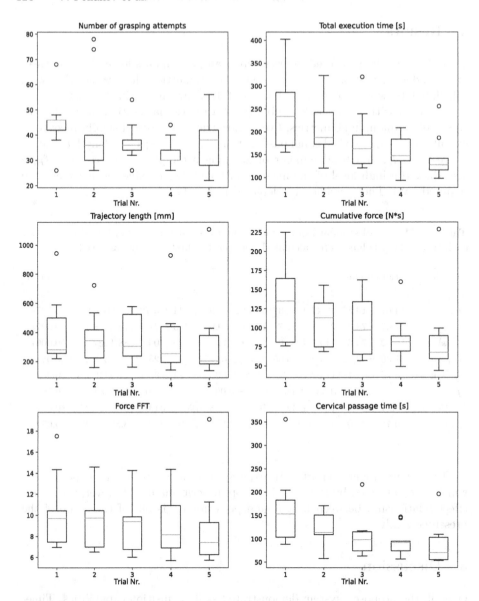

Fig. 5. Box plots showing minimum, maximum, median, and interquartile range values of the statistically significant metrics for each trial.

estimate the level of patient comfort and thus become an effective tool for cross-correlation assessment in the overall score.

Likewise, trajectory length and number of attempts exhibited gradual improvement over trials. However, the slope of the progress was not as smooth as in the case of time-based metrics (Fig. 5). The mean trajectory length of the second and third trials was higher compared to the first trial, whereas standard deviation and interquartile range also increased in values. This effect might be partially related to growing tiredness, as the drop of performance in these parameters was most observable in participants that reported to experience fatigue.

Opposed to the initial assumption of providing insights about the same phenomenon, tremor, force FFT and effective jerk behaved in a different manner. Whereas force FFT improved with each trial, effective jerk remained on the same level, although individual for each participant.

Contrarily to previous studies in VR hysteroscopic simulation with the same number of trials and non-expert participants [6,8], a plateau effect was not observed for the most number of statistically significant metrics. Mean and standard deviation of statistically significant metrics decreased with each trial without a significant change of slope. We can assume that this effect should take place with a higher number of repetitions, but additional research is required.

No significant change was observed in effective force over repetitions. This type of behaviour was somehow expected, as the exercise was designed for novice users and did not include the cases of a stenotic cervix. The authors assume that the situation might drastically change after augmenting the haptic interface with a mock-up of a hysteroscope. Due to introduction of a pivot point, motion in two rotational DOFs will be inverted and force perception will be partially reduced due to the lever effect.

6   Conclusion and Future Work

This paper presents some first results on the feasibility of VR training for office hysteroscopy. The developed platform aims to introduce an effective approach allowing medical students to sharpen their skills in performing outpatient hysteroscopic treatment. Employing physics-based rendering techniques along with realistic haptic feedback contributes to the level of realism and significantly improves the transfer of training. The preliminary results demonstrate the ability of the simulator to develop a trainee's dexterity in passage of the cervical canal and manipulation of hysteroscopic instruments. However, some of the presented metrics need further refinement.

Future work will focus on the face and content validity of the system. The hardware setup should be updated by adding a phantom of the female reproductive system, serving as the fulcrum point and contributing to visual resemblance between the simulation and the procedure. The haptic interface should be augmented with a mock-up of a real hysteroscopic instrumentation setup for higher content validity.

From the software perspective, the simulation also requires particular improvements. A graphical interface can enhance the usability of the system, making it easier to interact for a non-technical user. Another important consideration is to add variability by introducing new exercises and changing the simulation parameters in accordance with the level of complexity. Finally, the assessment system can be refined into a framework for effective overall evaluation and learning curve estimation. Introducing a complete solution for automatic assessment will serve as the foundation for adaptive training program, when the level of complexity grows over time with the level of a trainee's competence.

Overall, the proposed system has demonstrated its feasibility in VR surgical training for office hysteroscopy. Future studies will focus on further design and validation of the system with medical staff. These improvements will contribute to creating a useful surgical training system with a high level of realism and efficient transfer of skills characteristics.

References

1. Bettocchi, S., Selvaggi, L.: A vaginoscopic approach to reduce the pain of office hysteroscopy. J. Am. Assoc. Gynecol. Laparosc. **4**(2), 255–258 (1997). https://doi.org/10.1016/S1074-3804(97)80019-9. ISSN 10743804
2. Munro, M.G., Christianson, L.A.: Complications of hysteroscopic and uterine resectoscopic surgery. Clin. Obstet. Gynecol. **58**(4), 765–797 (2015). https://doi.org/10.1097/GRF.0000000000000146. ISSN 15325520
3. Erian, M.M., McLaren, G.R., Erian, A.M.: Advanced hysteroscopic surgery training. J. Soc. Laparoendosc. Surg. **18**(4) (2015). https://doi.org/10.4293/JSLS.2014.00396. ISSN 19383797
4. Faure, F., et al.: SOFA: a multi-model framework for interactive physical simulation. In: Payan, Y. (ed.) Soft Tissue Biomechanical Modeling for Computer Assisted Surgery, pp. 283–321. Springer, Heidelberg (2012). https://doi.org/10.1007/8415_2012_125
5. Google, Filament rendering engine. https://github.com/google/filament. Accessed 10 May 2020
6. Bajka, M., Tuchschmid, S., Fink, D., Székely, G., Harders, M.: Establishing construct validity of a virtual-reality training simulator for hysteroscopy via a multimetric scoring system. Surg. Endosc. **24**(1), 79–88 (2010). https://doi.org/10.1007/s00464-009-0582-4. ISSN 14322218
7. Hackethal, A., Immenroth, M., Burgerburger, T.: Evaluation of target scores and benchmarks for the traversal task scenario of the minimally invasive surgical trainer-virtual reality (MIST-VR) laparoscopy simulator. https://doi.org/10.1007/s00464-004-2224-1
8. Panel, P., Neveu, M.E., Villain, C., Debras, F., Fernandez, H., Debras, E.: Hysteroscopic resection on virtual reality simulator: what do we measure? J. Gynecol. Obstetrics Hum. Reprod. **47**(6), 247–252 (2018). https://doi.org/10.1016/j.jogoh.2018.02.005. ISSN 24687847
9. Anderson, T., Thomassee, M., Karhade, A., Peacock, J., Tolish, M., Young, F.: Development of a low cost, medium fidelity hysteroscopy simulator for spatial orientation training: proof of concept. J. Minimally Invasive Gynecol. **22**(6), S43 (2015). https://doi.org/10.1016/j.jmig.2015.08.118. ISSN 15534650
10. Bayona, S., Fernández-Arroyo, J.M., Martín, I., Bayona, P.: Assessment study of insight ARTHRO VR® arthroscopy virtual training simulator: face, content, and construct validities. J. Robotic Surg. **2**(3), 151–158 (2008). https://doi.org/10.1007/s11701-008-0101-y. ISSN 18632483
11. Singapogu, R.B., et al.: Salient haptic skills trainer: initial validation of a novel simulator for training force-based laparoscopic surgical skills. Surg. Endosc. **27**(5), 1653–1661 (2013). https://doi.org/10.1007/s00464-012-2648-y. ISSN 14322218

12. Horeman, T., Rodrigues, S.P., Willem Jansen, F., Dankelman, J., Van Den Dobbelsteen, J.J.: Force parameters for skills assessment in laparoscopy. IEEE Trans. Haptics **5**(4), 312–322 (2012). https://doi.org/10.1109/TOH.2011.60. ISSN 19391412

13. Savran, M.M., Nielsen, A.B., Poulsen, B.B., Thorsen, P.B., Konge, L.: Using virtual-reality simulation to ensure basic competence in hysteroscopy. Surg. Endosc. **33**(7), 2162–2168 (2018). https://doi.org/10.1007/s00464-018-6495-3

14. Munro, M.G., Behling, D.P.: Virtual reality uterine resectoscopic simulator: face and construct validation and comparative evaluation in an educational environment. J. Soc. Laparoendosc. Surg. **15**(2), 142–146 (2011). https://doi.org/10.4293/108680811X13071180406312. https://www.ncbi.nlm.nih.gov/pmc/articles/PMC3148859/. ISSN 10868089

15. Neis, F., et al.: Evaluation of the HystSim TM-virtual reality trainer: an essential additional tool to train hysteroscopic skills outside the operation theater. https://doi.org/10.1007/s00464-016-4837-6

16. Elessawy, M., et al.: Integration and validation of hysteroscopy simulation in the surgical training curriculum. J. Surg. Educ. **74**(1), 84–90 (2017). https://doi.org/10.1016/j.jsurg.2016.06.007. ISSN 18787452

17. Bajka, M., et al.: Evaluation of a new virtual-reality training simulator for hysteroscopy. Surg. Endosc. **23**(9), 2026–2033 (2009). https://doi.org/10.1007/s00464-008-9927-7. ISSN 14322218

18. Hernandez, A.U.: In-office hysteroscopy. In: Tinelli, A., Alonso Pacheco, L., Haimovich, S. (eds.) Hysteroscopy, pp. 33–40. Springer, Cham (2018). https://doi.org/10.1007/978-3-319-57559-9_4. ISBN 9783319575599

19. Ackerman, M.J.: The visible human project. Proc. IEEE **86**(3), 504–511 (1998). https://doi.org/10.1109/5.662875. ISSN 00189219

20. Schneider, C.A., Rasband, W.S., Eliceiri, K.W.: NIH Image to ImageJ: 25 years of image analysis, July 2012. https://doi.org/10.1038/nmeth.2089. https://www.nature.com/articles/nmeth.2089

21. Cignoni, P., Callieri, M., Corsini, M., Dellepiane, M., Ganovelli, F., Ranzuglia, G.: MeshLab: an open-source mesh processing tool. In: Scarano, V., Chiara, R.D., Erra, U. (eds.) Eurographics Italian Chapter Conference, pp. 129–136. The Eurographics Association (2008). https://doi.org/10.2312/LocalChapterEvents/ItalChap/ItalianChapConf2008/. ISBN 978-3-905673-68-5

22. Alliez, P., Fabri, A.: CGAL-the computational geometry algorithms library. In: ACM SIGGRAPH 2016 Courses, SIGGRAPH 2016. Association for Computing Machinery Inc, July 2016. https://doi.org/10.1145/2897826.2927362. ISBN 9781450342896

23. Omari, E.A., Varghese, T., Kliewer, M.A., Harter, J., Hartenbach, E.M.: Dynamic and quasi-static mechanical testing for characterization of the viscoelastic properties of human uterine tissue. J. Biomech. **48**(10), 1730–1736 (2015). https://doi.org/10.1016/J.JBIOMECH.2015.05.013. https://www.sciencedirect.com/science/article/pii/S0021929015002900. ISSN 0021-9290

24. Floater, M.S., Kosinka, J.: Barycentric interpolation and mappings on smooth convex domains. In: Proceedings - 14th ACM Symposium on Solid and Physical Modeling, SPM 2010, pp. 111–116. ACM Press, New York (2010). https://doi.org/10.1145/1839778.1839794. http://portal.acm.org/citation.cfm?doid=1839778.1839794. ISBN 9781605589848

25. 3DSystems: Geomagic openhatpics (2020). Accessed 10 May 2020. https://www.3dsystems.com/haptics-devices/openhaptics

Semantic Modeling of Virtual Reality Training Scenarios

Krzysztof Walczak[1]([✉]), Jakub Flotyński[1], Dominik Strugała[1],
Sergiusz Strykowski[1], Paweł Sobociński[1], Adam Gałązkiewicz[1], Filip Górski[2],
Paweł Buń[2], Przemysław Zawadzki[2], Maciej Wielgus[1],
and Rafał Wojciechowski[3]

[1] Poznań University of Economics and Business,
Niepodległości 10, 61-875 Poznań, Poland
`walczak@kti.ue.poznan.pl`
[2] Poznań University of Technology, Piotrowo 3, 60-965 Poznań, Poland
`filip.gorski@put.poznan.pl`
[3] Enea Operator sp. z o.o., Strzeszyńska 58, 60-479 Poznań, Poland

Abstract. Virtual reality can be an effective tool for professional training, especially in the case of complex scenarios, which performed in reality may pose a high risk for the trainee. However, efficient use of VR in practical everyday training requires efficient and easy-to-use methods of designing complex interactive scenarios. In this paper, we propose a new method of creating virtual reality training scenarios, with the use of knowledge representation enabled by semantic web technologies. We have verified the method by implementing and demonstrating an easy-to-use desktop application for designing VR scenarios by domain experts.

Keywords: Virtual reality · Semantic web · Training · Scenarios

1 Introduction

Progress in the quality and the performance of graphics hardware and software observed in recent years makes realistic interactive presentation of complex virtual spaces and objects possible even on commodity hardware. The availability of diverse inexpensive presentation and interaction devices, such as glasses, headsets, haptic interfaces, motion tracking and capture systems, further contributes to the increasing applicability of virtual (VR) and augmented reality (AR) technologies. VR/AR applications become popular in various application domains, such as e-commerce, tourism, education and training. Especially in training, VR offers significant advantages by making the training process more efficient and flexible, reducing the costs, and eliminating risks associated with training in a physical environment.

Employee training in virtual reality is becoming widespread in various industrial sectors, such as production, mining, gas and energy. However, building useful VR training environments requires competencies in both programming and

© Springer Nature Switzerland AG 2020
P. Bourdot et al. (Eds.): EuroVR 2020, LNCS 12499, pp. 128–148, 2020.
https://doi.org/10.1007/978-3-030-62655-6_8

3D modeling, as well as domain knowledge, which is necessary to prepare practical applications in a given domain. Therefore, this process typically involves IT specialists and domain specialists, whose knowledge and skills in programming and 3D modeling are usually low. Particularly challenging is the design of training scenarios, as it typically requires advanced programming skills, and the level of code reuse in this process is low. High-level componentization approaches commonly used in today's content creation tools are not sufficient, because the required generality and versatility of these tools inevitably leads to a high complexity of the content design process. Availability of appropriate user-friendly tools for domain experts to design VR training scenarios at the level of domain knowledge becomes therefore critical to enable reduction of the required time and effort, and consequently promote the use of VR in training.

A number of solutions enabling efficient modeling of 3D content using domain knowledge representation techniques have been proposed in previous works. In particular, semantic web provides standardized mechanisms to describe the meaning of any content in a way understandable to both users and software. However, it requires that the scenarios are designed by a knowledge engineering technician, which is not acceptable in practical VR training preparation. Thus, the challenge is to elaborate a method of creating semantic VR scenarios, which could be employed by users who do not have advanced knowledge and skills in programming and 3D modeling.

In this paper, we propose a new method of building VR training scenarios, based on semantic modeling techniques, with a user-friendly *VR Scenario Editor* (VRSEd) application implemented as an extension to Microsoft Excel, a tool commonly used by people in various domains. The editor enables domain experts to design scenarios using domain concepts described by ontologies. The presented approach takes advantage of the fact that in a concrete training scene and typical training scenarios, the variety of 3D objects and actions is limited. Therefore, it becomes possible to use a semantic database of available content elements and actions, and configure scenarios based on the existing building blocks using domain-specific concepts.

The work described in this paper has been performed within a project aiming at the development of flexible VR training system for electrical operators. All examples, therefore, relate to this application domain. However, the developed method and tools can be similarly applied to other domains, provided that relevant 3D objects and actions can be identified and semantically described.

The remainder of this paper is structured as follows. Section 2 provides an overview of the current state of the art in VR training applications, an introduction to the semantic web, and a review of approaches to semantic modeling of VR content. Section 3 describes our method of building VR training scenes. The proposed method of modeling training scenarios is described in Sect. 4. An example of a VR training scenario is presented in Sect. 5, while a discussion of the results is provided in Sect. 6. Finally, Sect. 7 concludes the paper and indicates possible future research.

2   Related Works

2.1   Training in VR

VR training systems enable achieving a new quality in employee training. With the use of VR it becomes possible to digitally recreate real working conditions with a high level of fidelity. Currently available systems can be categorized into three main groups: desktop systems, semi-immersive systems and fully immersive systems. Desktop systems use mainly traditional presentation/interaction devices, such as a monitor, mouse and keyboard. Semi-immersive systems use advanced VR/AR devices for presentation (e.g., HMD) or for interaction (e.g., motion tracking). Immersive systems use advanced VR/AR devices for both presentation and interaction. Below, examples of VR training systems within all of the three categories are presented.

The ALEn3D system is a desktop system developed for the energy sector by the Virtual Reality group of the Control Systems [23]. The system allows interaction with 3D content displayed on a 2D monitor screen, using a mouse and a keyboard [31]. The scenarios implemented in the system mainly focus on training the operation of power lines and include actions performed by a line electrician. The system consists of two modules: a VR environment and a course manager [22]. The VR environment can operate in three modes: virtual catalog, learning and evaluation. The course manager is a browser application that allows trainers to create courses, register students, create theoretical tests and monitor learning progress.

An example of a semi-immersive system is the IMA-VR system [19]. It enables specialized training in a virtual environment aimed at transferring motor and cognitive skills related to the assembly and maintenance of industrial equipment. The system was designed by CEIT and TECNALIA. The specially designed IMA-VR hardware platform is used to work with the system. The platform consists of a screen displaying a 3D graphics scene and a haptic device. This device allows a trainee to interact and manipulate virtual scene tools and components by touching while performing assembly and disassembly operations. The system provides various types of information during training, including a progress bar, technical descriptions of components and tools, meaningful information about operations and detailed error descriptions. In addition to the visual and haptic presentation, the most important information is also sent via audio messages. The system automatically records completed tasks and statistics (time taken, number of assists used and errors made, number of correct steps, etc.).

An example of a fully immersive AR system is the training system for the repairing electrical switchboards developed by Schneider Electric in cooperation with MW PowerLab [35]. The system is used to conduct training in operation on electrical switchboards and replacement of their parts. The system uses Microsoft HoloLens HMD. After a user puts on the HMD, the system scans the surroundings for an electrical switchboard. When a switchboard is located in the user's field of view, the system displays its name and is ready for operation.

The system can work in two ways: providing tips on a specific problem to be solved or providing general tips on operating or repairing the switchboard.

2.2 Semantic Web

The semantic web (the term proposed by Tim Berners-Lee [29]) provides a universal framework that allows data to be shared and reused across application, enterprise, and community boundaries. According to the WWW Consortium, the semantic web is a web of structured data, decoupling applications from data through a simple, abstract model for knowledge representation.

The basis of the semantic web are ontologies [42]. Ontology is a formal specification of a conceptualization of a given field, including the concepts used in that field, as well as the relationships between these concepts. The purpose of an ontology is to define uniform terminology and interpretation of terms [36]. Ontologies are sets of expressions that must be clearly understood and must be suitable for automatic processing by computer programs. Ontology instructions can either define general concepts or describe specific objects and events associated with them. Overall, an ontology consists of elements representing two different types of knowledge – terminology and assertions. Terminology, referred to as TBox (terminological box), is a formal representation of the classes and properties of objects in a given field, as well as the relationships between these classes and properties [10]. Assertions, referred to as ABox (assertional box), refer to specific objects (individuals, instances) in a specific fragment of the modeled reality, described by classes and properties specified in the TBox.

In 3D modeling, ontologies consisting of TBox instructions (TBox ontologies) correspond to 3D scene templates [18]. For example, a TBox ontology can specify classes of exhibitions in a virtual museum, with various categories of artifacts, such as statues, stamps and coins, as well as spatial properties of the artifacts [16]. 3D scene templates can describe many 3D scenes. Ontologies consisting of ABox instructions (ABox ontologies) describe individual 3D scenes or elements of 3D scenes. For example, an ABox ontology can describe a specific exhibition with artifacts in a virtual museum that meet the conditions set out in the TBox ontology – they belong to individual classes and are described by specific property values.

The basic element of the semantic web used to build ontologies is the Resource Description Framework (RDF) [43]. RDF is a data model that enables the creation of so-called resource expressions. It enables to describe resources available on the internet in a way "understandable" for computers (easily processable by computer programs). The Resource Description Framework Schema (RDFS) [44] and the Web Ontology Language (OWL) [41] are languages for building statements in RDF-based ontologies and knowledge bases.

RDF enables describing resources with expressions consisting of three elements: subject (resource described in the instruction), predicate (subject's property) and object (value of the property describing the subject) [43]. RDF also introduces basic concepts for describing resources, such as data types, sets and lists. RDF can be used with various types of content: text, graphic, audio and other documents. The RDFS and OWL standards extend RDF with the possibility of creating class hierarchies and properties, restrictions, properties of these restrictions and operations on sets. In turn, Semantic Web Rule Language (SWRL) extends OWL with rules.

2.3   Semantic Modeling of VR Content

A number of works have been devoted to ontology-based representation of 3D content, including a variety of geometrical, structural, spatial and presentational elements. A comprehensive review of the approaches has been presented in [18]. Existing methods are summarized in Table 1. Four of the methods address the low (graphics-specific) abstraction level, while six methods address a high (general or domain-specific) abstraction level. Three of those methods may be used with different domain ontologies.

Table 1. Comparison of semantic 3D content modeling methods

Approach	Level of abstraction	
	Low (3D graphics)	High (application domain)
De Troyer et al. [8,11,12,27,32]	✓	General
Gutiérrez et al. [20,21]	✓	Humanoids
Kalogerakis et al. [25]	✓	–
Spagnuolo et al. [2,3,34]	–	Humanoids
Floriani et al. [9,30]	✓	–
Kapahnke et al. [26]	–	General
Albrecht et al. [1]	–	Interior design
Latoschik et al. [14,28,46]	–	General
Drap et al. [13]	–	Archaeology
Trellet et al. [37,38]	–	Molecules
Perez-Gallardo et al. [33]	✓	–

The method proposed in [8,11,12,27,32] enables content creation at both the low and a high abstraction levels. Different 3D content ontologies connected by mapping are used at particular levels. Low-level ontologies may be created by graphic designers, while high-level ontologies may be created by domain experts. Mapping of low- to high-level ontologies adds interpretation to graphical components and properties. The approach also enables combination of primitive actions (e.g., move, turn, rotate, etc.) to complex behavior intelligible to end users without the knowledge of computer graphics.

The method proposed in [20,21] also enables 3D content creation at both low and high abstraction levels. Ontologies used in the method include graphical 3D content components (e.g., shapes and textures) and properties (e.g., coordinates and indices) as well as high-level domain-specific components (e.g., body parts) and properties (e.g., joint attributes, descriptors of articulation levels, 3D animations of face and body, and behavior controllers).

The method proposed in [25] enables 3D content creation at the low abstraction level. The used ontology provides components and properties that are equivalents of X3D nodes and attributes, e.g., textures, dimensions, coordinates and LODs. The method does not enable mapping between high- and low-level concepts, so it is unsuitable for modeling 3D content by domain experts.

A method of creating 3D humanoids has been proposed in [2,3,34]. After automatic segmentation of 3D models, the identified body parts are semantically annotated. Two modes of annotation have been developed. Automatic annotation is completed by software considering topological relations between content elements (e.g., orientation, size, adjacency and overlapping). Manual annotation is completed by a user equipped with a graphical tool.

The method proposed in [9,30] enables creation of non-manifold 3D shapes using low-level properties. Once 3D shapes are segmented, graphical properties are mapped to a shape ontology and form an ontology-based low-level shape representation. The ontology specifies diverse geometrical properties of shapes: non-manifold singularities (e.g., isolated points and curves), one-dimensional parts, connected elements, maximal connected elements, the number of vertices, the number of non-manifold vertices, the number of edges, the number of non-manifold edges and the number of connected elements. It permits representation of such objects as a spider-web, an umbrella with wires and a cone touching a plane at a single point.

The tool described in [26] leverages semantic concepts, services and hybrid automata to describe objects' behavior in 3D simulations. The tool has a client-server architecture. The client is based on a 3D browser, e.g., for XML3D, while the server is built of several services enabling 3D content creation. A graphical module maintains and renders 3D scene graphs. A scene module manages global scene ontologies, which represent the created simulations. A verification module checks spatial and temporal requirements against properties of content elements. An agent module manages intelligent avatars, e.g., their perception of the scene. The user interface enables communication with web-based and immersive virtual reality platforms. Ontology-based content representations are encoded in XML using the RDFa and OWL standards, and linked to 3D content encoded in XML3D.

In [1], a method of 3D content creation based on point clouds has been proposed. At the first stage of the method, an input point cloud is analyzed to discover planar patches, their properties (e.g., locations) and relations. Then an OWL reasoner processes a domain ontology, including conceptual elements that potentially match the analyzed patches. Next, matching elements are selected and configured to build a high-level representation in the interior design domain. Created representations are ontology-based equivalents to the input point clouds.

In [14,28,46], a general-purpose tool and a method of 3D content creation has been described. The method is based on actors and entities, which represent

3D content at a high level. They are described by shared state variables and are subject to events. In particular, the approach can be used in game design.

In [13], a method and software for representing underwater archaeological objects in 3D have been presented. In the approach, a Java-based application generates an ontology representing objects. Further, queries encoded in the SWRL language [40] can be used to select objects to build a 3D visualization.

In [37,38], an approach to semantic representation of 3D molecular models has been proposed. The approach combines different input (e.g., interaction using different haptic and motion tracking devices) and output (e.g., presentation in 2D and 3D) modalities to enable presentation and interaction suitable for particular content types and tasks to be done.

In [33], a system for 3D recognition of industrial spaces has been presented. The method used in the system recognizes objects in point clouds presenting interiors of factories. The recognized objects, their properties and relations, which are specific to 3D graphics, are further semantically represented using ontologies. On this basis, topological relations between objects are inferred.

The presented review indicates that there is a lack of a generic semantic method that could be used for creating interactive VR training scenarios in different application domains. The existing ontologies are either 3D-specific (with focus on static 3D content properties) or domain-specific (with focus on a single application domain). They lack domain-independent conceptualization of actions and interactions, which could be used by non-technical users in different domains to generate VR applications with limited help from graphics designers and programmers. In turn, the solutions focused on 3D content behavior, such as [15,17], use rules, which only to a limited extent fit the semantic web concept [40].

3 Building VR Training Scenes

3D VR training environments in our approach are created using a variety of hardware and software tools, including 3D laser scanners [45], CAD packages [6], 3D modeling software [5] and game engines [39], and are annotated using databases. The process consists of five main stages, as described below.

1. Physical elements of the training environment infrastructure are scanned into a polygon mesh. The mesh is encoded in STEP format [4] to enable further editing in subsequent stages. STEP is a standardized and widely used textual data format for CAD software (ISO 10303-21). It enables conversion of point clouds into CAD drawings without the risk of loosing relevant information. At this stage, the models contain no information about the hierarchy and semantics of particular elements.

2. Idealized and optimized 3D representations of the infrastructure elements are created using CAD software based on the scans. The main goal of this stage is to isolate groups of 3D model components, which will then be edited at the next stages. A designer performs the following steps: importing the STEP models into the CAD environment, dividing 3D models into components,

grouping 3D model components, and exporting the 3D models to DWG [7]. In case of the models presented in this paper, the AutoCAD environment was used due to its rich functionality and the ability to import non-standard file formats. An important advantage of this software is low CPU usage, which results in the possibility of editing complex objects. However, AutoCAD is primarily a design package and does not provide the functionality required for building visually appealing VR models.

3. 3D visual models of the infrastructure elements are created with the use of a 3D modeling environment. This stage aims to correct and optimize 3D models that contain unnecessary and repetitive elements and geometry defects. At this stage, the designer performs the following steps: importing 3D models into the modeling environment, removing repetitive components, correcting the geometry of 3D models, creating several LOD (Levels of Detail) for efficient rendering, and exporting the 3D models into the FBX format [24]. FBX is the primary 3D model format supported by game engines, in particular, the Unity 3D engine [39]. An example of a 3D modeling package, which can be used at this stage, is 3ds Max [5].

4. VR training scenes are assembled from the 3D visual models with the use of a 3D scene editor tool, built as an extension of a game engine IDE. The designer performs the following steps: importing 3D models saved in FBX format, creating a hierarchy of objects in the 3D scene, setting the spatial properties of 3D objects, configuring points and axes of rotation of 3D model components, assigning materials and textures to 3D models, and instantiating repetitive components of the scene model. The designer can use a 3D point cloud from the 3D scanning process as a reference in building the scene.

5. Databases of scene objects and equipment are created. The scene object database is specific to a particular VR training scene and describes the structure of objects (e.g., switchboard) and elements (e.g., switches and indicators) of the infrastructure that can be used in scenarios for the given scene. The database can be partially automatically generated based on the scene content and then extended by domain-experts using specifically designed interactive forms. Each element is associated possible states, in particular, boolean states (e.g., on, off), discrete states (e.g., gauge mode) and continuous states (e.g., voltage). The database of equipment includes elements shared by all scenarios, such as protective equipment and tools for performing particular types of works, and is created manually.

4   Modeling VR Training Scenarios

When the 3D model of a training scene together with the associated databases is available (cf. Sect. 3), the next important step is to design a training scenario. Scenario describes VR scene's behavior and interactivity, but is also a means of conveying the training material. Typically, programming scenarios is a complex and time-consuming process of writing scripts in a programming language supported by the game engine (C# in case of Unity 3D), which must be performed by a programmer.

Often, the same 3D training scene may be used with multiple different training scenarios. The scenarios may cover standard procedures to be performed or non-typical repair and maintenance actions. In each case, it should be possible to simulate malfunction of some of the elements to test subject's behavior in more complex situations. Moreover, simulation of different conditions (season, weather, daytime) or constraints (available equipment, time) may further improve the quality and versatility of the training process. Therefore, it becomes critical to permit the design of training scenarios in a quick and easy manner by domain experts without low-level programming in VR.

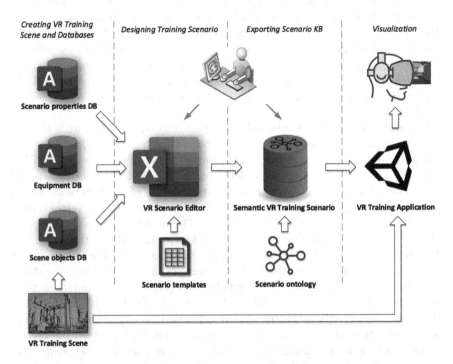

Fig. 1. Process of building a training scenario for a VR scene

4.1   Creating Training Scenarios

The process of creating a training scenario for a VR training scene in our approach is presented in Fig. 1. After a VR training scene and associated databases have been built, a training scenario can be created in three steps, as described below.

1. Designing a scenario using the VR Scenario Editor (VRSEd) application implemented as an extension to Microsoft Excel. The VRSEd editor provides several tools to support users in the design process. A scenario template is

imported to the editor. The template provides an overall structure and visual appearance of the scenario spreadsheet. Different templates may be used for different user groups or when the set of required attributes changes. Attribute values for selection lists in the scenario editor are retrieved from the scenario properties database. A scenario spreadsheet describes a sequence of training activities that should be executed by a single trainee, with possible trainee mistakes and system errors, e.g., lock the controller if possible, then switch off the transformer. The role of a trainer is reflected implicitly in the scenarios, by hints and comments shown to the trainee while training.

2. Exporting the scenario to a semantic VR scenario knowledge base, using a scenario exporter implemented in the VRSEd scenario editor. The knowledge base is encoded using RDF, RDFS and OWL standards and includes all information necessary for proper execution of the scenario in the VR Training Application. The knowledge base is an ABox compatible with the TBox scenario ontology. In other words, the scenario ontology specifies the terminology in the form of classes and properties, which is used in assertions specified in the scenario knowledge base. The generated scenario knowledge base consists of statements (RDF triples), which are counterparts to the particular rows of the scenario spreadsheet.

3. Importing the semantic VR scenario knowledge base into the VR Training Application implemented in the Unity 3D game engine. The scenario is loaded for a specific VR training scene described by the scenario. The correct assignment of the scene and the scenario is verified during the import. The knowledge base importer creates a hierarchy of script objects, which is then directly used during the scene runtime. One can import another scenario to the same VR training scene to provide different types of training.

4.2 Databases

The three databases shown in Fig. 1 provide all necessary data required by the VRSEd scenario editor to build a VR training scenario. All databases are currently implemented in Microsoft Access. In the next versions of the environment, in which remote access to databases will be required, the databases will be implemented in an SQL RDBMS.

Database of Scene Objects. For each VR training scene, a database of scene objects is created. The database contains 3 tables: *Objects*, *Elements* and *States*. The Objects table provides information about all infrastructure objects within the scene. The Elements table contains records corresponding to particular elements of objects, on which actions are performed or whose state depends on the user actions. The States table contains records representing all possible states of infrastructure objects' elements, on which actions can be performed.

Database of Equipment. The equipment database is common to all training scenarios created using the VRSEd scenario editor. The database contains information about protective equipment (such as a protective visor, gloves or helmet) and specific work equipment, which may be required to perform particular tasks. The database contains also information how information about the need to use the particular kind of equipment should be presented to a user, and the representation of the equipment in a VR scene.

Database of Scenario Properties. In addition to data specific to a given virtual training scene, such as infrastructure objects, object elements and object states, the scenario editor must have access to all possible values of their properties. The list of values is common for all scenarios and is stored in the database of scenario properties. These values are included in the drop-down lists, when a user selects a property value. In particular, these are properties containing information on the types of work performed, types of equipment required for performing particular types of work, and types of protective equipment. The scenario properties database contains two tables: *Attributes* and *Fields*. The Attributes table contains attributes in the scenario tables that can be supplemented by selecting fields from drop-down lists. An example attribute is "Item mapping fidelity". The Fields table contains all possible values of attributes. Each attribute may be associated with multiple field values. Field values for "Item mapping fidelity" can be "High", "Medium", and "Low".

4.3   VR Scenario Editor Application

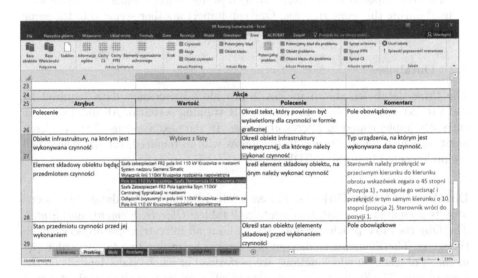

Fig. 2. The VR Scenario Editor implemented as extension to Microsoft Excel

The VR Scenario Editor (VRSEd) application has been implemented as an extension to Microsoft Excel (Fig. 2) to enable quick and efficient creation of training scenarios by non-IT-specialists. The main advantages of using MS Excel as the editor implementation platform include the popularity of the software, which eliminates the need to install additional programs, the availability of numerous well-documented add-ons and programming libraries, as well as a wide community of users.

On top of the window (Fig. 2), the VRSEd toolbar is visible. It provides tools for importing databases, loading a scenario template, and creating different types of entities that may be used in a scenario (steps, activities, actions, objects, elements, problems, etc.).

Individual scenario sheets (visible on the bottom) contain descriptions of basic scenario properties, the course of the scenario, errors and problems that may occur in the scenario, and different types of equipment to be used. Each sheet consists of different types of tables. The Scenario sheet contains general information about the scenario and the required equipment.

The main sheet of the workbook provides information about the course of the scenario. It describes the training in the form of a logical sequence of *steps*, *activities*, and *actions* to be performed by a trainee. In each scenario, at least one step must be defined. Steps are divided into activities. Each activity can be associated with a problem that may occur during the training, an error that can be made, and the necessary equipment. Within an activity, the trainee performs actions on infrastructure objects that are described using the Action table (visible in Fig. 2). The Action table lists the *objects* and *elements* of the infrastructure, on which the action is carried out, the way their states change as a result of the action, and how this change in state is reflected in the training. The sequential form of scenarios is sufficient for a vast majority of training scenarios in the selected domain, with possible side threads represented by trainee's mistakes and system errors.

Various types of errors may be made during a training session, which are described in the Errors sheet. Each error is described by properties that specify how to inform the trainee about the error and how the system responds to the error. The Problems worksheet contains the table Potential problem showing events that may occur during the training that disrupt the work course. A problem may be associated with elements of objects in the scene that depend on the problem, i.e., their state changes. For any potential problem, the trainee may make an error when trying to resolve it.

The structure of scenario spreadsheets, which is based on tables, matches the structure of scenario knowledge bases based on RDF triples (cf. Sect. 2.2). When a scenario is exported into a semantic VR scenario knowledge base, every table is exported to multiple triples. The table identifier designates the subject of a triple (e.g., action), the attribute name in a particular row in the first column designates the predicate (e.g., infrastructure object id), and the attribute value in the row in the second column designates the predicate value (e.g., a particular object id selected from the list)—Fig. 2.

4.4   Ontology and Semantic Scenario Knowledge Base

A formal *scenario ontology* has been designed to enable semantic description of training scenarios in VR. The scenario ontology is a TBox, which specifies the classes and properties used to describe training scenarios (ABox), as well as relationships between these classes and properties. The scenario ontology has been implemented using the RDF, RDFS and OWL standards.

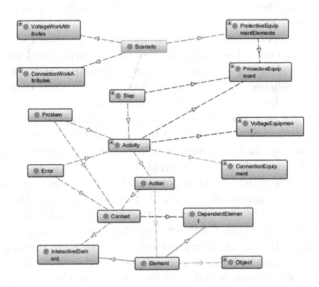

Fig. 3. Ontology of VR training scenarios

The entities specified in the scenario ontology, as well as the relations between them, are depicted in Fig. 3. The entities encompass classes (rectangles) and properties (arrows) that fall into three categories describing: the workflow of training scenarios, objects and elements of the infrastructure, and equipment necessary to execute actions on the infrastructure.

Every *scenario* is represented by an individual of the *Scenario* class. A scenario consists of at least one *Step*, which is the basic element of the workflow, which consists of at least one *Activity*. Steps and activities correspond to two levels of generalization of the tasks to be completed by training participants. Activities specify equipment required when performing the works. In the VR training environment, it can be presented as a toolkit, from which the user can select the necessary tools. Steps and activities may also specify protective equipment. *Actions*, which are grouped into activities, specify particular indivisible tasks completed using the equipment specified for the activity. Actions are executed on infrastructural components of two categories: *Objects* and *Elements*, which form two-level hierarchies. A technician, who executes an action, changes the *State* of an object's element (called *Interactive Element*), which may affect elements of this or other objects (called *Dependent Elements*). For example, a control panel of a dashboard is used to switch on and off a transformer, which is announced on the panel and influences the infrastructure. N-ary relations between different entities in a scenario are represented by individuals of the *Context* class, e.g., associated actions, elements, and states. Non-typical situations in the workflow are modeled using *Errors* and *Problems*. While errors are due to the user, e.g., a skipped action on a controller, problems are due to the infrastructure, e.g., a controller's failure.

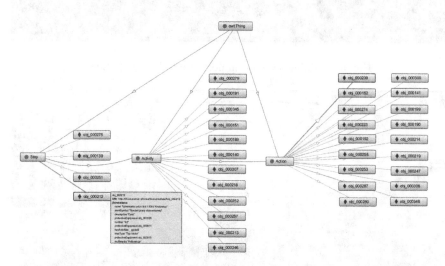

Fig. 4. VR training scenario described as a semantic knowledge base (fragment)

The scenario knowledge base is an ABox specifying a specific training scenario consisting of steps, activities and actions, along with its elements and infrastructure objects, which are described by classes and properties specified in the scenario ontology (Fig. 4). Scenario knowledge bases are encoded in OWL/Turtle. A scenario knowledge base is generated based on the scenario Excel workbook by the VRSEd KB exporter module. It is then imported into the VR Training Application by an importer module, which – based on the scenario KB – generates the equivalent object model of the scenario.

5 Example VR Training Scenario

A VR training scenario designed with VRSEd can be imported into the VR Training Application. In Fig. 5, a training scenario imported into the Unity 3D IDE is presented. On the left, the training scene is visible with scenario objects highlighted. On the right, three levels of the scenario, together with their properties, can be seen.

In Fig. 6 and 7, the VR Training Application, as seen by a trainee in the VR mode, is presented. The trainee can place hand in the walkie-talkie area and

Fig. 5. Training scenario imported into Unity 3D IDE

Fig. 6. VR Training Application – execution of Step 1 Activity 1

press the controller button to display information about the step, activity and action to be performed (Fig. 8).

By changing the scenario in VRSEd, a designer can modify all attributes of any step, activity and action of the scenario. In Fig. 9, a scenario is presented that starts with the working area not properly marked. Marking of the work area is one of the mandatory steps before the real work can start. Therefore, the first step for the trainee will be to mark the area with an appropriate sign. In Fig. 10, the same scenario, but with the modified initial state, is presented. The working area is already clearly marked, which is visible in the model, and the trainee does not have to perform the action of marking. This change in VRSEd requires only selecting a different initial state from a list in one of the scenario rows. Performing this change directly in Unity 3D model and code would be a difficult and time-consuming operation.

Fig. 7. VR Training Application – execution of Step 1 Activity 2

Fig. 8. Avatar and walkie-talkie used to activate displaying of scenario commands

6   Results and Discussion

Training of employees in practical industrial environments requires the ability to design new and modify existing training scenarios efficiently. In practice, the number of scenarios is by far larger than the number of training scenes. In the case of training electrical operators of high-voltage installations, typically one 3D model of an electrical substation is associated with at least a dozen of different scenarios. These scenarios include learning daily maintenance operations, reactions to various problems that may occur in the installation as well as reactions to infrastructure malfunction.

The training scenarios are typically very complex. The "Karczyn" scenario used as an example in this paper covers only preparation for a specific maintenance work and consists of 4 steps, 11 activities, and 17 actions. For each action,

Fig. 9. Initial scenario state set to "Work Area Not Marked"

Fig. 10. Initial scenario state set to "Work Area Marked"

there are dependent objects (44 in case of this scenario). For each step, activity, action and object, the scenario provides specific attributes (9–10 for each item). For each attribute, the name, value, command and comment are provided. In total, the specification of the course of the scenario consists of 945 rows in Excel. In addition, there are 69 rows of specifications of errors and 146 rows of specification of problems. The scenario also covers protective equipment, specific work equipment, and others.

The generic scenario ontology (TBox) encoded in OWL takes 1,505 lines of code and 55,320 bytes in total. The "Karczyn" scenario saved in Turtle (which is a more efficient way of encoding ontologies and knowledge bases) has 2,930 lines of code and 209,139 bytes in total.

Implementation of the "Karczyn" scenario directly as a set of Unity 3D C# scripts would lead to very complex code, difficult to verify and maintain even by a highly-proficient programmer. The design of such a scenario is clearly beyond the capabilities of most domain experts dealing with everyday training of electrical workers.

The use of the VRSEd tool, together with a formal ontology described in this paper, enables concise representation of the scenario, and provides means of editing and verification of scenario correctness with a user-friendly and familiar tool. Moreover, by using different scenario templates, the tool can be customized for different user groups, providing branding, explanatory graphics, automation, hints and custom fields further simplifying the scenario design process.

An important aspect to consider is the size of the scenario representations. The total size of the "Karczyn" Unity 3D project is 58 GB, while the size of the executable version is only 1.8 GB. Storing 20 scenarios in editable form as Unity projects would require 1.16 TB of disk space. Storing 20 scenarios in the form of semantic knowledge bases requires only 4 MB of storage space (plus the size of the executable application). Such scenario representations can be easily exchanged over the network between different training sites.

The ability to save scenarios at any stage of their development in the form of Excel files further contributes to the increased solution's usability. The "Karczyn" scenario saved as an XLSX file requires 447 KB. One can easily create and store multiple versions of multiple scenarios on a typical laptop computer.

7 Conclusions and Future Works

The method of semantic modeling of VR training scenarios presented in this paper enables flexible and precise modeling of scenarios at a high level of abstraction using concepts specific to a particular application domain instead of forcing the designer to use low-level programming with techniques specific to computer graphics. The presented VRSEd editor, in turn, enables efficient creation and modification of the scenarios by domain experts. Hence, the method and the tool make the development of VR applications, which generally is a highly technical task, attainable to non-technical users allowing them to use in the design process concepts of their domains of interest.

Future works include several elements. First, the environment will be extended to support collaborative creation of scenarios by distributed users. It will require changing the document-based database implementation (currently with Microsoft Access) with a full relational SQL database management system supporting transactions and concurrent access of multiple users. Second, we plan to extend the training application to support not only the training mode, but also the verification mode of operation with appropriate scoring based on user's performance. Finally, we plan to extend the scenario ontology with concepts of parallel sequences of activities, which can be desirable for multi-user training, e.g., in firefighting.

Acknowledgments. The research work presented in this paper has been supported by the European Union from the European Regional Development Fund within the Smart Growth Operational Programme 2020–2024. The project is executed within the priority axis "Support for R&D Activity of Enterprises" of the National Centre for Research and Development under the contract POIR.01.01.01-00-0463/18.

References

1. Albrecht, S., Wiemann, T., Günther, M., Hertzberg, J.: Matching CAD object models in semantic mapping. In: Proceedings ICRA 2011 Workshop: Semantic Perception, Mapping and Exploration, SPME (2011)
2. Attene, M., Robbiano, F., Spagnuolo, M., Falcidieno, B.: Semantic annotation of 3D surface meshes based on feature characterization. In: Falcidieno, B., Spagnuolo, M., Avrithis, Y., Kompatsiaris, I., Buitelaar, P. (eds.) SAMT 2007. LNCS, vol. 4816, pp. 126–139. Springer, Heidelberg (2007). https://doi.org/10.1007/978-3-540-77051-0_15
3. Attene, M., Robbiano, F., Spagnuolo, M., Falcidieno, B.: Characterization of 3D shape parts for semantic annotation. Comput. Aided Des. **41**(10), 756–763 (2009). https://doi.org/10.1016/j.cad.2009.01.003
4. Autodesk: STEP (STP, STEP) Files (2019). https://knowledge.autodesk.com/support/3ds-max/learn-explore/caas/CloudHelp/cloudhelp/2020/ENU/3DSMax-Data-Exchange/files/GUID-B5F0FE98-B42C-48EC-AC94-0D1B25AD97F2-htm.html
5. Autodesk: 3ds Max (2020). https://www.autodesk.pl/products/3ds-max/overview
6. Autodesk: AutoCAD Civil 3D (2020). http://www.autodesk.com/products/autocad-civil-3d/overview
7. Autodesk: DWG Format (2020). https://www.autodesk.com/products/dwg
8. Bille, W., De Troyer, O., Pellens, B., Kleinermann, F.: Conceptual modeling of articulated bodies in virtual environments. In: Thwaites, H. (ed.) Proceedings of the 11th International Conference on Virtual Systems and Multimedia (VSMM), Archaeolingua, Ghent, Belgium, pp. 17–26 (2005)
9. De Floriani, L., Hui, A., Papaleo, L., Huang, M., Hendler, J.: A semantic web environment for digital shapes understanding. In: Falcidieno, B., Spagnuolo, M., Avrithis, Y., Kompatsiaris, I., Buitelaar, P. (eds.) SAMT 2007. LNCS, vol. 4816, pp. 226–239. Springer, Heidelberg (2007). https://doi.org/10.1007/978-3-540-77051-0_25
10. De Giacomo, G., Lenzerini, M.: TBox and ABox reasoning in expressive description logics. In: Proceedings of the Fifth International Conference on the Principles of Knowledge Representation and Reasoning (KR 1996), vol. 1996, pp. 37–48 (1996)
11. De Troyer, O., Kleinermann, F., Mansouri, H., Pellens, B., Bille, W., Fomenko, V.: Developing semantic VR-shops for e-Commerce. Virtual Reality **11**(2–3), 89–106 (2007)
12. De Troyer, O., Kleinermann, F., Pellens, B., Bille, W.: Conceptual modeling for virtual reality. In: Grundy, J., Hartmann, S., Laender, A.H.F., Maciaszek, L., Roddick, J.F. (eds.) Tutorials, Posters, Panels and Industrial Contributions at the 26th International Conference on Conceptual Modeling - ER 2007. CRPIT, vol. 83, pp. 3–18. ACS, Auckland, New Zealand (2007)

13. Drap, P., Papini, O., Sourisseau, J.-C., Gambin, T.: Ontology-based photogrammetric survey in underwater archaeology. In: Blomqvist, E., Hose, K., Paulheim, H., Ławrynowicz, A., Ciravegna, F., Hartig, O. (eds.) ESWC 2017. LNCS, vol. 10577, pp. 3–6. Springer, Cham (2017). https://doi.org/10.1007/978-3-319-70407-4_1

14. Fischbach, M., et al.: SiXton's curse - simulator X demonstration. In: Hirose, M., Lok, B., Majumder, A., Schmalstieg, D. (eds.) Virtual Reality Conference (VR), pp. 255–256. IEEE (2011). http://dx.doi.org/10.1109/VR.2011.5759495

15. Flotyński, J., Krzyszkowski, M., Walczak, K.: Semantic composition of 3D content behavior for explorable virtual reality applications. In: Barbic, J., D'Cruz, M., Latoschik, M.E., Slater, M., Bourdot, P. (eds.) EuroVR 2017. LNCS, vol. 10700, pp. 3–23. Springer, Cham (2017). https://doi.org/10.1007/978-3-319-72323-5_1

16. Flotyński, J., Walczak, K.: Customization of 3D content with semantic meta-scenes. Graph. Models **88**, 23–39 (2016). https://doi.org/10.1016/j.gmod.2016.07.001

17. Flotyński, J., Walczak, K.: Knowledge-based representation of 3D content behavior in a service-oriented virtual environment. In: Proceedings of the 22nd International Conference on Web3D Technology, Brisbane (Australia), 5–7 June 2017, p. Article No. 14. ACM, New York (2017). https://doi.org/10.1145/3055624.3075959

18. Flotyński, J., Walczak, K.: Ontology-based representation and modelling of synthetic 3D content: a state-of-the-art review. Comput. Graph. Forum **35**, 329–353 (2017). https://doi.org/10.1111/cgf.13083

19. Gavish, N., et al.: Evaluating virtual reality and augmented reality training for industrial maintenance and assembly tasks. Interact. Learn. Environ. **23**(6), 778–798 (2015). https://doi.org/10.1080/10494820.2013.815221

20. Gutiérrez, M.: Semantic virtual environments, EPFL (2005)

21. Gutiérrez, M., Thalmann, D., Vexo, F.: Semantic virtual environments with adaptive multimodal interfaces. In: Chen, Y.P.P. (ed.) MMM, pp. 277–283. IEEE Computer Society (2005)

22. Hoffman, H., Vu, D.: Virtual reality: teaching tool of the twenty-first century? Acad. Med.: J. Assoc. Am. Med. Coll. **72**(12), 1076–1081 (1997). https://doi.org/10.1097/00001888-199712000-00018

23. Instituto Nacional de Electricidad y Energías Limpias: Sala de prensa (2017). https://www.ineel.mx/detalle-de-la-nota.html?id=38

24. Jeong, T., Kim, Y.: A new lightweight file format based on FBX for efficient 3D graphics resource processing. J. Theor. Appl. Inf. Technol. **97**, 2393–2403 (2018)

25. Kalogerakis, E., Christodoulakis, S., Moumoutzis, N.: Coupling ontologies with graphics content for knowledge driven visualization. In: VR 2006 Proceedings of the IEEE Conference on Virtual Reality, Alexandria, Virginia, USA, pp. 43–50, March 2006

26. Kapahnke, P., Liedtke, P., Nesbigall, S., Warwas, S., Klusch, M.: ISReal: an open platform for semantic-based 3D simulations in the 3D internet. In: Patel-Schneider, P.F., et al. (eds.) ISWC 2010. LNCS, vol. 6497, pp. 161–176. Springer, Heidelberg (2010). https://doi.org/10.1007/978-3-642-17749-1_11

27. Kleinermann, F., De Troyer, O., Mansouri, H., Romero, R., Pellens, B., Bille, W.: Designing semantic virtual reality applications. In: Proceedings of the 2nd Intuition International Workshop, Senlis, pp. 5–10 (2005)

28. Latoschik, M.E., Tramberend, H.: Simulator X: a scalable and concurrent software platform for intelligent realtime interactive systems. In: Proceedings of the IEEE VR 2011 (2011)

29. Lugrin, J.L.: Alternative reality and causality in virtual environments. Ph.D. thesis, University of Teesside, Middlesbrough, United Kingdom (2009)

30. Papaleo, L., De Floriani, L., Hendler, J., Hui, A.: Towards a semantic web system for understanding real world representations. In: Proceedings of the Tenth International Conference on Computer Graphics and Artificial Intelligence (2007)
31. Patoni, R.: Alen 3D. https://www.scribd.com/document/245796121/ALEN-3D
32. Pellens, B., De Troyer, O., Bille, W., Kleinermann, F., Romero, R.: An ontology-driven approach for modeling behavior in virtual environments. In: Meersman, R., Tari, Z., Herrero, P. (eds.) OTM 2005. LNCS, vol. 3762, pp. 1215–1224. Springer, Heidelberg (2005). https://doi.org/10.1007/11575863_145
33. Perez-Gallardo, Y., Cuadrado, J.L.L., Crespo, Á.G., de Jesús, C.G.: GEODIM: a semantic model-based system for 3D recognition of industrial scenes. In: Alor-Hernández, G., Valencia-García, R. (eds.) Current Trends on Knowledge-Based Systems. ISRL, vol. 120, pp. 137–159. Springer, Cham (2017). https://doi.org/10.1007/978-3-319-51905-0_7
34. Robbiano, F., Attene, M., Spagnuolo, M., Falcidieno, B.: Part-based annotation of virtual 3D shapes. In: 2013 International Conference on Cyberworlds, pp. 427–436 (2007)
35. Schneider Electric: HoloLens Application on Premset (2017). https://www.youtube.com/watch?v=RpXyagutoZg
36. Sikos, L.F.: Description Logics in Multimedia Reasoning. Springer, Cham (2017). https://doi.org/10.1007/978-3-319-54066-5
37. Trellet, M., Ferey, N., Baaden, M., Bourdot, P.: Interactive visual analytics of molecular data in immersive environments via a semantic definition of the content and the context. In: 2016 Workshop on Immersive Analytics (IA), pp. 48–53. IEEE (2016)
38. Trellet, M., Férey, N., Flotyński, J., Baaden, M., Bourdot, P.: Semantics for an integrative and immersive pipeline combining visualization and analysis of molecular data. J. Integr. Bioinform. **15**(2), 1–19 (2018)
39. Unity Technologies: Unity (2020). http://unity.com/
40. W3C: SWRL: A Semantic Web Rule Language Combining OWL and RuleML (2004). http://www.w3.org/Submission/SWRL/
41. W3C: OWL 2 Web Ontology Language Structural Specification and Functional-Style Syntax (Second Edition) (2012). https://www.w3.org/TR/owl2-syntax/
42. W3C: Building the Web of Data (2013). http://www.w3.org/2013/data/
43. W3C: RDF 1.1 Concepts and Abstract Syntax (2014). https://www.w3.org/TR/rdf11-concepts/
44. W3C: RDF Schema 1.1 (2014). https://www.w3.org/TR/rdf-schema/
45. Walczak, K., Flotyński, J.: Inference-based creation of synthetic 3D content with ontologies. Multimedia Tools Appl. **78**(9), 12607–12638 (2019). https://doi.org/10.1007/s11042-018-6788-5
46. Wiebusch, D., Latoschik, M.E.: Enhanced decoupling of components in intelligent realtime interactive systems using ontologies. In: Software Engineering and Architectures for Realtime Interactive Systems (SEARIS), Proceedings of the IEEE Virtual Reality 2012 Workshop, pp. 43–51 (2012)

Exploiting Extended Reality Technologies for Educational Microscopy

Helena G. Theodoropoulou[1] , Chairi Kiourt[2(✉)] , Aris S. Lalos[1] ,
Anestis Koutsoudis[2] , Evgenia Paxinou[3] , Dimitris Kalles[3] ,
and George Pavlidis[2]

[1] Industrial Systems Institute, Athena-Research and Innovation Center in Information,
Communication and Knowledge Technologies, Patra, Greece
hetheod@gmail.com, lalos@isi.gr
[2] Institute for Language and Speech Processing, Athena-Research and Innovation
Center in Information, Communication and Knowledge Technologies, Xanthi, Greece
{chairiq,akoutsou,gpavlid}@athenarc.gr
[3] School of Science and Technology, Hellenic Open University, Patra, Greece
paxinou.evgenia@ac.eap.gr, kalles@eap.gr

Abstract. Exploiting extended reality technologies in laboratory training enhances both teaching and learning experiences. It complements the existing traditional learning/teaching methods related to science, technology, engineering, arts and mathematics. In this work, we use extended reality technologies to create an interactive learning environment with dynamic educational content. The proposed learning environment can be used by students of all levels of education, to facilitate laboratory-based understanding of scientific concepts. We introduce a low-cost and user-friendly multi-platform system for mobile devices which, when coupled with edutainment dynamics, simulation, extended reality and natural hand movements sensing technologies such as hand gestures with virtual triggers, is expected to engage users and prepare them efficiently for the actual on-site laboratory experiments. The proposed system is evaluated by a group of experts and the results are analyzed in detail, indicating the positive attitude of the evaluators towards the adoption of the proposed system in laboratory educational procedures. We conclude the paper by highlighting the capabilities of extended reality and dynamic content management in educational microscopy procedures.

Keywords: Extended reality · STEAM education · Interactive technologies · Mobile extended reality · Human-computer interactions

1 Introduction

A key element of teaching content derived from Science, Technology, Engineering, Arts and Mathematics (STEAM), is the availability of laboratory infrastructure as it offers the opportunity to acquire skills and a deeper understanding of natural phenomena [1]. In 1989, Nersessian [2] stressed that, *"practical experience is the heart of science learning"*, which indicates the importance of having practical laboratories procedures within the

© Springer Nature Switzerland AG 2020
P. Bourdot et al. (Eds.): EuroVR 2020, LNCS 12499, pp. 149–162, 2020.
https://doi.org/10.1007/978-3-030-62655-6_9

educational process. Nonetheless, the installation of laboratory infrastructure requires space, personnel and time, while its operation and maintenance can often raise costs at a prohibitive level [3]. Considering this and the evolution of all disciplines, there has been a growing need for innovative and low-cost methods/techniques/systems to be introduced when teaching STEAM [4–7]. Information and Communication Technology (ICT) has been introducing tools and systems for years now to complement laboratory training. Nowadays, with the introduction of cutting-edge technologies such as Extended Reality (XR), ICT has shown promising future outcomes towards the enhancement of the "hands-on labs" (physically involved in laboratory performed activities) approach, by overcoming obstacles related to budget, distance and availability.

The main contribution of this paper is the introduction of an innovative and interactive educational mobile XR tool/system based on dynamic content for assisting learners in laboratory instrument manipulation. To demonstrate our approaches, we make use of a microscope (and its components) as it composes one of the fundamental instruments of laboratories related to Biology, Physics and Chemistry (Science), which are also known as "wet labs" [8–11]. Within this framework, the proposed system aims to instruct learners about a microscope's main components and functionalities. Additionally, it enables users to learn about various laboratory procedures by interacting with the microscope using hand gestures over virtual triggers (single camera-based motion sensing technologies). Understanding the need and the importance of the dynamic management of educational content [12], this system introduces a Web based interface based on link data technologies [13]. It must be stressed that the proposed system also aims at the exploitation of edutainment approaches [14–17], setting the standards for increased immersion and presence in the XR environment, stimulating the user's senses, leading to better understanding of educational material and new skill development [16].

The rest of this paper is organized as follows. The following section covers a brief literature review of related works while indicating the novelties of the proposed system. The third section offers a detailed analysis of the system's architecture and components. The fourth section provides the educational approaches, while the fifth focuses on the system's objective evaluation. The paper concludes by summarizing the key points of the proposed system and sets out future directions.

2 Background

The evolution of Virtual Reality (VR) technologies combined with low cost equipment has allowed the emergence of innovative laboratory training solutions [18]. By using simulation techniques, researchers attempt to overcome cost, time and spatial obstacles thus changing the setting of STEAM education through the application of virtual laboratories [19, 20]. Studies have shown that students, who perform experiments in a virtual environment, become familiar with the laboratory instruments and, therefore, can be more actively involved in the physical lab training process [8].

Researchers pinpointed that the use of XR in STEAM education results in an increase of user achievement [21], engagement and motivation to accept change [22] as well as improved knowledge acquisition while amplifying both pleasure and enjoyment of being involved. The use of XR in laboratory training can provide efficient, safe, convenient, flexible and portable educational tools. Such tools allow users to access them easily, anytime and remotely (from any computer system that access the Web) [23]. Therefore, they can help prepare students for the on-site hands-on laboratory experience. Over the years, several studies have been conducted on the use of VR technology in laboratory training. Onlabs is a standalone 3D virtual reality biology laboratory that provides a high-level realistic environment for higher education students [20]. Becerra et al. [4] developed and evaluated a low-cost VR application for understanding of movement in physics by using gamification techniques. Bogusevschi and Muntean [6] introduced a VR application for experimental laboratory simulations of "Water Cycle in Nature" for primary school students. In the terms of learners' experience and application usability, the results were very encouraging.

Additionally, edutainment is often used, which is the combination of fun and education [16] that can be achieved either by incorporating elements of entertainment into a learning scenario or vice versa. The goal of edutainment is to make learning enjoyable, by enabling an interesting and engaging experience, transforming the learning process into an event, supporting the active participation [17]. Nowadays, technology provides the media that can stimulate learners' senses in order to maximize their engagement and understanding of the educational material, while enables the instructors to easily personalize and communicate the content of their teaching [24]. Aksakal [16], referring to the education expert David Buckingham said that when edutainment is based on visual context, constitutes "*the game of describing with least word*". Edutainment is widely applied through VR technology, with many future promising results through XR applications, since XR technology supports interaction, personalization and fun, through the undoubtfully interesting and engaging ability to simultaneously explore real and virtual elements in the same environment. Nevertheless, Okan [14] aptly states that during the design process of an edutainment application "*the question is how much "edu" and how much "tainment"* [25] *should be included*". Thus, the design of an edutainment software should be focused on the efficient communication of the educational content and the user should not be distracted by the enrichment content.

Nowadays, even though "physical" laboratories are still the fundamental core of STEAM laboratory education, researchers aim to develop systems and tools using XR technologies. However, the creation of a user-friendly enjoyable multilingual system/tool with personalized content which can be used in all levels of education is a challenging task especially when the corresponding effectiveness is required to remain unaffected by geographical, financial and time constraints. The proposed system constitutes a part of the integrated system XRLabs which explores the development of STEAM educational systems/tools based on conventional laboratory training procedures for students of all educational levels [7, 26]. The proposed system aims at allowing users to practice remotely without time and sources restrictions, focusing on skill acquisition and better understanding of laboratory procedures, by using a low-cost, user-friendly mobile XR solution for every education level.

3   User-Centric Extended Reality Based Framework

One of the most essential and frequently used instruments in hard science laboratories is the microscope. In our study we choose to make use of a photonic stereo microscope to exploit the capabilities of XR in STEAM education. The proposed system is structured on three main components (sub-systems): the dynamic management of the educational content, the implementation of AR/MR as part of the XR technology and the use of hand gestures as an interaction method (virtual buttons triggering).

Figure 1 depicts the system's main architecture. It clearly indicates that the educational part of the system appeals to many different user levels. The demonstration of the educational content takes place via the XR sub-system using mobile devices. Moreover, the educational content and the scenarios are managed by expert users (e.g. trainers) through a Web-based Graphical User Interface (GUI). On the other hand, it should be highlighted that users without Internet access may exploit some local content (considered as default).

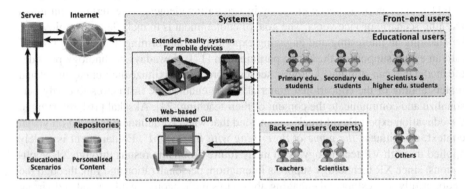

Fig. 1. System's architecture overview

3.1   Dynamic Content Management (DCM)

The first sub-system implements a Dynamic Content Management (DCM) application of the educational content using a Web-based GUI. The ability to add new user groups (different levels) as well as editing existing groups is the first step that experts (trainers etc.) should perform. Furthermore, they can select a list of target groups and assign to them appropriate educational content according to their interests. In addition, a system for registering users and logging in to the platform has been implemented to manage the users of the system (trainers and learners), enabling personalization. All content of the XR systems can be managed through the DCM sub-system in real-time. The application supports multiple languages, but the demonstration has been implemented to support English and Greek. Figure 2 depicts screenshots of the DCM.

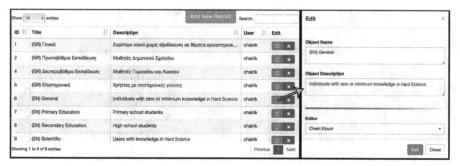

Fig. 2. Web-based dynamic content interface snapshots.

3.2 XR Sub-system

The second sub-system (XR) is aimed for mobile devices, Android and iOS smartphones and tablets, exploiting the advanced capabilities of the Unity game engine and the Vuforia SDK. Two different tracking methods are being exploited serving different purposes. Firstly, we exploit image marker tracking (marker-based methods) [27] to present the virtual laboratory instrument (3D microscope) on a real surface (e.g. table). To be more specific, when the device's camera detects a specially designed image (in our case composed of multiple QR codes) which operates as a marker, it triggers the display of the necessary virtual elements (microscope, virtual buttons) on top of it. This approach constitutes a version of the educational tool that aims to enable distance training when the real instrument is not available to the learner. Secondly, we exploit an advanced object recognition technique, based on model target detection, using the available 3D model of an object, in our case the microscope. In this case the user has the ability to superimpose information on top of the actual instrument. Specifically, when the camera detects the real microscope (physical laboratory instrument) and a pointer (dot) in the center of the screen aims at some component on the real microscope, that component is highlighted, and the relevant educational content appears next to it.

Both approaches can run independently or simultaneously. When applied together, the user has the opportunity to enhance her/his learning skills, by visually matching the focused part of the virtual microscope, with the corresponding part of the real microscope. Additionally, MR features are applied, like virtual triggers being responsive to environment (hand movements) and occlusion handling [28] (the real microscope hides the virtual one when the latter is placed behind the real) as it is expected in the actual reality according to the position of the two objects.

The system also applies in stereoscopic mode, where the user can use special low-cost AR glasses. Therefore, it is important to stress that smartphones have a significant advantage over tablet devices. Because of their size, they can be easily attached on a head-mounted stereo view cardboard (a low-cost solution for VR/AR/MR applications) and improve the immersive attributes of the educational process. Figure 3 depicts snapshots of the XR user experience, illustrating the simultaneous viewing of the two different versions where the user can visualize and understand the real components that correspond to the virtual components of the microscope.

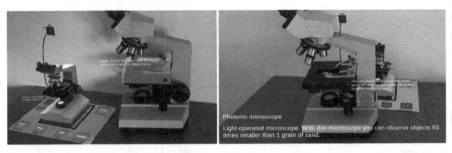

Fig. 3. Simultaneous display of both detection methods showing MR features

Given the fact that many studies have highlighted the problem of motion sickness in virtual environments [29, 30], the deployment of the XR sub-system in two different view modes: stereoscopic view and full-screen view, enables the user to personalize his/her experience according to his/her needs, preferences and possible physical discomforts.

3.3 Interaction Sub-system

For the implementation of the interaction sub-system, we exploit motion sensing technologies, single camera-based hand-tracking method via the emerging technology of marker based Virtual Triggering (VT). Simply put, the latter technology allows users to move their hand over a specific marker in the camera's field-of-view and the system returns the corresponding action. Figure 4 acts as a representation of the hand motion tracking mechanism over the area of a virtual button (small QR codes) in the camera's field-of-view. The red ray indicates the connection between virtual microscope and the mobile device camera. The yellow and green rays refer to exiting/entering system and view modes, while blue rays refer to the interactions with the virtual microscope and its components (training material). The right image of Fig. 4 depicts an example where the user interrupts the communication between the camera and the most bottom-right QR code, resulting in a real-time interaction with the light of the microscope.

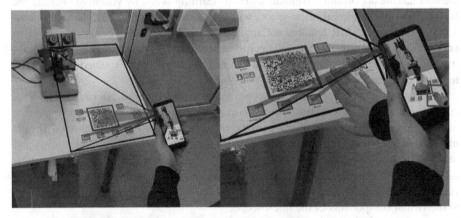

Fig. 4. Single camera based virtual buttons triggering methods

It is important to stress that we choose to use the marker-based AR technology, to take advantage of VT approaches, in order to create a unified system that will exploit the same interaction method in both stereoscopic and full screen mode, enhancing the application's user friendliness. Thus, the trainee will not be obliged to become familiar with different interaction methods depending the view mode they choose.

The proposed method, composes a natural low-cost way of interacting with the virtual object by exploiting hand moves, aiming to increase immersion and improve the educational experience without the need of expensive equipment. For example, in the "Microscopy" mode, when the user moves his/her hand over the virtual button "Interaction", the user simultaneously can interact (rotate, press, etc.) with the targeted microscope component, thus simulating its real functionality.

Table 1 summarizes the functionality of each virtual button placed on the image marker in addition to the mode and view being activated.

Table 1. Virtual buttons functionality summarize

Virtual button functionality		Mode*	View**
EXIT	Exit stereoscopic view	Both	Stereo
Mono/Stereo	Toggle Full screen/Stereoscopic view	Both	Both
General info	Enable/Disable startup general information	Both	Both
Back	Return to the previous step of the microscopy process	Microscopy	Both
Next	Go to the next step of the microscopy process	Microscopy	Both
Interaction	Interact with the targeted microscope component	Microscopy	Both

*Microscope Exploration or Microscopy or Both
**Full Screen or Stereo or Both

For the clarity of the experience, the elements being selected (components of the microscope) are highlighted with Red color, while in the "Microscopy" mode, the elements that the user interacts with, are highlighted in green. Figure 5 presents snapshots of the system. In particular, it illustrates the 3D model of the microscope, which with the use of the image marker, spawns on the real surface next to the real microscope. Furthermore, the top right image shows the appropriate highlighting while individual components are in focus (red color) or being interacted with (green color). All text content is obtained dynamically from the repositories. Additionally, the bottom image of Fig. 5 depicts the stereoscopic view mode.

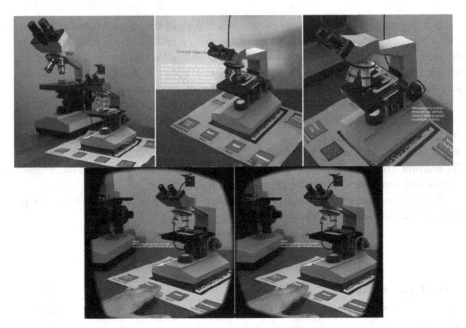

Fig. 5. Extended Reality based training in microscope manipulation. (Color figure online)

4 Educational Approach

In laboratory training, it is of great importance that the learner is familiar in advance with the basic functions of the laboratory instrument, in order to avoid unnecessary costs, wasted time and resources due to misuse and lack of experience [8]. Additionally, simulation in education, increases student engagement and motivation utilizing an Edutainment environment. Moreover, with the outbreak of the pandemic (Coronavirus disease 2019, COVID-19)[1], many countries around the world were forced to impose quarantine, thus highlighting the necessity of the existence of infrastructure for distance work and education. As a result, the possibility of developing systems that enhance the remote laboratory training for educational science programs where the performance of hands-on activities is crucial, is very promising and welcomed.

The system we propose is a low-cost solution which can supplement or be an alternative to real skills training, exploiting edutainment mechanisms. First of all, the trainers can intervene in the education procedure by introducing the educational material dynamically and enable the learners to self-practice remotely as many times as needed to understand the subject. As mentioned in the previous session, one of the fundamental principles of edutainment is personalization, which allows trainees to acquire knowledge for the same subject at their own pace [17]. The main purpose of the proposed system is to: (i) provide general technical information about a laboratory instrument, (ii) focus on

---

[1] Covid-19 of the SARS-CoV-2 virus, which was first detected in the Chinese city of Wuhan at the end of 2019.

the components of a microscope and their functionalities and (iii) interactively demonstrate the basic steps of a complete microscopy procedure. System usage flowchart for learners is depicted in Fig. 6.

Fig. 6. The main flowchart of system usage

When the application is launched, the user is prompted to login to the system using credentials acquired by their trainer. Next, the user selects the appropriate language followed by the selection of the appropriate educational content based on his/her skill level. Thus, we have created different educational content for different target groups, such as (i) Primary education, (ii) Secondary education, (iii) Higher education and scientists, and (iv) others. At this point, it should be highlighted that the trainer may create specific content for a given user group. As a next step, the user selects the preferred training mode ("Microscope Exploration" or "Microscopy"), based on the needs of the educational course. The last step involves the selection of view mode (Stereoscopic or Full-screen). Users without head-mounting or users with tablet-based devices are recommended to use the full-screen mode.

The deployment[2] provides two different training scenarios to learners. In the first mode ("Microscope exploration") the user can turn the camera around the virtual or/and (or if available) the real microscope, pointing it at individual components of the instrument and get information about its functionalities (see footnote 2). The second mode ("Microscopy") is the sequential demonstration of the microscopy process in a step by step manner. In this mode, the user can interact with the components of the virtual microscope by using the necessary virtual triggers to manipulate it in real-time. Individual steps need to be followed to complete the microscopy procedure (see footnote 2). The design of the use of virtual buttons that trigger the sequence of microscopy steps (Next, Back), does not allow user errors (the interaction with the microscope through the virtual button is enabled only if the previous step is successfully completed), which enhances the user-friendliness of the application.

When the real microscope is available, the learner can use the acquired knowledge to perform the microscopy using the real instrument, having real-time empirical knowledge thus minimizing the possibility of mishandling it. Therefore, knowledge is better communicated through imitation and repetition. In the classroom where material, time and laboratory instruments availability are important, the system allows all students to simultaneously practice using the virtual version on their mobile device, while the teacher demonstrates the microscopy process on the real microscope. Hence, the learner

---

[2] Deployment as well as all the additional support material: http://www.ceti.gr/chairiq/xrlabs/.

takes an active role in her/his learning, acquiring knowledge and having fun through empiric learning.

In developing the system for training different target groups on microscopy, the learning theories of how knowledge is constructed, were taken into consideration. With the Microscope Exploration Mode and based on the behaviorism [31], the system teaches facts and gives essential information for understanding the new concept of microscopy and acquiring the knowledge through repetition. In the Microscopy Mode, we considered the Cognitive Load Theory [32] and as we acknowledged that the microscopy experiment has an inherent difficulty, we divided this experiment into 14 steps in order to lower the high intrinsic cognitive load [33]. The extraneous load was also limited to a minimum, by avoiding unnecessary information and confusing instructions [34]. Finally, as constructivism declares, we designed an application that engages actively the learner as it includes observation, reflection, data collection and interaction. Aiming to increase enjoyment through learning, we combine personalization, interaction and simulation technology, thus the system stimulates the student's instinctive curiosity to learn through experience. Providing the opportunity for distance training, we enable students to practice continuously, thus increasing their confidence in understanding the process, enjoying the satisfaction of good student performance.

The combination of XR technologies and hand gestures based interactive methods provides a pleasant and interesting educational environment for the users. The entertaining aspects of the proposed system (interactive educational scenarios, simulation, graphical, visual and personalized content) are offered to attract and engage learners to enjoy the laboratory training process. However, the incorporation of the graphical elements into the system (information pointers, highlight shapes, colors) are used carefully, without unnecessary effects, aiming to emphasize to the educational content, without distracting the learner. Thus, combined with personalization and interaction, the system motivates the learners to get in touch and understand the subject through stimulating their curiosity and their senses, aiming at learning and not just having fun with the application [14]. The development of educational scenarios through the DCM is controlled by the trainers, providing them the important capability of customization of the educational scenarios/procedures or the development of new ones. For example, instructors through DCM can change the educational text content that want to communicate each time or select samples for microscopy that will be available to the trainee as images, depending on the actual experiment they want to present to him/her. Additionally, trainers may exploit the proposed system as a laboratory procedure demonstration that offers enhanced experience through a screen sharing plugin of the mobile device. This leads to a worldwide real-time connection among trainers and learners. To sum up, the exploitation of the proposed system by the learner in educational processes focuses on three different aspects:

- Home practicing: as a preparation tool before the interaction with the physical laboratory instruments, which allows learners to repeat the experiment without constraints.
- Instrument guide: the learner may exploit the XR systems during the real experiment in the physical laboratory for further information or to recall some elements of the instrument.

– Continuous knowledge update/lifelong learning: without any restrictions, out of courses or training sessions and available for anyone.

5   System Evaluation

In order to study the effectiveness of the proposed system, eleven laboratory (Hard Science) experts (Researchers/University Teachers) and computer graphics (Computer Science) experts (Researchers/University Teachers) are employed to evaluate it, based on a short questionnaire in accordance with evaluation rules pointed out by Guimaraes and Martins [35]. The evaluation procedure was as follows: first the experts watched an instruction video, then they had the opportunity to test the system by themselves and at the end they answered the questionnaire. The analysis of the results confirms the positive impression of scientists in combining XR technologies with educational content. Overall, the system was well-rated and judged as very useful supplementary tool for demonstrating and teaching laboratory instrument functionalities.

Some statistical results of the experts' evaluation are depicted in Fig. 7 where the top-left graph presents the experience of the experts in AR/MR systems, from very low to very high [1, 5]. It should be highlighted that moderate to low experience experts are laboratory experts, while the rest are computer graphics experts. Considering that the system mainly focuses on educating learners, it is critical to exploit XR technology and create an interesting and fun learning tool without distracting the user from the educational process. The evaluation process gave satisfactory results with 81,9% of the respondents ("agree" and "strongly agree", columns 4 and 5) that they were not distracted from the educational subject (Fig. 7 graph b). On the other hand, the interaction system (Fig. 7 graph c) and the user instructions (Fig. 7 graph d) were accepted quite widely. Furthermore, 72,7% of the experts, preferred the full-screen mode instead of stereoscopic mode. Nevertheless, exploring these results, we have set as one of our future goals to focus on improving the usability of stereo mode.

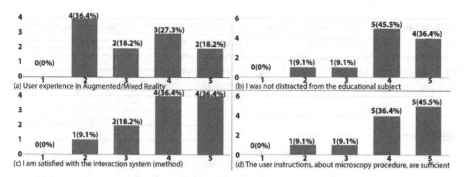

Fig. 7. Statistical results of the experts' evaluation.

6 Conclusions

The main scope of the proposed system is to introduce a low-cost, innovative, dynamic and interactive educational XR based tool, for assisting users in laboratory training (both in handling equipment and carrying out experimental processes). The tool is considered as a part of the STEAM education toolkit and it is addressed to all educational levels. Thus, we aim to attempt an approach to laboratory instruction, utilizing simulation and XR technology, combined with dynamic data management and interaction techniques, that can exploit ideally all user senses. Unlike the traditional science lab, this system does not require a specific physical space or dedicated room and simply assumes the availability of a mobile device (smartphone or tablet), thus solving problems of laboratory equipment availability, cost, maintenance, possible instrument's misuse and user safety. Additionally, learners are given the opportunity to practice as much as they want without restrictions such as time, cost, availability, distance as well as safety issues. In addition, using this system reduces the repair costs and the risks of misusing the laboratory facilities, as misuse can cause considerable damage to expensive and sensitive equipment. Similarly, students' safety can be improved as they become aware of the possible laboratory hazards (equipment and consumables) at a virtual while inexpensive level. Furthermore, the adoption of a dynamic management system of the educational content allows flexibility and enhances the creation of a multilingual educational system.

In the future, we aim to develop an upgraded system, exploiting marker-less XR techniques to eliminate the need of special printed image markers. Moreover, we will explore cutting-edge interaction methods such as the use of special sensor devices to achieve higher levels of gesture estimation accuracy in order to engage the learner in a more realistic and natural experience. Furthermore, we will approach the enrichment of the enjoyment of the system using gamified elements. Finally, we will focus on assessing the effectiveness of the system by assessing the learners experience, with pretests and post-test based on learning analytics methodologies. In general, the main goal will be to succeed in creating an educational playful platform that attracts both trainers and learners and engage them in utilizing entertainment and rewarding motives.

Acknowledgments. This work is supported by the project XRLabs -Virtual laboratories using interactive technologies in virtual, mixed and augmented reality environments (MIS 5038608) implemented under the Action for the Strategic Development on the Research and Technological Sector, co-financed by national funds through the Operational program of Western Greece 2014–2020 and European Union funds (European Regional Development Fund).

References

1. Sypsas, A., Kalles, D.: Virtual laboratories in biology, biotechnology and chemistry education: a literature review. In: Proceedings of the 22nd Pan-Hellenic Conference on Informatics, PCI 2018, p. 70. ACM, New York (2018)
2. Nersessian, N.J.: Conceptual change in science and in science education. Synthese (1989). https://doi.org/10.1007/BF00869953
3. Rambli, D.R.A., Nayan, M.Y., Sulaiman, S.: A Portable Augmented Reality Lab. Ist Int. Malaysian Educ. Technol. Conv. (2007)

4. Becerra, D.A.I., et al.: Evaluation of a gamified 3D virtual reality system to enhance the understanding of movement in physics. In: CSEDU 2017 - Proceedings of the 9th International Conference on Computer Supported Education, no. 1, pp. 395–401. INSTICC, SciTePress (2017)

5. Shin, J.M., Jin, K., Kim, S.Y.: Investigation and evaulation of a virtual reality vocational training system for general lathe. In: CSEDU 2019 - Proceedings of the 11th International Conference on Computer Supported Education, no. 2, pp. 440–445. INSTICC, SciTePress (2019)

6. Bogusevschi, D., Muntean, G.M.: Water cycle in nature – an innovative virtual reality and virtual lab: Improving learning experience of primary school students. In: CSEDU 2019 - Proceedings of the 11th International Conference on Computer Supported Education, no. 1, pp. 304–309. INSTICC, SciTePress (2019)

7. Kiourt, C., et al.: XRLabs: extended reality interactive laboratories. In: Proceeding of the 12th International Conference on Computer Supported Education (CSEDU 2020) (2020)

8. Paxinou, E., Zafeiropoulos, V., Sypsas, A., Kiourt, C., Kalles, D.: Assessing the impact of virtualizing physical labs. In: 27th EDEN Annual Conference, European Distance and E-Learning Network, pp. 17–20 (2018)

9. Heradio, R., De La Torre, L., Galan, D., Cabrerizo, F.J., Herrera-Viedma, E., Dormido, S.: Virtual and remote labs in education: a bibliometric analysis. Comput. Educ. **98**, 14–38 (2016). https://doi.org/10.1016/j.compedu.2016.03.010

10. Karakasidis, T.: Virtual and remote labs in higher education distance learning of physical and engineering sciences. In: IEEE Global Engineering Education Conference, EDUCON, pp. 798–807 (2013)

11. Bonde, M.T., et al.: Improving biotech education through gamified laboratory simulations. Nat. Biotechnol. **32**(7), 694–697 (2014). https://doi.org/10.1038/nbt.2955

12. Kiourt, C., Koutsoudis, A., Pavlidis, G.: DynaMus: a fully dynamic 3D virtual museum framework. J. Cult. Heritage **22**, 984–991 (2016). https://doi.org/10.1016/j.culher.2016.06.007

13. de Vries, L.E., May, M.: Virtual laboratory simulation in the education of laboratory technicians–motivation and study intensity. Biochem. Mol. Biol. Educ. **47**(3), 257–262 (2019). https://doi.org/10.1002/bmb.21221

14. Okan, Z.: Edutainment: is learning at risk? Br. J. Educ. Technol. **34**, 255–264 (2003). https://doi.org/10.1111/1467-8535.00325

15. Corona, F., Cozzarelli, C., Palumbo, C., Sibilio, M.: Information technology and edutainment: education and entertainment in the age of interactivity. Int. J. Digit. Lit. Digit. Competence **4**, 12–18 (2013). https://doi.org/10.4018/jdldc.2013010102

16. Aksakal, N.: Theoretical view to the approach of the edutainment. Procedia Soc. Behav. Sci. **186**, 1232–1239 (2015). https://doi.org/10.1016/j.sbspro.2015.04.081

17. Anikina, O.V., Yakimenko, E.V.: Edutainment as a modern technology of education. Procedia Soc. Behav. Sci. **166**, 475–479 (2015). https://doi.org/10.1016/j.sbspro.2014.12.558

18. Brown, A., Green, T.: Virtual reality: low-cost tools and resources for the classroom. TechTrends **60**(5), 517–519 (2016). https://doi.org/10.1007/s11528-016-0102-z

19. Zagoranski, S., Divjak, S.: Use of augmented reality in education. In: IEEE Region 8 EUROCON 2003: Computer as a Tool - Proceedings, no. 2, pp. 339–342 (2003)

20. Zafeiropoulos, V., Kalles, D., Sgourou, A.: Adventure-style game-based learning for a biology lab. In: Proceedings - IEEE 14th International Conference on Advanced Learning Technologies, ICALT 2014, pp. 665–667 (2014)

21. Estapa, A., Nadolny, L.: The effect of an augmented reality enhanced mathematics lesson on student achievement and motivation. J. STEM Educ. **16**(3), 40 (2015)

22. Ferrer-Torregrosa, J., Torralba, J., Jimenez, M.A., García, S., Barcia, J.M.: ARBOOK: development and assessment of a tool based on augmented reality for anatomy. J. Sci. Educ. Technol. **24**(1), 119–124 (2014). https://doi.org/10.1007/s10956-014-9526-4

23. Ma, J., Nickerson, J.V.: Hands-on, simulated, and remote laboratories: a comparative literature review. ACM Comput. Surv. **38**(3) (2006). https://doi.org/10.1145/1132960.1132961

24. Makarius, E.E.: Edutainment: using technology to enhance the management learner experience. Manag. Teach. Rev. **2**(1), 17 (2017). https://doi.org/10.1177/2379298116680600

25. Mann, D.: Serious play. Teach. Coll. Rec. **97**(3), 419–469 (1996). https://doi.org/10.1075/japc.13.2.02cha

26. Lalos, S., Kiourt, C., Kalles, D., Kalogeras, A.: Personalized interactive edutainment in extended reality (XR) laboratories. ERCIM News Educ. Technol. **120**, 29–30 (2020)

27. Siltanen, S.: Theory and applications of marker-based augmented reality (2012)

28. Walton, D.R., Steed, A.: Accurate real-time occlusion for mixed reality. In: Proceedings of the ACM Symposium on Virtual Reality Software and Technology, VRST, pp. 1–10 (2017)

29. LaViola, J.J.: A discussion of cybersickness in virtual environments. ACM SIGCHI Bull. **32**, 47–56 (2000). https://doi.org/10.1145/333329.333344

30. Weech, S., Kenny, S., Barnett-Cowan, M.: Presence and cybersickness in virtual reality are negatively related: a review (2019)

31. Watson, J.B.: Psychology as the behaviourist views it. Psychol. Rev. (1913). https://doi.org/10.1037/h0074428

32. Piaget, J.: Origins of Intelligence in the Child. Routledge and Kegan Paul, London (1936)

33. Diederen, J., Gruppen, H., Hartog, R., Voragen, A.G.J.: Design and evaluation of digital learning material to support acquisition of quantitative problem-solving skills within food chemistry. J. Sci. Educ. Technol. **14**, 495–507 (2005). https://doi.org/10.1007/s10956-005-0224-0

34. de Jong, T.: Cognitive load theory, educational research, and instructional design: some food for thought. Instr. Sci. **38**, 105–134 (2010). https://doi.org/10.1007/s11251-009-9110-0

35. De Paiva Guimarães, M., Martins, V.F.: A checklist to evaluate augmented reality applications. In: Proceedings - 2014 16th Symposium on Virtual and Augmented Reality, SVR, pp. 45–52 (2014)

Tracking and Rendering

Improved CNN-Based Marker Labeling for Optical Hand Tracking

Janis Rosskamp[1]([✉]), Rene Weller[1], Thorsten Kluss[2], Jaime L. Maldonado C.[2], and Gabriel Zachmann[1]

[1] Computer Graphic and Virtual Reality, University of Bremen, Bremen, Germany
J.Rosskamp@cs.uni-bremen.de
[2] Cognitive Neuroinformatics, University of Bremen, Bremen, Germany

Abstract. Hand tracking is essential in many applications reaching from the creation of CGI movies to medical applications and even real-time, natural, physically-based grasping in VR. Optical marker-based tracking is often the method of choice because of its high accuracy, the support for large workspaces, good performance, and there is no wiring of the user required. However, the tracking algorithms may fail in case of hand poses where some of the markers are occluded. These cases require a subsequent reassignment of labels to reappearing markers. Currently, convolutional neural networks (CNN) show promising results for this re-labeling because they are relatively stable and real-time capable. In this paper, we present several methods to improve the accuracy of label predictions using CNNs. The main idea is to improve the input to the CNNs, which is derived from the output of the optical tracking system. To do so, we propose a method based on principal component analysis, a projection method that is perpendicular to the palm, and a multi-image approach. Our results show that our methods provide better label predictions than current state-of-the-art algorithms, and they can be even extended to other tracking applications.

Keywords: Hand tracking · Motion capturing · Marker labeling

1 Introduction

The human hand is the most versatile tool of the human body to interact with the surrounding world, e.g., by grasping or pointing at objects. In order to allow for this most natural interaction method in virtual environments, too, it is necessary to track the human hands and transfer their movements and poses into the VR world to control a virtual hand. A wide variety of different tracking methods have been developed and some commercial products, such as the Oculus Quest, already feature built-in markerless tracking. While tracking methods using single cameras are easy to set up, they can only track the user's hand with moderate accuracy. This is sufficient for basic interactions in virtual environments. Our motivation for developing a high-precision tracking pipeline is the investigation

© Springer Nature Switzerland AG 2020
P. Bourdot et al. (Eds.): EuroVR 2020, LNCS 12499, pp. 165–177, 2020.
https://doi.org/10.1007/978-3-030-62655-6_10

of natural grasping behavior of humans with its variety of complex manipulations and the capability to flexibly adapt to unexpected situations, in order to provide models that enable a more natural grasping behavior in robotics. Thus, high precision tracking is a crucial precondition for the quality of the underlying datasets that will be generated with human participants.

In general, high precision hand tracking is essential in all scenarios where physically-based grasping is needed to enable dexterous manipulation of objects [21]. Here, hand deformation and friction is taken into account, and accurate hand poses are necessary for a realistic force estimation to guarantee the stability of grasps. High precision tracking is also necessary in other fields like immersive medical training or interactive virtual prototyping that require a precise recognition of hand poses, too.

The only technology available today that can generate the required accuracy is optical marker-based tracking using a multi-camera setup, such as *Optitrack* systems, which can deliver an accuracy in the sub-millimeter range with high frame rates. Typical optical tracking systems like Optitrack usually only track the positions of individual passive markers in 3D; connectivity information has to be computed from these marker positions algorithmically. Initially, *labels* can be assigned to the markers in order to relate them to their semantic positions, e.g., the tip of the thumb or the palm. The human hand, which has 27 degrees of freedom in a relatively small space, requires a dense marker set, especially for high-precision tracking. On the one hand, denser marker sets reduce tracking errors. On the other hand, due to the complex geometry and motion of the hand, markers are often occluded due to self-occlusion. In this case, reappearing markers must be *relabeled* to transfer the motion correctly to a virtual hand in the virtual environment. Especially for virtual reality applications, this relabeling process has to be performed in real-time and should be highly accurate. So, we cannot take subsequent motions into account, which is possible in mo-cap post-processing.

Han et al. [10] have formulated the labeling of dense marker sets as an image keypoint problem. Their basic idea was to solve it using a convolutional neural network (CNN). CNNs work very well for 2D images, but for unstructured 3D problems, CNNs are difficult to apply in real-time. Hence, they decided to project the 3D positions of the markers, delivered by the tracking system, onto a 2D plane and input this 2D image to the CNN. They report remarkable results with a real-time performance.

In this paper, we present several significant improvements over this state-of-the-art labeling prediction. Our main approach is to optimize the transformation of the 3D marker positions to the 2D planes. We propose three methods to optimize this crucial step. First, an obvious idea is to use several random directions instead of a single one and evaluate them in parallel. We combined this idea with an optimization algorithm to identify the best result. Second, we applied a principal component analysis (PCA) on the dense marker set to predict depth images with optimal spatial distributions. Our third method takes into account that typically the palm is easy to identify and unlikely to be occluded. Hence, we chose a projection perpendicular to the palm to increase the labeling prediction. In addition, with the additional knowledge about the projection direction in case of the palm projection and the PCA, we hypothesized that a CNN trained specifically for this case could achieve better results than the original CNN that was trained for random projections. Consequently, we generated new CNNs for these cases.

We have tested our algorithms with synthetic data and in a real-world hand tracking application. Our results show significant improvements over the current state-of-the-art labeling prediction. Even more so, we were able to increase dramatically the number of tracking frames where *all* marker labels are predicted correctly. This is important measure of assessing labeling accuracy in cases where many markers were occluded and need to be relabeled when they reappear at the same time (e.g., in a motion from fist to open hand). Also, in case of small tracking volumes, the hand can temporarily leave that volume and must be relabeled completely when re-entering. The same can happen for complicated hand poses with a low number of cameras, where many self occlusions occur. In this paper, we have focused on hand tracking, but our methods can be easily generalized to other labeling problems as well.

2   Related Work

Optical motion capturing is used in many areas, for instance, in animation for games and movies, medical studies [6] or virtual assembly [22]. Labeling of passive markers on non-rigid structures is an active field of research. In general, it can be broadly categorized into two categories: tracking of sparse and dense markersets. Sparse markers are often used for large capture volumes and full-body tracking. Compared with dense markers where 19 markers are used for hand tracking, labeling is easier, but small nuances in movement are hard to track with 13 or fewer markers [1].

Meyer et al. [13] used key poses for labeling and a least-squares method to track marker positions to recover from occlusions. Schubert et al. [18] relaxed the requirement for an initial pose and allows nearly arbitrary poses. Aristidou and Lasenby [2] predict positions of occluded markers using a Variable Turn Model within an unscented Kalman filter without assuming any skeleton model. In Alexanderson et al. [1], Gaussian mixture models are used to track sparse markersets in large capture volumes. They do not require any key poses, and the system is stable even when the user leaves and enters the capture volume. After initializing labels, reappearing markers are relabeled in real-time using inverse kinematics (IK) in Maycock et al. [12]. They predict positions of non-critical occluded markers during run time. Ghorbani et al. [8] use permutation learning to automatically label markers without manual initialization for full body tracking. Han et al. [10] use a CNN to label dense markersets by creating depth images from 3D marker positions.

There exist many hand tracking methods besides passive optical marker tracking. Pavllo et al. [16] are using active markers and IMUs to predict motion even when occlusions happen. While this method is accurate, it requires a heavy glove with cables. Sensor-based tracking using stretch-sensing [9] or bend-sensing gloves [23] is easy to set up, without occlusions and usable in nearly every environment. However, they usually require cables or batteries and the average error of joint angles is 6–8°, even after a user-specific calibration. Recently IMU-based gloves were developed for medical evaluations [5,11]. Hand tracking with single RGB cameras [14,19,20] or depth cameras [3,7] are the most obtainable methods. In [15] even tightly interacting hands can be tracked. However, they are not suitable for applications that need high precision tracking.

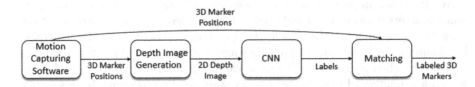

Fig. 1. Overview of our labeling pipeline (adapted from [10]).

3   Our Approach

Optical motion capturing software uses multiple cameras, often in the infrared spectrum, to track a set of reflective markers and computes their 3D positional data. Tracked data is accurate but often suffers from occlusion of markers. In hand tracking, a typical example of occlusions are markers that are too close to the body; hence, cameras cannot see them. When markers become visible again, correct labels must be assigned to every reappearing marker. For instance, the markers on the tip of the index finger must be differentiated from the tip marker on the middle finger but also from the index fingers' carpus marker to avoid wrongly detected hand poses. For the online labeling of markers, [10] proposed a method based on convolutional neural networks for relabeling. We will give a short recap of this method because our approach is inspired by it.

3.1   Recap: CNN-Based Marker Labeling

The main idea presented by [10] to solve the relabeling problem is to use CNNs. An outline of the labeling pipeline is shown in Fig. 1. In practice, 3D CNNs are too slow for real-time applications [17]; hence, the authors decided to use a network with 2D convolutions. To do that, they transform the 3D marker positions delivered by the tracking software into a 2D image using orthographic projection. The direction of the projection axis is found by creating a random point and determining the direction to the weighted center of the point cloud from this position. Values along the projection axis can be understood as depth values and are normalized in the range $[0.1, 1.0]$. By splatting the markers on the image, their relative depth is preserved. The resulted image (Fig. 2b)) is used as input for the actual CNN, which predicts a vector of 3D marker positions. The vector elements' order is fixed and corresponds to a label; for instance, the fourth vector element corresponds to the marker on the thumb tip. To assign these labels to the original markers, matching of the predicted 3D positions to the markers' real 3D positions is done by solving a minimum weight bipartite matching problem. The most important step to influence the quality of the resulting label is the generation of the 2D image from the 3D points, i.e., mainly the choice of the projection direction. In [10], the authors simply created ten 2D images using random projection axes (RPA) to label a single frame of markers positions. From these ten images, the one with the highest spatial spread is selected and fed into the CNN. In the following, we propose three methods for image generation which all improve the labeling results compared to RPA.

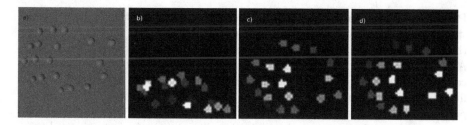

Fig. 2. Image a) shows the point cloud data of the tracked markers for a flat hand pose (small joint angles). To label the 3D positional data, a depth image is created from a). In b), the depth image was created from a random projection direction. Image c) uses a projection axis generated with the PCA method. Image d) was created using a projection axis perpendicular to the palm (PalmP). The depth information is visualized as pixel intensities.

3.2   Our Projection Methods

As mentioned above, the main idea for the improvement of the labeling quality is the choice of an optimized projection direction. We propose three methods that we will detail in the following.

Multi Images - Minimal Cost. The RPA method creates ten images from the point cloud but feds only one of them for labeling into the CNN. A straight forward idea for the improvement would be to feed them all into the CNN and choose the best result from the *output* of the network. This consideration is the basis of our *multi images - minimal cost method (Multi)*. Obviously, this requires an appropriate rating function. Moreover, the method can be generalized to create n depth images and choose an optimum number of projection directions based on results from experiments which we will discuss in Sect. 4. Finally, we decided to generate the directions for the n images not completely randomly but distribute them uniformly on a sphere around the point cloud's center. All images pass through the network, and we get n vectors of 3D marker data. We use minimum weight bipartite matching to solve the minimum-cost flow problem for all output vectors. In the minimum-cost flow problem, the edges between the initial and predicted 3D marker positions represent distances. Subsequently, selecting the solution with the lowest C corresponds to a matching where the euclidean distance between initial and predicted markers is minimal:

$$\min(C^{(1)}, \ldots, C^{(n)}) \quad \text{with} \quad C^{(i)} = \sum_{j=1} \left\| y_j^{(i)} - x_{M(j)}^{(i)} \right\|_2. \tag{1}$$

Consequently, we select the set of labels with the lowest matching cost C to get the best fitting solution.

Principal Component Analysis. Instead of selecting the highest spatial spread out of a random set of images, we can also calculate a projection plane that yields an image with a high spatial spread for the given marker positions. A traditional method to find such a projection axis is to compute a principal component analysis (PCA) for the 3D points. More precisely, using PCA, we can find the three principal axes of our point cloud. The first two principal axes are pointing in the direction of the highest variance, also called the spatial spread. Consequently, we have chosen the projection direction as the last principal axis. In detail: Our projection vector v is given by the eigenvector $v_i, i = 1\ldots3$ which corresponds to the smallest eigenvalue λ of the covariance matrix of the point cloud:

$$p = v_i \quad \text{with} \quad \lambda_i = \min(\lambda_1, \lambda_2, \lambda_3). \tag{2}$$

Figure 2c) shows a depth image created by the PCA method.

Palm Prediction. While the previously proposed methods can be generalized easily to arbitrary labeling problems, our final method is based on the domain knowledge that we are actually tracking a human hand. The idea is to find a projection axis that will lead to similar images independent of the actual hand poses. We decided to define a projection perpendicular to the palm. To get the palm's orientation in our marker point cloud, we require that the markers attached on the back of the hand are identified. Our glove has three rigidly attached markers on the back of the hand (see Fig. 7). We can then easily determine these markers under the assumption that the distance between them does not change. Figure 2d) show an image created with our *palm prediction method (PalmP)*.

3.3   CNN Training

In principle, we could simply reuse the original CNN network proposed by [10]; all our methods are compatible. However, this network is trained with random projection directions and hence would deliver the best results with this kind of input. In the case of our PCA and especially the Palm Prediction projections, that partly consider domain knowledge, the specifically trained neural network could provide better results which is also supported by our experiments (see Sect. 4). Hence, we decided to train the network with specifically generated input images for these particular methods.

4   Results

We have evaluated the performance as well as the quality of our CNN-based labeling methods. We have them with both, synthetic data but also in a real VR hand tracking environment. All our experiments were performed on a Linux-PC running Ubuntu 20.04 with an Intel Core i7 3.5 GHz, 16 GByte of main memory, and an NVIDIA GTX 1080 Ti GPU with Tensorflow 1.13.1.

4.1   CNN Architecture and Training

In order to guarantee a fair comparison of our methods with the current state-of-the-art labeling method, we decided to use the same network architecture and training data as proposed by [10]. They used a VGG-style neural network with several 3×3 convolutional layers followed by a fully connected layer. As input for the CNN, they used depth images of size 52×52. There is also a training set of 168691 frames of labeled hand configurations available (please note, in [10], there were 170330 frames used), which were synthetically generated from real hand motion of five different users. In [10], the network was trained using random depth images. To increase the labeling accuracy of PCA and PalmP we decided to additionally use networks trained with depth images generated from the PCA and PalmP methods. This increased the accuracy by more than 40% points compared to the network trained with random sampling. To avoid overfitting, we split the data into a training and validation set for PCA and PalmP networks, which reduces the training set to 137357 frames. In the following, we evaluate all methods using this synthetic validation data set.

4.2   Synthetic Data

We first evaluated the labeling performance of our networks on the synthetic data set provided by [10]. The results are summarized in the left plot of Fig. 3. In comparison to the original RPA projection, our labeling methods improve the number of correctly labeled markers in all cases. For instance, PCA increases the labeling accuracy to 90%, which is an improvement of 14% points. It can be directly applied on the point cloud data without the need to know any marker labels beforehand. When labels for the markers for the palm are known, we can apply the PalmP method, which improves the accuracy up to 97%. The accuracy of the Multi method with 20 images is 95%, which is slightly lower than the PalmP results. Similar to PCA, no marker labels or geometric information is needed. Instead, we pass as many images as possible to the CNN and select the output with the lowest matching cost as our solution. This leads to higher run times, which are investigated in Sect. 4.4.

Interestingly, our implementation of the orig. RPA method was not able to reproduce the results from [10], where an accuracy of 85–99% was reported. To minimize the chance of implementation errors, we implemented a number of tests for our code and tried both the original released pre-trained network and our own trained network. Even with these discrepancies between the results, it is clear that our projection methods improved the results.

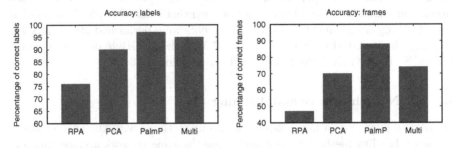

Fig. 3. Using the synthetic validation set, the labeling accuracy of all methods is compared. The left image shows the percentage of correctly labeled markers. The right image shows the percentage of frames, where every marker has the correct label. All our methods improve the current state-of-the-art (RPA). For the Multi method 20 images were used.

We further evaluate the capacity of the networks to label *all* markers in a frame correctly. This is important in cases where many markers are occluded simultaneously, and all must be relabeled from scratch. As an example, consider the case where only two markers were mislabeled. We would still have a labeling accuracy of 89%, but labels of the two markers are mixed up and hand pose reconstruction would fail. The results are shown in the right of Fig. 3. Our methods label between 70% (PCA) and 88% (PalmP) of all frames entirely correctly. This is an improvement of up to 41% points compared to the original RPA method.

PalmP. In the PalmP method, we use a projection perpendicular to the palm. However, we could also choose other markers to define a coordinate system for the projection, it is not obvious that the projection perpendicular to the palm is best. An example of an alternative would be an axis perpendicular to the plane containing two markers from the back of the hand and one from the thumb tip. To find the optimal projection, we have trained the CNN using other projections and computed the labeling accuracy. Figure 4 shows the results. Indeed, we achieve the best accuracy for the palm projection. We get slightly lower results for a plane containing two palm markers and one at a fingertip. A plane constructed from

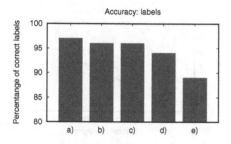
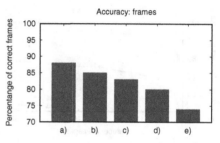

Fig. 4. The labeling accuracy for different image planes for the PalmP method is shown. In a) the three markers on the back of the hand are used. For b)–d) a combination of a marker on the fingertip and two markers on the back of the hand is used: b) is the index finger tip, c) is the thumb tip, and d) the pinky tip. In e) the tips of the thumb, index and pinky finger are used for the image plane.

three fingertip markers produces the worst results. The projection axis using the palm not only produces the best results, but the markers are also the easiest to identify in the point cloud if we use a marker setup, as shown in Fig. 7. Here, the three markers are rigidly attached, so the distance between them remains constant.

Multi. The Multi method uses multiple CNN predictions to label a single frame of motion capture data. In this section, we investigate the dependency of the labeling accuracy and the number of predictions. Obviously, the accuracy increases with an increasing number of predictions. Figure 5 shows the labeling accuracy in relation to the number of CNN passes. For a small number of CNN calls, accuracy improves fast, and, if we use five instead of only two calls, our results improve by 6% points. On the other hand, the results only change by less than 2% points if we use 40 instead of 30 calls. Using 20 CNN passes, we obtain an accuracy of 95% and can still run our labeling step in real-time (see Sect. 4.4).

4.3   Real Data

We also evaluate the labeling performance of our methods on 1927 frames of real motion capture data. The data was created using a setup of six Optitrack cameras and the glove shown in Fig. 7. We decided to use a relatively small number of cameras in order to increase the number of occlusion cases and, thus, stress our hand tracking. Markers on our glove are placed between joints on top of the phalanges to decrease slipping if joints are rotated. An additional inverse kinematics step is necessary to compute the joint angles. Moreover, inverse kinematic is used to check if the labels predicted by the CNN are correct. We use a standard damped least-squares inverse kinematics method [4]. The labeling accuracy for all methods is shown in Fig. 6. Similar to the validation with synthetic data,

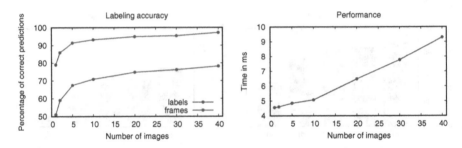

Fig. 5. These plots show the influence of the number of CNN calls on the labeling accuracy (left) and the run-time (right) is investigated for the Multi method. In the left plots, the blue curve denotes the percentage of all correctly labeled markers. The red curve shows the percentage of correct frames, where all markers were assigned a correct label. (Color figure online)

we observe that PCA, PalmP, and Multi outperform the standard random projections method. The labeling performance on real data is very similar to the results from synthetic data.

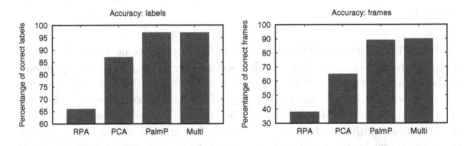

Fig. 6. Using real motion capture data, the labeling accuracy of all methods is compared. The left image shows the percentage of correctly labeled markers. The right image shows the percentage of frames, where every marker has the correct label. For the Multi method 20 images were used.

4.4   Performance

A complete labeling step with PCA or PalmP takes approximately 4.5 ms, where image generation and marker matching take around 0.05 ms, and the CNN prediction approximately 4.45 ms. The Multi method uses multiple CNN calls. The right image of Fig. 5 shows the performance of the Multi method with respect to the number of CNN passes. For 40 calls, the prediction requires around 9.3 ms. This is only twice the time used for single image labeling and can be explained by batching in the prediction step. Often a dedicated computer for tracking is used, and the joint angles are streamed to the VR application. Hence, the Multi method runs in real-time with 60 Hz, even if 20 images are used for labeling.

Fig. 7. A glove attached with 19 markers for tracking with optical motion capture systems. The three markers on the back of the hand have a fixed distance and can be interpreted as a rigid body.

5   Conclusions and Future Works

We have presented three new methods for CNN-based marker labeling for optical hand tracking. The approach was to transform 3D marker positions into 2D depth images that can be input into a convolutional neural network. The goal was to maximize the spread of the marker positions in the image to achieve best labeling accuracy. To do that, we proposed methods based on PCA, a multi image approach, and a method that also considers domain knowledge for the case of hand tracking (PalmP). Moreover, we have trained two CNNs for the PCA and the PalmP method to further improve the quality of the tracking. Our results show that the PCA method increases the accuracy to 90%, which is an improvement of 14% points compared to the state-of-the-art method. It can be applied to every marker set and does not increase runtime. If we have prior knowledge of some marker labels, in our case, the back of the hand, labeling accuracy improves to up to 97% with our PalmP method. If no information about the marker set is available, our multi-projection method achieves similar results to the PalmP method, depending on the number of projections. It also allows for an easy trade-off between performance and accuracy.

Our work also offers interesting avenues for future works: for instance, we want to investigate the labeling accuracy of our methods on non-hand mark-ersets. Transferring the PCA or Multi method to other markersets is straight forward. Using the PalmP method requires a proper projection direction based on domain knowledge for optimal results. Additionally, we want to investigate simultaneous marker labeling of two interacting hands. At the moment, the hands are separated using clustering and then labeled individually using the CNN. An open challenge is the prediction of 3D marker positions of occluded markers during online tracking.

Acknowledgment. The research reported in this paper has been (partially) sup-ported by the German Research Foundation DFG, as part of Collaborative Research Center (Son-derforschungsbereich) 1320 "EASE - Everyday Activity Science and Engi-neering", University of Bremen (http://www.ease-crc.org/). The research was con-ducted in subproject H01 <Acquiring activity models by situating people in virtual environments>.

References

1. Alexanderson, S., OSullivan, C., Beskow, J.: Real-time labeling of non-rigid motion capture marker sets. Comput. Graph. **69**(C), 59–67 (2017). https://doi.org/10.1016/j.cag.2017.10.001

2. Aristidou, A., Lasenby, J.: Real-time marker prediction and CoR estimation in optical motion capture. Vis. Comput. **29**(1), 7–26 (2013). https://doi.org/10.1007/s00371-011-0671-y

3. Baek, S., Kim, K.I., Kim, T.K.: Augmented skeleton space transfer for depth-based hand pose estimation. In: 2018 IEEE/CVF Conference on Computer Vision and Pattern Recognition. pp. 8330–8339. IEEE, Salt Lake City, June 2018. https://doi.org/10.1109/CVPR.2018.00869. https://ieeexplore.ieee.org/document/8578967/

4. Buss, S.R.: Introduction to inverse kinematics with Jacobian transpose, pseudoinverse and damped least squares methods, p. 19

5. Connolly, J., Condell, J., O'Flynn, B., Sanchez, J.T., Gardiner, P.: IMU sensor-based electronic goniometric glove for clinical finger movement analysis. IEEE Sens. J. **18**(3), 1273–1281 (2018). https://doi.org/10.1109/JSEN.2017.2776262

6. Galna, B., Barry, G., Jackson, D., Mhiripiri, D., Olivier, P., Rochester, L.: Accuracy of the microsoft kinect sensor for measuring movement in people with Parkinson's disease. Gait Posture **39**(4), 1062–1068 (2014). https://doi.org/10.1016/j.gaitpost.2014.01.008

7. Ge, L., Cai, Y., Weng, J., Yuan, J.: Hand PointNet: 3D hand pose estimation using point sets. In: 2018 IEEE/CVF Conference on Computer Vision and Pattern Recognition, pp. 8417–8426, June 2018. https://doi.org/10.1109/CVPR.2018.00878. iSSN: 2575-7075

8. Ghorbani, S., Etemad, A., Troje, N.F.: Auto-labelling of markers in optical motion capture by permutation learning. In: Gavrilova, M., Chang, J., Thalmann, N.M., Hitzer, E., Ishikawa, H. (eds.) CGI 2019. LNCS, vol. 11542, pp. 167–178. Springer, Cham (2019). https://doi.org/10.1007/978-3-030-22514-8_14

9. Glauser, O., Wu, S., Panozzo, D., Hilliges, O., Sorkine-Hornung, O.: Interactive hand pose estimation using a stretch-sensing soft glove. ACM Trans. Graph. **38**(4), 1–15 (2019). https://doi.org/10.1145/3306346.3322957. http://dl.acm.org/citation.cfm?doid=3306346.3322957

10. Han, S., Liu, B., Wang, R., Ye, Y., Twigg, C.D., Kin, K.: Online optical marker-based hand tracking with deep labels. ACM Trans. Graph. **37**(4), 1–10 (2018). https://doi.org/10.1145/3197517.3201399. http://dl.acm.org/citation.cfm?doid=3197517.3201399

11. Lin, B.S., Lee, I.J., Yang, S.Y., Lo, Y.C., Lee, J., Chen, J.L.: Design of an inertial-sensor-based data glove for hand function evaluation. Sensors (Basel) **18**(5) (2018). https://doi.org/10.3390/s18051545. https://www.ncbi.nlm.nih.gov/pmc/articles/PMC5982580/

12. Maycock, J., Rohlig, T., Schroder, M., Botsch, M., Ritter, H.: Fully automatic optical motion tracking using an inverse kinematics approach. In: 2015 IEEE-RAS 15th International Conference on Humanoid Robots (Humanoids), pp. 461–466, November 2015. https://doi.org/10.1109/HUMANOIDS.2015.7363590

13. Meyer, J., Kuderer, M., Müller, J., Burgard, W.: Online marker labeling for fully automatic skeleton tracking in optical motion capture. In: 2014 IEEE International Conference on Robotics and Automation (ICRA), pp. 5652–5657, May 2014. https://doi.org/10.1109/ICRA.2014.6907690. iSSN: 1050-4729

14. Mueller, F., et al.: GANerated hands for real-time 3D hand tracking from monocular RGB. In: 2018 IEEE/CVF Conference on Computer Vision and Pattern Recognition. pp. 49–59. IEEE, Salt Lake City, June 2018. https://doi.org/10.1109/CVPR.2018.00013. https://ieeexplore.ieee.org/document/8578111/

15. Mueller, F., et al.: Real-time pose and shape reconstruction of two interacting hands with a single depth camera. ACM Trans. Graph. **38**(4), 1–13 (2019). https://doi.org/10.1145/3306346.3322958. http://dl.acm.org/citation.cfm?doid=3306346.3322958

16. Pavllo, D., Porssut, T., Herbelin, B., Boulic, R.: Real-time finger tracking using active motion capture: a neural network approach robust to occlusions. In: Proceedings of the 11th Annual International Conference on Motion, Interaction, and Games, MIG 2018, pp. 1–10. Association for Computing Machinery, New York, November 2018. https://doi.org/10.1145/3274247.3274501

17. Riegler, G., Ulusoy, A.O., Geiger, A.: OctNet: learning deep 3D representations at high resolutions. In: 2017 IEEE Conference on Computer Vision and Pattern Recognition (CVPR), pp. 6620–6629. IEEE, Honolulu, July 2017. https://doi.org/10.1109/CVPR.2017.701. http://ieeexplore.ieee.org/document/8100184/

18. Schubert, T., Gkogkidis, A., Ball, T., Burgard, W.: Automatic initialization for skeleton tracking in optical motion capture. In: 2015 IEEE International Conference on Robotics and Automation (ICRA), pp. 734–739, May 2015. https://doi.org/10.1109/ICRA.2015.7139260. iSSN: 1050-4729

19. Simon, T., Joo, H., Matthews, I., Sheikh, Y.: Hand keypoint detection in single images using multiview bootstrapping, pp. 4645–4653, July 2017. https://doi.org/10.1109/CVPR.2017.494

20. Spurr, A., Song, J., Park, S., Hilliges, O.: Cross-modal deep variational hand pose estimation. In: 2018 IEEE/CVF Conference on Computer Vision and Pattern Recognition, pp. 89–98. IEEE, Salt Lake City, June 2018. https://doi.org/10.1109/CVPR.2018.00017. https://ieeexplore.ieee.org/document/8578115/

21. Verschoor, M., Lobo, D., Otaduy, M.: Soft hand simulation for smooth and robust natural interaction, pp. 183–190, March 2018. https://doi.org/10.1109/VR.2018.8447555

22. Vélaz, Y., Lozano-Rodero, A., Suescun, A., Gutiérrez, T.: Natural and hybrid bimanual interaction for virtual assembly tasks. Virtual Reality **18**(3), 161–171 (2014). https://doi.org/10.1007/s10055-013-0240-y. http://link.springer.com/10.1007/s10055-013-0240-y

23. Wang, Y., Neff, M.: Data-driven glove calibration for hand motion capture. In: Proceedings of the 12th ACM SIGGRAPH/Eurographics Symposium on Computer Animation - SCA 2013, p. 15. ACM Press, Anaheim (2013). https://doi.org/10.1145/2485895.2485901. http://dl.acm.org/citation.cfm?doid=2485895.2485901

Volumetric Medical Data Visualization for Collaborative VR Environments

Roland Fischer[✉], Kai-Ching Chang, René Weller, and Gabriel Zachmann

University of Bremen, Bremen, Germany
{rfischer,weller,zach}@cs.uni-bremen.de, kchang@uni-bremen.de
https://cgvr.informatik.uni-bremen.de

Abstract. In clinical practice, medical imaging technologies, like computed tomography, have become an important and routinely used technique for diagnosis. Advanced 3D visualization techniques of this data, e.g. by using volume rendering, provide doctors a better spatial understanding for reviewing complex anatomy. There already exist sophisticated programs for the visualization of medical imaging data, however, they are usually limited to exactly this topic and can be hardly extended to new functionality; for instance, multi-user support, especially when considering immersive VR interfaces like tracked HMDs and natural user interfaces, can provide the doctors an easier, more immersive access to the information and support collaborative discussions with remote colleagues. We present an easy-to-use and expandable system for volumetric medical image visualization with support for multi-user VR interactions. The main idea is to combine a state-of-the-art open-source game engine, the Unreal Engine 4, with a new volume renderer. The underlying game engine basis guarantees the extensibility and allows for easy adaption of our system to new hardware and software developments. In our example application, remote users can meet in a shared virtual environment and view, manipulate and discuss the volume-rendered data in real-time. Our new volume renderer for the Unreal Engine is capable of real-time performance, as well as, high-quality visualization.

Keywords: Volume rendering · Medical visualization · Virtual Reality · Collaborative VR · Computed tomography · Unreal Engine

1 Introduction

Computed tomography (CT) is a vital examination tool in medicine, especially for radiologists, and widely used in clinical practice. Its use cases range from diagnosis and therapeutics to preventive medicine and screening of diseases. CT images are, for example, commonly used for visualization purposes in tumor board reviews or for postmortem imaging in forensic pathology. 3D visualization of the CT data is rarely taken advantage of yet. However, it is slowly getting more important. Due to rising processing power and continuous research in algorithms and rendering techniques, faster and more advanced 3D visualization techniques

© Springer Nature Switzerland AG 2020
P. Bourdot et al. (Eds.): EuroVR 2020, LNCS 12499, pp. 178–191, 2020.
https://doi.org/10.1007/978-3-030-62655-6_11

are developed. The main benefit is the more intuitive, three-dimensional visualization of the data. This makes it easier and faster to get an overview of the data and an understanding of the spatial relations, volumes, and general layout of the depicted objects. This is helpful for analyzing complex anatomy or conveying medical situations in an easy-to-understand way. Typical 3D visualization techniques are maximum/minimal intensity projection (MIP/MinIP), surface shaded display (SSD), also called indirect volume rendering, and direct volume rendering (DVR). SSD shows opaque three-dimensional surfaces, called isosurfaces, of specific objects or organs in the volume data determined by a density-dependent segmentation. DVR accounts for the possibility of multiple tissue types per voxel and maps the densities to opacities and colors using transfer functions. This results in a semi-transparent rendering [8,9].

Currently, both 2D and 3D CT reconstructions are typically viewed on 2D screens or projectors, which limits the advantages of volumetric visualizations. On the other hand, Virtual Reality (VR) devices such as the HTC Vive become popular in many fields as they provide immersive stereoscopic visualizations with intuitive user interfaces and novel cooperative multi-user capabilities. VR offers a natural progression over previous 2D telepresence tools and leads to a new quality of collaborative work, as users can meet and intuitively interact with virtual objects as well as with each other in a shared virtual 3D environment. This makes VR an important tool for the entertainment industry but also industrial, educational, and medical applications. For example, a current trend is to use VR for simulators in which users can be trained and educated realistically and in a safe virtual environment (e.g. laparoscopy, heart surgery, and even orthopedic operations [15]). These benefits and the increasing display resolutions of newer headsets make VR in general, and multi-user VR particularly, well suited for use cases like inspection and discussion of volumetric medical data and corresponding 3D visualizations as part of diagnosis or pre-operative planning [21].

VR applications and their virtual environments are typically created and powered by 3D graphics engines like Unity or the Unreal Engine which provide features such as high-quality graphics and automatic VR integration. However, they are usually mesh/polygon-based and, out of the box, do not support volume rendering.

We propose a system based on the Unreal Engine 4 in which multiple users can collaboratively inspect and interact with volume-rendered CT data in real-time within a VR environment resembling an operating room. For this purpose, we combine mesh- and volume rendering into an immersive multi-user application. This includes a custom direct volume renderer for the Unreal Engine and several optimization and lighting techniques to achieve real-time performance as well as a good visualization quality. Additionally, we have developed a custom pipeline for processing CT images allowing easy and effective visualization of multiple windows in parallel.

2   Related Work

Volume rendering is a promising tool for medical visualization as it proved to be useful for planning of surgical treatment of nasal bone fractures [27], acetabular fractures [29], virtual endoscopy [16] or the visualization of complex anatomy such as the ossicular chain in chronic suppurative otitis media [12]. Recently, a direct volume rendering approach for serial PET–CT scans that preserves anatomical consistency was presented [14]. The high computational effort of direct volume rendering can be mitigated by algorithmic optimizations, e.g., early ray termination and empty space skipping [25]. Also, the visual quality can be improved, e.g., by applying local ambient occlusion [13]. Berger et al. [2] have shown that the novel, more complex cinematic rendering technique provides a superior visualization to the classic volume rendering using ray casting, however, the significantly slower computation is still a challenge. Brucks [3] developed a custom volume rendering implementations for the Unreal Engine 4, however, it is only rudimentary and not designed for medical data, leading to artifacts.

Several evaluations show that VR can be beneficial in a wide range of medical applications, foremost simulators for training of different surgical procedures [17,23]. Often, medical imaging plays a central role in these applications: e.g., Maloca et al. [19] proposed an OpenGL-based immersive VR system for real-time volume rendering of Optical Coherence Tomography data. An accompanying study suggested that it could be helpful for education and preoperative planning. Similarly, Scholl et al. [26] developed a medical VR application for 3D visualization based on volume rendering. Real-time performance is achieved by the use of several acceleration and optimization techniques. Adams et al. [1] used the Unity 3D engine to develop an immersive VR application for medical imaging in which CT images and corresponding, segmented 3D models can be viewed and manipulated. Magdics et al. [18] also used Unity to develop an educational VR application in which volume rendering is used for visualizing Nasal Cavities. Faludi et al. [11] presented a VR application that uses not only direct volume rendering but also haptic rendering of medical data. However, non of these systems support multiple users or collaborative work, which is another popular and promising research area.

Regarding collaborative medical VR, Cecil et al. [4] developed a system for orthopedic surgery. Similarly, Paiva et al. [22] presented a VR simulator for surgical team training. Chheang et al. [5] proposed a promising collaborative VR system for planning and simulation of laparoscopic liver surgery, Christensen et al. [6] positively evaluated the feasibility of team training in VR for robot-assisted minimally invasive surgery, and Elvezio et al. [10] designed a VR system for collaborative symmetric and asymmetric interactions and found that low latencies (below 15 ms) are crucial for effective collaboration. These works, however, do not feature 3D visualization of CT data.

3   Our Approach

The goal of our system is to combine the benefits of collaborative VR and medical 3D visualization to an immersive, interactive application based on a modern, extensible open-source 3D game engine, specifically the Unreal Engine 4. As the engine does not support volume rendering out of the box, we have developed and integrated a ray-marching-based volume renderer, based on Ryan Brucks' rudimentary implementation [3], focusing on a good trade-off between speed and visual quality.

We have decided to use the Unreal Engine 4 for several reasons: first, it is known for its high graphical fidelity, second, it supports most available VR devices like the HTC Vive with a platform independent interface, and it has networking capabilities included. Moreover, due to its open-source implementation, it can be easily extended with native C++ programming but also offers an easy graphical programming interface via Blueprints. We decided to directly benefit from Unreal's networking architecture, hence, we use a client-server model enabling users to host and join sessions via a lobby system, whereby the first client acts also as a server. An overview of the whole system design is shown in Fig. 1.

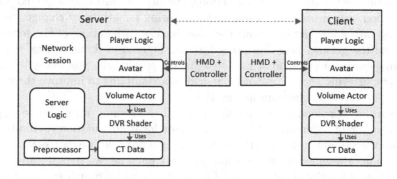

Fig. 1. System architecture of our application. The first client acts also as a server.

The CT data requires a preprocessing step to be loaded into the Unreal Engine. The processed data can be rendered seamlessly into the polygonal scene using our shader-based direct volume rendering solution. Our DVR approach achieves real-time performance guaranteeing a smooth VR experience. In the following, we will describe the individual parts of our system in detail.

3.1   Direct Volume Rendering

In order to visualize the CT data in our Unreal Engine-based virtual environment, we opted for a direct volume rendering approach based on ray marching. Our pipeline is specifically designed for the visualization of CT data, thus, the first step is to read and process the CT DICOM files in a preprocessing phase. To map the density to opacity, we employ multiple, freely adjustable, default windows with corresponding transfer functions. The advantage of having multiple windows is that each feature captured by a window can be visualized with high contrast. To store the windows in a single grayscale image (8 bit) we decided to blend the windows similar to the RADIO algorithm by Mandell et al. [20], which maintains the relative attenuation relationships between the fundamental anatomic densities and thus accommodates radiologists and their expectations. Figure 2 depicts the underlying concept. However, any other blending algorithm would be compatible too. Additionally, the volumetric data set has to be transformed into a format suitable for import and further processing in the Unreal Engine, therefore, we arrange the individual 2D slices of the volume sequentially into sequence maps (see Fig. 3).

We have implemented the ray casting directly in a pixel shader. We use a unit cube as a geometrical proxy mesh and reconstruct the volume coordinates from the generated sequence maps. In order to avoid artifacts of box-aligned samples (left diagram in Fig. 4), we align the first sampling points to stacked view-aligned planes instead (middle diagram in Fig. 4). Additionally, we precompute the sampling step length and the maximal number of samples fitting in the volume outside of the ray casting loop to reduce overhead. The calculation is based on the CT data set's proportions, the ray's accordingly adjusted starting position, and a user-adjustable factor allowing for arbitrary changes to the sampling rate. More details about the aforementioned handling of the sequence maps and the general sampling procedure can be read in Ryan Brucks' volume rendering guide for the Unreal Engine 4 [3]. We provide the possibility to apply stochastic jittering and a 2×2 ordered grid supersampling to improve the visual quality (see the right diagram in Fig. 4).

Regarding convincing yet fast shading and shadowing, we opted to implement a couple of different and not too complex local illumination methods and compare the visual results. Firstly, at each sample position, we cast shadow rays to determine the amount of occlusion. For this purpose, we dynamically track the position of multiple light sources. This method enables proper self-shadowing from multiple dynamic lights, however, is rather computational expensive. Therefore, we lower the shadow rays' sampling frequency in contrast to the primary

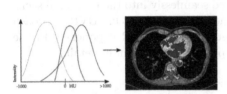
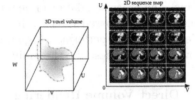

Fig. 2. Window blending according to the RADIO algorithm. Left: bone, lung, soft tissue windows. Right: blended CT image.

Fig. 3. Right: sequence map of CT slices. Left: corresponding reconstruction in the shader.

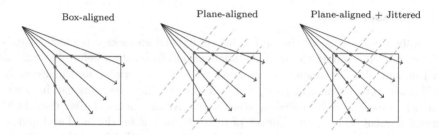

Fig. 4. Sampling positions in the volume. Left: in the naive approach the start sample positions align with the box mesh and cause patterned artifacts throughout the volume. Middle: sampling positions on equidistant view-aligned planes. Right: the sample positions are additionally jittered along the ray axis.

rays'. Secondly, we implemented the classic Blinn-Phong shading model that is evaluated at each sampling position. It is rather cheap to compute and enables local lighting approximation by diffuse and specular reflections which can be configured on a per-material-basis. We approximate the needed surface normals, which are not present in CT data, based on the local gradient using the central differences technique in the preprocessing phase. Lastly, we also implemented volumetric local ambient occlusion (LAO). Here, the sampling point is shaded based on the amount of occlusion, which is estimated by the opacities of the local neighborhood. This method can be used to prevent full shadows, which may obscure fine details. Another advantage is that it is not based on gradients, which are often not well defined (e.g. in homogeneous regions) and susceptible to noise. Algorithm 1 outlines the raycasting process.

To increase the performance, we reduce the number of samples being taken by early ray termination and empty space skipping using an octree. We construct the octree using a pointer-free branch-on-need strategy and encode it in a texture during the preprocessing phase, as the data is static. During sampling, the octree is traversed top-down similar to the parametric approach described in [24].

Algorithm 1. Shader-Based Raycasting

---

for each *pixel* (in parallel) **do**
    compute *firstSamplePos* and *maxSamples*
    while *maxSamples* not reached and *accumOpacity* below 1 **do**
        sample position using opacity sequence map
        calculate base color depending on opacity
        update *accumOpacity* by composition with sample opacity
        evaluate selected lighting method(s) and update color
        update *accumColor* by composition with sample color
        increment sample position

3.2   Collaborative VR

Generally, we made use of Unreal Engines polygonal and stereo rendering capabilities and VR support to build our application. To create a believable virtual environment, thus, enhancing the immersion and the experience for the users, we build a 3D scene resembling an operation room in which the users can interact. Similarly, users are represented by static mesh avatars modeled after doctors in a medical outfit. Our avatars consist of separate models for the head and hands; their corresponding positions are tracked directly by the HMD and the accompanying controllers. To avoid issues with possibly faulty and distracting animations by inverse kinematics, we refrain from using whole-body skeletal meshes. Each user can be identified by a personal name shown over the avatar. Figure 5 shows a session with three users inspecting the CT data in the virtual operating room.

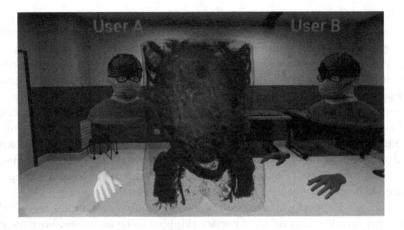

Fig. 5. Several networked users inspecting the 3D visualized CT data in a shared virtual environment.

We included a lobby system with which users can create or search for active sessions, or alternatively join one via a known IP, thus, enabling multiple of these virtual shared environments to exist in parallel. Also, although VR usage is our main focus, VR and non-VR users can mix and collaborate without restriction as we have implemented movement and interaction metaphors for both of them. For example, we implemented physical 3D buttons placed in the scene for VR users and keyboard shortcuts for non-VR users to manipulate properties of the 3D visualization. To reduce the latency between user input and perceived action, which has been shown to be crucial for a positive user experience in previous studies [28], all (inter)actions from users are executed locally first, before being sent and replicated on the server, from which they are finally broadcasted to all remaining users. Furthermore, the Unreal Engine provides some additional latency optimization techniques which help to minimize and stabilize the time needed for communication between client and server.

As a locomotion metaphor for VR users, we decided to use the classical teleportation approach, in combination with room-scale locomotion, as it minimizes the occurrence of motion sickness [7]. A problem arising from using teleportation in a multi-user environment is that the actual process of vanishing and reemerging somewhere else will be confusing for observers as it resembles the typical effects of a slow network connection or network errors. Therefore, we have implemented a particle effect, to highlight the deliberate action of the teleportation process.

To allow for collaborative work between users, we replicate not only their avatars but also the complete state of the 3D visualization of the CT data, making it a single shared object in the scene which is rendered from the individual users' viewpoint. It can be grabbed, moved, and rotated freely and naturally using the controller for optimal (re)view (see Fig. 6). Non-VR users, however, can rotate the object via an orbiting mode. To keep it simple, we do not restrict concurrent manipulation, which internally would be executed sequentially, as users can coordinate themselves. The replicated hands in VR make it easy to point specific spots or areas in the 3D visualization and to make gestures, which help in discussing the data, show findings, or plan interventions.

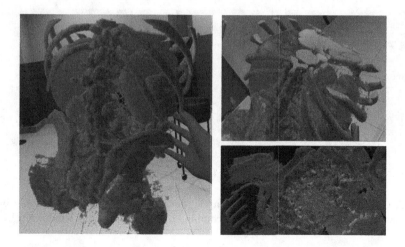

Fig. 6. Several images illustrating how the 3D visualization can be grabbed and freely be moved and rotated for a better view. The background was hidden in the image in the bottom-right.

In addition to the 3D visualization of the medical data, users in our application have the possibility to view accompanying 2D images, e.g. the raw CT data, on a virtual TV in the operating room scene. This may be useful if there is a need to quickly check for specific fine details not visible in the 3D visualization. Finally, the complete scene bar the 3D visualization can be dynamically hidden, resulting in a black background, for an undistracted contrast-rich view.

4   Results

We have evaluated the quality as well as the performance of the main aspects of our approach. In order to show the quality of our volumetric renderer, we visually compare our results to two competing visualization tools. Additionally, we did extensive measurements regarding the performance under various conditions, e.g. different lighting models and optimization methods. For the evaluations, we used several real-world CT data sets obtained by a hospital. The number of slices varies between the data sets and ranges from 47 to 317. We have developed and tested our work based on the Unreal Engine 4.22. Figure 7 shows our volume renderer with different active windows. In the left image, only the bone window is applied. The middle image depicts, among others, inner structures of the liver, small intestine, colon, and skin. Finally, in the right image, all three windows (the third one being soft tissue) are simultaneously visualized. Our DVR is able to effectively render single materials like the bone as well as compositions of multiple materials simultaneously, and thus, the complete range of CT data. This helps in conveying the spatial relationships between organs and getting a good understanding of the data.

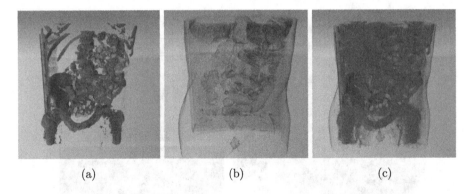

(a)   (b)   (c)

Fig. 7. Our volume renderer applied to a CT data set using different windows: bone (a), bowel and skin (b), and soft tissue, combined with the previous windows (c).

Figure 8 depicts our renderer with the different lighting settings. The left image shows a bone window using only shadow rays. Self-shadowing can be seen which helps in conveying depth, however, because of the limited sampling rate for shadow rays, the shadows are coarse and imprecise. In the middle image, we switched on the Blinn-Phong lighting model. A possible issue with this technique is, that, depending on the position of the light source relative to the visualized object, areas may lie completely in the shadows, and thus, can be hard to inspect if no additional ambient lighting is applied. The right image, however, shows the combination with the local ambient occlusion technique. This combination circumvents the problem of full shadows and results in the best lighting. The transition between being in complete light and full shadow is the most fine-granular and accounts for the local neighborhood providing the best depth perception and understanding of object shapes.

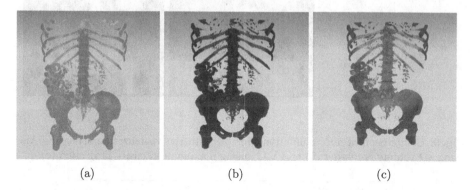

(a)   (b)   (c)

Fig. 8. Our volume renderer using different illumination methods: shadow rays (a), additional Blinn-Phong lighting (b), both combined with LAO (c). As can be seen, the latter enhances the depth perception by superior shadowing.

Figure 9 illustrates a comparison of our renderer (first image) with the common visualization tools RadiAnt DICOM Viewer in the standard 3D volume rendering mode (second image), and the Visualization Toolkit (VTK) with maximum intensity projection as a composition scheme (third image). The comparison shows that our renderer generates visualizations which are very effective in conveying a perception of depth and giving a clear and understandable overview of the data set as a whole. At the same time, our renderer produces precise, plastic visualizations of the individual materials. VTK uses MIP which results in relatively flat images with missing details. The advanced lighting and shading of our renderer make the assessment of the spatial relations between the objects easy. Although the results by RadiAnt are very good too, they tend to exhibit slightly stronger artifacts and a simpler shading is used.

A performance evaluation was done on a PC with Windows 10, Intel Core i7 4790 CPU, Nvidia Titan V graphics card, 32 GB of system memory, and a Full HD monitor. To perform the measurements, we used the native GPU profiler of the Unreal Engine and took the average of multiple runs.

Figure 10 shows the performance of our renderer and the influence of factors such as the number of slices and different lighting methods. In all cases, our renderer outperforms the rudimentary volume rendering solution by Ryan Brucks [3], independent of the chosen lighting models. Actually, we achieve real-time performance for VR in all our test cases.

Additionally, we have evaluated the efficiency of our octree implementation for empty space skipping. With the octree, we measured performance improvements for all test data sets of up to 49.4%. The average improvement was 14.7%, while the empty space ratio varied between roughly 45% and 55%, except for one

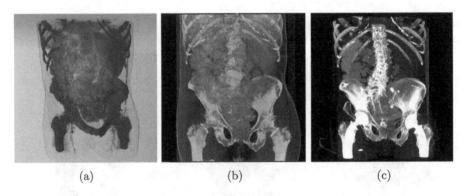

(a)   (b)   (c)

Fig. 9. Comparison of our volume renderer (a) with the visualization tools RadiAnt using 3D volume rendering (b) and VTK using maximum intensity projection (c).

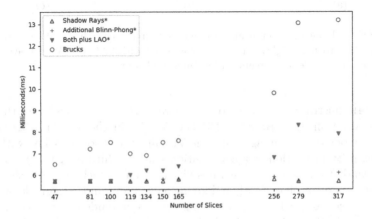

Fig. 10. The performance using different lighting models and data sets with a varying amount of slices. Our methods are marked with asterisks, "Brucks" is a rudimentary volume rendering integration in Unreal. Even though advanced lighting models increases the computational time, or renderer is real-time capable in all cases and significantly faster than the implementation by Brucks.

data set with only 36%. This shows that our octree implementation is effective in increasing the performance, especially for high-slice data sets.

Finally, we have measured the network performance, specifically the latency. However, in order to get objective and comparable results, we avoided a real internet transmission that is highly dependent on individual factors such as the connection quality or the distance. Instead, we set up client and server on two different computers which were connected via a router and measured the round time of the network messages from client to server and back. The average time was 16.8 ms with a standard deviation of 1.6 ms that is added by our system. Obviously, in case of an internet connection, additional latency have to be added. To conclude, our application is very well suited for collaborative work as actions form other users are replicated quickly. Accordingly, the user feedback, regarding the multi-user VR experience as well as the medical visualization, is very positive so far.

5 Conclusion and Future Work

We have presented a multi-user virtual reality system for medical visualization based on a state-of-the-art game engine that is capable of 3D visualizing computed tomography data in real-time and in a high visual quality. This is achieved by our custom ray-marching-based direct volume renderer which we have implemented using shaders and integrated into the Unreal Engine. Our renderer supports different lighting models, transfer functions selection, and artifact-reducing methods. Our evaluation shows that we achieve VR capable framerates of more than 100 Hz even for complex data sets consisting of more than 300 slices and with advanced lighting features such as ambient occlusion enabled. Our system includes a multi-user component and is designed as a shared virtual environment resembling a real operation room, thus, enabling immersive collaborative work between co-located or remote users. Thanks to the combination of the sophisticated game engine, VR, and our fast high-quality direct volume renderer, users can interact with each other and the shared visualized CT data in an immersive virtual environment and (re)view and discuss the 3D data in a comprehensive natural way. This makes our system ideally suited for pre-operative planning, possibly tumor boards, post-operative evaluation, or patient education.

For the future we plan to expand the interaction possibilities with the volume visualization, specifically, we are looking at integrating a dynamic clipping plane for a better view of internal regions and a volumetric drawing tool allowing for quick sketches and annotations inside the volume. Other improvements would be a direct integration and parallelization of the preprocessing part to speed up the workflow and allowing for a dynamic adjustment of the transfer functions. To improve the visualization of complex structures and organs that involve multiple materials support for multi-dimensional transfer functions could be added.

Acknowledgment. This work was partially funded by the German Federal Ministry of Education and Research (BMBF) under the grant 16SV8077.

References

1. Adams, H., Shinn, J., Morrel, W.G., Noble, J., Bodenheimer, B.: Development and evaluation of an immersive virtual reality system for medical imaging of the ear. In: Medical Imaging 2019: Image-Guided Procedures. Robotic Interventions, and Modeling, vol. 10951, pp. 265–272. International Society for Optics and Photonics, SPIE (2019)
2. Berger, F., Ebert, L.C., Kubik-Huch, R.A., Eid, K., Thali, M.J., Niemann, T.: Application of cinematic rendering in clinical routine CT examination of ankle sprains. Am. J. Roentgenol. **211**(4), 887–890 (2018)

3. Brucks, R.: Creating a volumetric ray marcher. https://shaderbits.com/blog/creating-volumetric-ray-marcher (2016). Accessed 17 July 2020
4. Cecil, J., Ramanathan, P., Rahneshin, V., Prakash, A., Pirela-Cruz, M.: Collaborative virtual environments for orthopedic surgery. In: 2013 IEEE International Conference on Automation Science and Engineering (CASE), pp. 133–137 (2013)
5. Chheang, V., et al.: Collaborative virtual reality for laparoscopic liver surgery training (10 2019)
6. Christensen, N., et al.: Feasibility of team training in virtual reality for robot-assisted minimally invasive surgery, pp. 1–4 (04 2018)
7. Christou, C.G., Aristidou, P.: Steering versus teleport locomotion for head mounted displays. In: De Paolis, L.T., Bourdot, P., Mongelli, A. (eds.) AVR 2017. LNCS, vol. 10325, pp. 431–446. Springer, Cham (2017). https://doi.org/10.1007/978-3-319-60928-7_37
8. Dappa, E., Higashigaito, K., Fornaro, J., Leschka, S., Wildermuth, S., Alkadhi, H.: Cinematic rendering - an alternative to volume rendering for 3D computed tomography imaging. Insights Imaging **7**, 849–856 (2016)
9. Ebert, L.C., et al.: Forensic 3D visualization of CT data using cinematic volume rendering: a preliminary study. Am. J. Roentgenol. **208**(2), 233–240 (2017)
10. Elvezio, C., Ling, F., Liu, J.S., Feiner, S.: Collaborative virtual reality for low-latency interaction. In: The 31st Annual ACM Symposium on User Interface Software and Technology Adjunct Proceedings, pp. 179–181, October 2018
11. Faludi, B., Zoller, E.I., Gerig, N., Zam, A., Rauter, G., Cattin, P.C.: Direct visual and haptic volume rendering of medical data sets for an immersive exploration in virtual reality. In: Shen, D., et al. (eds.) MICCAI 2019. LNCS, vol. 11768, pp. 29–37. Springer, Cham (2019). https://doi.org/10.1007/978-3-030-32254-0_4
12. Guo, Y., Liu, Y., Lu, Q.H., Zheng, K.H., Shi, L.J., Wang, Q.J.: CT two-dimensional reformation versus three-dimensional volume rendering with regard to surgical findings in the preoperative assessment of the ossicular chain in chronic suppurative otitis media. Eur. J. Radiol. **82**(9), 1519–1524 (2013)
13. Hernell, F., Ljung, P., Ynnerman, A.: Local ambient occlusion in direct volume rendering. IEEE Trans. Vis. Comput. Graph. **16**(4), 548–559 (2010)
14. Jung, Y., Kim, J., Bi, L., Kumar, A., Feng, D.D., Fulham, M.: A direct volume rendering visualization approach for serial PET-CT scans that preserves anatomical consistency. Int. J. Comput. Assist. Radiol. Surg. **14**(5), 733–744 (2019)
15. Kaluschke, M., et al.: Hips - a virtual reality hip prosthesis implantation simulator. In: 2018 IEEE Conference on Virtual Reality and 3D User Interfaces (VR), March 2018
16. Krüeger, A., Kubisch, C., Strauss, G., Preim, B.: Sinus endoscopy - application of advanced GPU volume rendering for virtual endoscopy. IEEE Trans. Vis. Comput. Graph. **14**, 1491–1498 (2009)
17. Larsen, C., Strandbygaard, J., Ottesen, B., Sorensen, J.: The efficacy of virtual reality simulation training in laparoscopy: a systemic review of randomized trials. Acta Obstetricia Gynecol. Scand. **91**, 1015–28 (2012)
18. Magdics, M., White, D., Marks, S.: Extending a virtual reality nasal cavity education tool with volume rendering. In: 2018 IEEE International Conference on Teaching, Assessment, and Learning for Engineering (TALE), pp. 811–814 (2018)
19. Maloca, P.M., et al.: High-performance virtual reality volume rendering of original optical coherence tomography point-cloud data enhanced with real-time ray casting. Transl. Vis. Sci. Technol. **7**(4), 2 (2018)

20. Mandell, J.C., et al.: Clinical applications of a CT window blending algorithm: radio (relative attenuation-dependent image overlay). J. Digit. Imaging **30**(3), 358–368 (2017)
21. Nguyen, B.J., et al.: Evaluation of virtual reality for detection of lung nodules on computed tomography. Tomogr. (Ann. Arbor Mich.) **4**(4), 204–208 (2018)
22. Paiva, P., Machado, L., Valença, A., Batista, T., Moraes, R.: SimCEC: a collaborative VR-based simulator for surgical teamwork education. Comput. Entertain. **16**, 1–26 (2018)
23. Pulijala, Y., Ma, M., Pears, M., Peebles, D., Ayoub, A.: Effectiveness of immersive virtual reality in surgical training - a randomized control trial. J. Oral Maxillofacial Surg. **76**, 1065–1072 (2017)
24. Revelles, J., Ureña, C., Lastra, M., Lenguajes, D., Informaticos, S., Informatica, E.: An efficient parametric algorithm for octree traversal, May 2000
25. Ruijters, D., Vilanova, A.: Optimizing GPU volume rendering. J. WSCG **14**(1–3), 9-+ (2006)
26. Scholl, I., Bartella, A., Moluluo, C., Ertural, B., Laing, F., Suder, S.: MedicVR. In: Handels, H., Deserno, T., Maier, A., Maier-Hein, K., Palm, C., Tolxdorff, T. (eds.) Bildverarbeitung für die Medizin 2019, pp. 152–157. Springer, Wiesbaden (2019). https://doi.org/10.1007/978-3-658-25326-4_32
27. Song, S.W., Jun, B.C., Chae, S.R., Kim, B.G.: Clinical utility of three-dimensional facial computed tomography in the treatment of nasal bone fractures: a new modality involving an air-bone view with a volume rendering technique. Indian J. Otolaryngol. Head Neck Surg.: Off. Publ. Assoc. Otolaryngol. India **65**(Suppl 2), 210–215 (2013)
28. Waltemate, T., et al.: The impact of latency on perceptual judgments and motor performance in closed-loop interaction in virtual reality. In: Proceedings of the 22nd ACM Conference on Virtual Reality Software and Technology, VRST 2016, pp. 27–35. Association for Computing Machinery, New York (2016)
29. Wang, H., et al.: Application of an innovative computerized virtual planning system in acetabular fracture surgery: a feasibility study. Injury **47**(8), 1698–1701 (2016)

Viewing-Direction Dependent Appearance Manipulation Based on Light-Field Feedback

Toshiyuki Amano[1]([✉]) [iD] and Hiroki Yoshioka[2]

[1] Graduate School of Systems Engineering, Wakayama University, Wakayama, Japan
amano@wakayama-u.ac.jp
[2] Panasonic Industrial Devices Systems and Technology, Co., Ltd.,
Nagaokakyo, Japan

Abstract. We propose a novel light-field feedback system that achieves appearance manipulation depending on the viewing-direction. Our method employs a reflection model using multiple projectors and cameras. It produces stable light-field feedback in the multiple-input and multiple-output system with decoupling using a pseudo-inverse. Through experiments, we confirmed that our method successfully enabled viewing-direction dependent appearance manipulation on the mirror reflection and the retro-reflection surface. Additionally, we verified that our method achieves robust appearance manipulation against disturbances, such as ambient light change.

Keywords: Spatial augmented reality · Light field · Optical feedback · Adaptive radiometric compensation

1 Introduction

Spatial augmented reality (SAR), also known as projection mapping, is used in various entertainment shows and attractions at amusement parks. Shader lamps, a pioneering work in SAR, enabled texture mapping using shadow animations of 3D building models. Since then, many projection techniques such as adaptive geometric calibration [1,2], inter-reflection compensation through light transport analysis [3], dynamic projection mapping [4,5], and projection onto deformable objects [6,7] were developed. Besides, novel projection techniques such as high dynamic range projection [8], high-speed projection [9], multi-spectrum projection [10], and light-field projection [11] have been proposed. Light-field projection enables auto-stereoscopic and structural color display on a retro-reflective screen [15]. Potentially, it could also alternate apparent color for each viewing-direction using bidirectional reflectance distribution function (BRDF) analysis.

Amano et al. demonstrated an adaptive appearance manipulation that generates different colors depending on each viewing-direction by using a multiple projector–camera feedback system [12]. In this research, four pairs of projector–camera feedback units are employed, and each unit alternates apparent color

© Springer Nature Switzerland AG 2020
P. Bourdot et al. (Eds.): EuroVR 2020, LNCS 12499, pp. 192–205, 2020.
https://doi.org/10.1007/978-3-030-62655-6_12

with optical feedback [16] for each viewing-direction. The system enables the perceptual material appearance of metallic textiles to transform into the structural color or silky material. This approach realizes adaptive manipulation without reflectance analysis and compensation of the manipulation error owing to changes in environmental illumination. However, it requires a trial and error approach because the independently working projector–camera units do not care projected illumination from the other units in their projection calculations.

Murakami et al. proposed an alternative method for viewing-direction dependent appearance manipulation based on the reflectance matrix [13]. The matrix describes response among multiple projectors and cameras that is equivalent to rough sampled BRDF. It achieves the desired level of directional appearance manipulation through the pre-measurement of the directional reflection property. However, since the images are previously optimized for a particular illumination environment, the result is affected by environmental illumination.

To solve the aforementioned problems and take advantage of both Murakami's and Amano's methods, we propose a novel viewing-direction dependent appearance manipulation method based on light-field feedback (LFFB) combined with Murakami's and Amano's methods. The LFFB system consists of multiple cameras and projectors as well as diffused reflection surfaces and other complex reflection surfaces. Therefore, it can be thought of as a multiple-input and multiple-output (MIMO) system, requiring signal decoupling for successful control. However, the mixing process varies according to the surface reflection property. Especially in the case of Lambertian reflectance, decoupling is impossible. Therefore, we require an adaptive decoupling strategy adapted to each reflection property at the manipulation point.

2   Direction Dependent Appearance Manipulation

2.1   Multiple Projector–Camera Feedback System

Amano et al. [12] proposed a system that directionally alters the object's apparent color using four pairs of independently operating projector–camera feedback units. Each projector–camera feedback unit adjusts its projection illumination based on the model predictive appearance control and alternates the apparent surface color. Complex appearance manipulation can be achieved by simultaneously operating multiple projector–camera feedback units. For altering structural color, color phase shifting is implemented in the HSV color space, and a different degree of phase shift is set for each unit. In [12], the manipulation is working in stable is confirmed. However, the system is not suitable for retro-reflection or leaning surface because the camera and projector in each unit are placed on the mirror symmetry position.

2.2   Light-Field Projection from Reflectance Analysis

Murakami et al. [13] proposed a light-field projection for viewing-direction dependent appearance manipulation with reflectance analysis.

When illumination $\mathbf{p}_v = (p_v^r, p_v^g, p_v^b)^T$ is projected from the projector $v = 1, 2, \ldots, V$ onto the manipulation point S, the illumination of the manipulation point S is observed by the cameras placed along each viewing-direction $\mathbf{c}_u = (c_u^r, c_u^g, c_u^b)^T$ and is written as

$$\mathbf{c}_u = \sum_{v=1}^{V} k_{uv} m_{uv} \mathbf{p}_v + \mathbf{f}_u, \tag{1}$$

where $k_{uv} \in \mathbb{R}^{3 \times 3}$ is reflectance

$$k_{uv} = \begin{pmatrix} \kappa^{rr} & \kappa^{rg} & \kappa^{rb} \\ \kappa^{gr} & \kappa^{gg} & \kappa^{gb} \\ \kappa^{br} & \kappa^{bg} & \kappa^{bb} \end{pmatrix}_{uv}, 0 \leq \kappa^{ij} \leq 1, \tag{2}$$

$m_{uv} \in \mathbb{R}^{3 \times 3}$ is a color mixing matrix between the projector Prj$v$ that compensates for the color sensitivity difference between each pair of cameras and projectors, $\mathbf{f}_u \in \mathbb{R}^3$ is the environmental illumination observed on Cam$u$. Both m_{uv} and $\mathbf{f}_u$ are obtained by prior color calibration.

For appearance manipulation, the projection illumination from each projector $\mathbf{p}_v$ is obtained by non-negative optimization based on the optical response with the user providing the manipulation reference for each direction. The illumination simultaneously projected from all the projectors onto S achieves the desired adjustment of the viewing-direction dependent appearance. It should be noted that a non-Lambertian surface reflection is required for its manipulation. The desired directional color is displayed with this approach, but the illumination error due to environmental illumination changes cannot be compensated.

3 Proposed Method

3.1 Light-Field Feedback Model

Our light-field feedback (LFFB) system is designed to compensate for the manipulation error due to environmental illumination change by the expansion of the appearance manipulation framework [16], as shown in Fig. 1. We put manipulation reference for each direction without reflectance estimation for simplifying. Therefore the system attempts multiple view radiometric compensation instead of adaptive appearance manipulation. The LFFB shown in Fig. 1 consists of 4 projectors (Prj1, ..., Prj4) and 4 cameras (Cam1, ..., Cam4), but it is not limited in the number of devices.

To achieve viewing-direction dependent appearance manipulation, the LFFB performs the following operations:

1. Capture an image on each camera Cam1, ..., Cam4.
2. Calculate the control error from the reference image Ref$i$ for all Cam$i$.
3. Reshape Cam$i$ by pixel mapping C2C and unify the geometrical shape.
4. Apply demixing by K^{-1} and update each projection image by Σ.

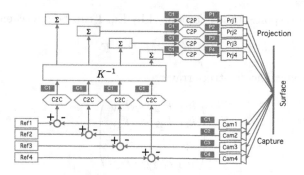

Fig. 1. Proposed light-field feedback model for the MIMO system. We employ signal decoupling K^{-1} for adapting to the various reflection types. C1, ... and P1, ... denote the image geometry of each camera or projector. C2C and C2P denote the geometrical conversion between these images. Ref1, ... are the references for each viewing-direction.

5. Project each projection image from the projector Prj$i$ after the geometrical reshaping by C2P is completed.

It should be noted that the labels C1, ..., C4 and P1, ..., P4 denote the image coordinate system corresponding to each camera or projector. The pixel value in the projection image $\mathbf{p_v}(t) \in ([\mathbf{0}, \mathbf{1}], [\mathbf{0}, \mathbf{1}], [\mathbf{0}, \mathbf{1}])^{\mathbf{T}}$ for projector v is updated by expansion to the Amano method's vector feedback, as follows:

$$\mathbf{p}_v(t+1) = \sum_{u=1}^{4} k_{vu}^* (1 - \alpha) \{\mathbf{r}_u - \mathbf{c}_u(t)\}$$

$$./(\mathbf{c}_{full,u} - \mathbf{c}_{0,u}) + \mathbf{p}_v(t) \tag{3}$$

where $\mathbf{c}_u(t) \in ([0, 1], [0, 1], [0, 1])^T$ denotes the pixel values in the image captured by camera u at processing step t and α is the trade-off parameter between stability and performance, ./ is the channel-wise division of RGB color.

The matrix k_{vu}^*, the block matrix of K^{-1} shown in Fig. 1, is a manipulation gain for $\mathbf{p}_v(t+1)$. We attempted the decoupling of the captured projected illumination of the MIMO system by applying this block matrix and achieved the optimal LFFB for various reflection types. Its design is discussed in the following section.

3.2   Decoupling of MIMO System Based on Reflectance Matrix

Since the contribution of each projection image to the captured image depends on the reflection property, suitable decoupling is required to stabilize the LFFB. Assume that the captured image values $\mathbf{c}_u, u = 1, \ldots, U$ and projection image values $\mathbf{p}_v, v = 1, 2, \ldots, V$ respectively are as follows:

$$C = (\mathbf{c}_1, \mathbf{c}_2, \cdots, \mathbf{c}_u)^T,$$
$$P = (\mathbf{p}_1, \mathbf{p}_2, \cdots, \mathbf{p}_v)^T. \tag{4}$$

The optical response that is produced by Eq. 1 can be rewritten as follows:

$$C = (K \circ M)P + F \tag{5}$$

where K is a reflectance matrix array

$$K = \begin{pmatrix} k_{11} & k_{12} & \cdots & k_{1V} \\ k_{21} & k_{22} & \cdots & k_{2V} \\ \vdots & \vdots & \ddots & \vdots \\ k_{U1} & k_{U2} & \cdots & k_{UV} \end{pmatrix}. \tag{6}$$

M is an array of color mixing matrices m_{uv} that compensates for the color sensitivity difference between each pair of cameras and projectors, and F is the environmental illumination component that aligns $\mathbf{f}_u$. The operator $\circ$ denotes a block-wise product. For simplicity, we assume that each m_{uv} is included in k_{uv}, and we remove M from Eq. 7. Then, the optical response can be rewritten as

$$C = KP + F. \tag{7}$$

The reflectance matrix array K is a rough sampling of the BRDF, and it expresses the optical contribution that is how the surface reflects each projected illumination in each camera direction. In this sense, k_{vu}^* is obtained from the block matrix of K^{-1}.

4   Decoupling for LFFB

4.1   Hardware Setup

To explore a suitable inverse matrix for the decoupling, we assembled our LFFB system with four projectors and four cameras, as shown in Fig. 2. Each projector–camera pair was placed in a horizontally at 40° intervals. We employed four Ximea MQ013CG-E2 cameras with a resolution of 1280 × 1024 pixels for Cam1, ..., Cam4, two EPSON EB-1761W projectors with a resolution of 1280 × 800 for Prj2 and Prj3, and two EPSON EB-1780W projectors with a resolution of 1280 × 800 for Prj1 and Prj4. These devices were connected to an iMacPro with a 3.2 GHz 8core CPU. We employed Prj5 (EPSON EB-1761W) additionally to change the environmental illumination in our experiments.

4.2 Naive Inverse Reflection Matrix

Since the reflectance matrix describes the mixing relation for the projected illumination in each captured image, a naive inverse of the reflectance matrix may
be a decoupling solution for the MIMO system. For the experiment, we used a
woven Nishijin textile with gold and silver leaves shown in Fig. 3(a). Firstly, we
obtained images with RGB color projection for all combinations and calculated
the reflectance matrix K using Murakami's method [13]. Next, we generated
a manipulation reference using monochrome conversion applied to the target

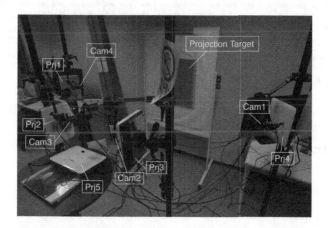

Fig. 2. Equipment setup for the proposed LFFB system. The system consists of four
projectors (Prj1, ..., Prj4) and four cameras (Cam1, ..., Cam4). The projector (Prj5)
provides additional environmental illumination for evaluation.

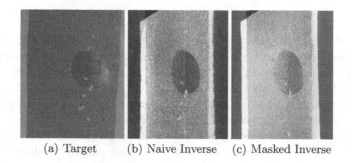

(a) Target   (b) Naive Inverse   (c) Masked Inverse

Fig. 3. Manipulation target and results of viewing-direction dependent appearance
manipulation. Our masked inverse procedure (right) eliminates the salt-and-pepper
noise that appears with decoupling using naive inverse (middle).

captured image with white illumination from all viewing-directions. From this, the appearance manipulation results shown in Fig. 3(b) was derived. A smooth achromatic appearance was expected to demonstrate successful manipulation results. However, colorful salt-and-pepper noise was produced. To understand the cause of this problem, we investigated the reflectance matrix in detail.

(a) Reflectance Matrix

K	p1			p2			p3			p4		
c1	0.93	0.21	0.08	0.82	0.18	0.10	0.20	0.04	0.02	0.12	0.02	0.00
	0.36	0.94	0.39	0.30	0.72	0.36	0.04	0.16	0.08	0.03	0.08	0.03
	0.07	0.28	0.96	0.08	0.28	0.97	0.00	0.04	0.19	-0.01	0.02	0.11
c2	0.10	0.01	0.01	0.40	0.09	0.04	0.88	0.18	0.05	0.08	0.02	0.01
	0.03	0.09	0.03	0.09	0.29	0.12	0.17	0.61	0.22	0.02	0.09	0.05
	0.00	0.01	0.10	0.01	0.06	0.35	0.02	0.11	0.72	-0.01	0.01	0.10
c3	0.04	0.00	-0.01	0.06	0.01	0.01	0.15	0.02	0.00	0.19	0.04	0.02
	0.01	0.04	0.01	0.00	0.05	0.01	0.05	0.15	0.07	0.06	0.20	0.07
	0.00	0.00	0.05	0.00	0.01	0.10	0.00	0.03	0.28	-0.01	0.05	0.35
c4	0.08	0.01	0.00	0.04	0.01	0.01	0.06	0.01	0.00	0.26	0.06	0.02
	0.01	0.06	0.03	-0.01	0.03	0.01	0.00	0.04	0.02	0.07	0.20	0.10
	0.00	0.01	0.06	0.00	0.01	0.04	0.00	0.00	0.04	0.00	0.05	0.26

(b) Naive Inverse

K^{-1}	c1			c2			c3			c4		
p1	-0.58	-1.38	15.31	-0.77	1.01	-71.8	16.06	6.09	217.6	-11.7	10.74	-276
	3.75	11.46	-30.4	-9.11	-44.4	144.4	17.11	213.8	-455	-2.72	-249	617
	-1.83	2.46	-10	10.71	-10.5	49.41	-95.5	43.02	-155	70.8	-56.8	205.4
p2	2.28	1.64	-19.6	0.7	-2.53	91.88	-21.7	-0.82	-279	15.45	-20.7	355.1
	-6.03	-15.1	44.5	12.58	65.98	-215	-16.7	-320	677.7	-2.14	372.5	-919
	2.34	-1.81	8.76	-12	5.81	-37.2	100.2	-19.1	115.5	-73.1	29.95	-151
p3	-0.91	-0.44	6.95	0.86	-0.02	-32.6	8.56	3.12	99.03	-6.34	4.69	-126
	2.27	5.96	-17.9	-4.78	-24.7	86.05	1.63	129	-273	4.76	-151	370.7
	-0.81	0.85	-3.77	4.36	-3.01	17.16	-36.9	9.78	-48.5	27.06	-14.1	63.25
p4	-0.08	0.86	-4.88	0.68	-2.24	22.87	-12	8.17	-70.2	13.47	-15.1	90.95
	-0.45	-2.85	7.45	0.94	10.29	-35.1	6.46	-50.7	110.8	-8.69	65.7	-152
	0.33	-0.12	0.71	-1.76	0.78	-4.25	14.03	-2.26	12.61	-9.91	2.33	-12.1

(c) Masked Inverse

K'^{-1}	c1			c2			c3			c4		
p1	1.19	-0.28	0.02	0	0	0	0	0	0	0	0	0
	-0.48	1.33	-0.51	0	0	0	0	0	0	0	0	0
	0.06	-0.38	1.19	0	0	0	0	0	0	0	0	0
p2	0	0	0	2.68	-0.82	-0.04	0	0	0	0	0	0
	0	0	0	-0.90	3.96	-1.27	0	0	0	0	0	0
	0	0	0	0.10	-0.70	3.05	0	0	0	0	0	0
p3	0	0	0	0	0	0	7.02	-1.15	0.25	0	0	0
	0	0	0	0	0	0	-2.33	7.43	-1.80	0	0	0
	0	0	0	0	0	0	0.15	-0.84	3.83	0	0	0
p4	0	0	0	0	0	0	0	0	0	4.21	-1.27	0.13
	0	0	0	0	0	0	0	0	0	-1.63	6.00	-2.24
	0	0	0	0	0	0	0	0	0	0.30	-1.10	4.27

Fig. 4. Reflectance matrix and two inverse strategies. The naive inverse matrix (b) produces negative or saturated values. These extreme values caused saturation or vibration in the projection images. By contrast, the inverse calculation using the masked reflectance matrix (c) produced no extreme values and achieved noiseless manipulation.

Figure 4(a) shows the reflectance K at the center of the red square in Fig. 3(a). Elements in the diagonal block matrices contain large values, unlike the off-diagonal blocks. From this, we infer that the reflection tends toward being mirror-like. Some elements have negative values. These variables are optically illegal but reasonable when we assume image noise due to subtracting environmental illumination. Figure 4(b) shows an inverse of (a) K^{-1} that is used for a naive approach. A serious problem is that some of the blocks have negative or saturated values. We can easily conclude that these excessive values cause the saturation or vibration in $p_v(t+1)$ and result in the salt-and-pepper projections, as shown in Fig. 3(b).

4.3   Blocks Masked Inverse

In [12], Amano et al. organized a system that consists of four pairs of independent optical feedback units. In each unit, the camera is placed in a position that mirrors the projector under the assumption of surface mirror reflection. This setup is equivalent to the design of our reflectance matrix model for

$$K' = \begin{pmatrix} k_{11} & 0 & 0 & 0 \\ 0 & k_{22} & 0 & 0 \\ 0 & 0 & k_{44} & 0 \\ 0 & 0 & 0 & k_{44} \end{pmatrix}. \tag{8}$$

When we applied the zero matrices to the off-diagonal blocks shown in the figure, the inverted matrix K^{-1} had no extreme values, as shown in Fig. 4(c) and achieved the noiseless manipulation shown in Fig. 3(c).

The main reason for this improvement may be that the projectors corresponding to the off-diagonal blocks do not contribute to illumination manipulation, and this unnecessary connection caused projection noise. However, correspondings are highly dependent on surface reflection property. For instance, the corresponding pairs can be move with a surface normal or microstructure. For ideal retro-reflection, the anti-diagonal blocks should have large values. Therefore, we propose the following block masking procedure:

1. Calculate absolute determinants $a_{uv} = |\det k_{uv}|$ for all blocks.
2. **while** $max(a_{uv}) \neq 0$ **do**
3. $(u', v') = \arg max_{u,v}(a_{uv})$
4.   Replace k_{uv} for $\{(u, v)|u = u'$ and $v \neq v'\}$.
5.   in the 0 matrix and for $\{(u, v)|u = u'$ or $v = v'\}$ put $a_{uv} = 0$.
6. **end while**

To avoid $\det K' = 0$ in the process, we took care during selection that the same column should not be selected for other rows.

4.4   Decoupling of Color Mixing

Each block k_{uv} in the reflectance matrix K involves color mixing [14], not only the reflection property. In other words, it describes how the RGB illumination from the projection affects each of the RGB components of the captured image. Thus, its decoupling should be considered for optimal feedback. Inverse transformation k_{uv}^{-1} may be a solution. However, it is not always optimal since the value of the projected image cannot be negative.

To explore the best approach, we compared the responses using a simple inverse matrix k_{uv}^{-1} (Full Elements) and the inverse diagonal matrix $(k_{uv} \odot I_3)^{-1}$, where $I_3 \in \mathbb{R}^{3 \times 3}$ is an identity matrix $\odot$ denotes the Hadamard product (Diagonal). The fall distance(Steps reach 10% of initial MAE) using the naive inverse matrix (Full Elements) was 107 steps. By contrast, the fall distance using the inverse diagonal matrix (Diagonal) was 76 steps, and it achieved higher convergence performance than the naive inverse. Therefore, we employed an inverse diagonal matrix for the K^{-1} block in addition to the masked inverse algorithm.

5   Evaluation

5.1   Adaptivity for Various Reflection Surface

In [12], four pairs of projector–camera units are employed and placed at mirror symmetry positions. This achieved viewing-direction dependent appearance manipulation for a shiny object. However, it does not account for other reflections such as asymmetry reflection and retro-reflection. By contrast, our proposed method adaptively configures the cameras by K^{-1}, and this enables LFFB on such reflective surfaces. To validate our method, we attempted viewing-direction dependent appearance manipulation of the color phase shift on a scene consisting of a mirror reflection (Nishijin textile with gold and silver leaves), a diffuse reflection (picture printed on matte photo paper), and retro-reflection (3M retro-reflection sheet 680–10 of color bars drawn with permanent marker) shown on the left in Fig. 5.

Figure 6 shows the block selection results at each manipulation point. As we can see, the type1 reflection matrix that infers mirror reflection occupied the textile region. For the retro-reflection sheet region, the type10 matrix with block matrices aligned anti-diagonally occupied the entire region. Conversely, various matrices types were selected in the matte photo paper region.

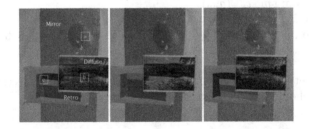

Fig. 5. Manipulation scene and references. We placed three different types of reflection materials for mirror reflection, retro reflection, and diffuse reflection in the manipulation area (left). For the control reference, we applied a color shift of $-50°$ of the original image for Cam1 and Cam2 (middle) and of $+50$th$°$ for Cam3 and Cam4 (right).

Next, we calculated the K^{-1} for each manipulation point and attempted the viewing-direction dependent color phase shifting with our LFFB system. We set the references shown on the middle image of Fig. 5 for Cam1 and Cam2 and the right image of Fig. 5 for Cam3 and Cam4. Then we obtained the manipulation result shown in Fig. 7(a). Figure 7 shows the color phase manipulation results of both methods. When we compare these results, we can see a similar manipulation result in the textile region. Because the system consists of four projectors, the insufficient angular resolution cannot adapt the small surface normal change on the curve in both results. Some of the erroneous block selection creates noise at the edge of the tapestry. However, our method successfully manipulates the color phase, similar to Amano's method. The main advantage of our method

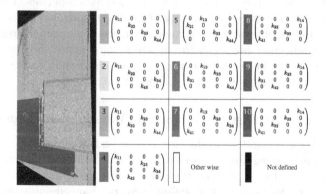

Fig. 6. Reflectance matrix block selection result. The color in the map (left) represents selected type shown in the legend (right). We can see some selection errors on the textile edge, but the most results on the textile and retro-reflection sheets are correct.

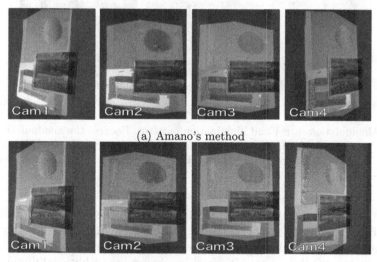

Fig. 7. Color phase manipulation results for various reflections. From left to right, each image is shown as it appears on Cam1, Cam2, Cam3, and Cam4, respectively. Since Amano's method assumes mirror reflection for the projector camera feedback, we can see the opposite color phase shift on the retro-reflection sheet. By contrast, our method manipulated successfully because of the decoupling based on the reflection property.

is its adaptivity that changes the corresponding pair by means of projector-camera feedback according to the perceived reflective properties. Therefore we can manipulate apparent color correctly not only for mirror reflection but also for retro-reflection. Conversely, since Amano's method assumed mirror reflection as the surface reflection property, the opposite color phase shift on the retro-reflection sheet could be seen. However, we have no method to manipulate its color phase on the diffuse surface for its optical nature.

5.2   Robustness Against Environmental Illumination Change

We conducted a comparative evaluation of our and Murakami's methods [13] to confirm robustness against changes in environmental illumination. Since our method employs feedback based on the reflectance matrix, the radiometric error on the object's surface due to a modeling error or changed environmental illumination conditions may be compensated for. The textile that we used consists of colorful silk and silver threads and is shown on the left in Fig. 8. Both the silk and silver threads are shiny and exhibit a different appearance that changes by viewing-direction and light-field projection.

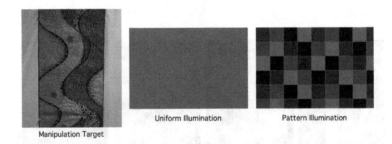

Fig. 8. Manipulation target and illumination patterns. Because the manipulation target (left) is made of colorful silk and silver threads, it is glossily reflective. Illumination patterns (middle, right) are projected from Prj5 as additional environmental illumination for evaluation.

First, we measured the reflectance matrix K and the environmental illumination $\mathbf{F}$ for all surface points on the textile under environmental lighting with additional uniform illumination projection shown in the center of Fig. 8. Its pixel value is 125, and Prj5 projected it. Next, we changed the additional illumination to pattern illumination, as shown on the right in Fig. 8. Each pixel value in the bight area is 125, 83, 42, and 0. The viewing-direction dependent color phase shift was performed using both methods. We can see that the color phase of the flowers changed with the viewing-direction in both results shown in Fig. 9. Most parts of the textile are comprised of silver thread. In these portions, therefore, we cannot expect an impressive color change with a color phase shift. However, since we used the same brightness image for all viewing-directions as a manipulation reference, the material's appearance changed to that of a matte fabric.

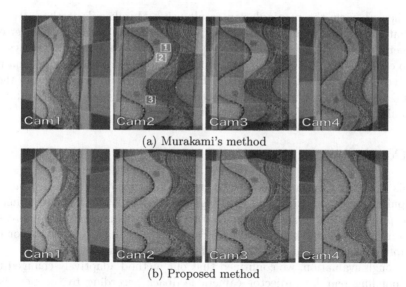

(a) Murakami's method

(b) Proposed method

Fig. 9. Viewing-direction dependent appearance manipulation results. We applied a different color phase shift for each viewing-direction. The apparent color of the flowers changed with the viewing-direction, and the glossiness of the silver strings was removed in both results. The remaining overlaid illumination with Murakami's method (top) is removed by proposed method (bottom).

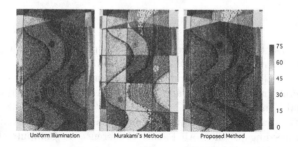

Fig. 10. Visualization of the appearance manipulation error from Cam3 view. The pseudo color shows the absolute pix value error from the reference for each color channel. The proposed method (right) successfully removed the patterned illumination that remained in Murakami's method (middle).

Table 1. Averaged manipulation error

	Region 1	Region 2	Region 3
Uniform	8.57	8.23	7.88
Murakami's	12.0	7.41	20.7
Proposed	5.51	7.40	6.16

When we view the manipulation result using Murakami's method, we can see that the illumination pattern projected by Prj5 has remained. Conversely, our method successfully eliminated the pattern. The superiority of our system is also confirmed by the visualized manipulation error shown in Fig. 10 and the averaged manipulation error marked in Fig. 9(a) shown in Table 1. From these results, we can also confirm that our method achieved the equivalent quality as manipulation under uniform environmental illumination.

6   Conclusion

In this study, we proposed a novel viewing-direction dependent appearance manipulation method using the LFFB system. The LFFB required decoupling of mixed projected illumination in the captured image. This relation is expressed by the reflectance matrix; however, we cannot simply apply its inverse for the decoupling. We proposed a block masked inverse procedure as a solution.

Through evaluation, we confirmed that our method adaptively changed the corresponding pair by projector–camera feedback according to the perceived reflective properties. It then correctly manipulated the color phase for both the retro-reflection and mirror reflection areas. Additionally, we also confirmed that our method achieved the same quality of viewing-direction dependent appearance manipulation for pattern illumination as well as uniform environmental illumination.

References

1. Okatani, T., Deguchi, K.: Autocalibration of a projector-camera system. IEEE Trans. Pattern Anal. Mach. Intell. **27**(12), 1845–1855 (2005)
2. Tehrani, M.A., Gopi, M., Majumder, A.: Automated geometric registration for multi-projector displays on arbitrary 3D shapes using uncalibrated devices. IEEE Trans. Visual Comput. Graphics. https://doi.org/10.1109/TVCG.2019.2950942
3. Wetzstein, G., Bimber, O.: Radiometric compensation through inverse light transport. In: Proceedings of the 15th Pacific Conference on Computer Graphics and Applications, pp. 391–399 (2007)
4. Resch, C., Keitler, P., Klinker, G.: Sticky projections - a new approach to interactive shader lamp tracking. In: IEEE International Symposium on Mixed and Augmented Reality (ISMAR), pp. 151–156 (2014)
5. Siegl, C., et al.: Real-time pixel luminance optimization for dynamic multi-projection mapping. ACM Trans. Graph. **34**(6), 237:1–237:11 (2015)
6. Punpongsanon, P., Iwai, D., Sato, K.: SoftAR: visually manipulating haptic softness perception in spatial augmented reality. IEEE Trans. Visual Comput. Graphics **21**(11), 1279–1288 (2015)
7. Fujimoto, Y., et al.: Geometrically-correct projection-based texture mapping onto a deformable object. IEEE Trans. Visual Comput. Graphics **20**(4), 540–549 (2014)
8. Pjanic, P., Willi, S., Grundhofer, A.: Geometric and photometric consistency in a mixed video and galvanoscopic scanning laser projection mapping system. IEEE Trans. Visual Comput. Graphics **23**(11), 2430–2439 (2017)

9. Narita, G., Watanabe, Y., Ishikawa, M.: Dynamic projection mapping onto deforming non-rigid surface using deformable dot cluster marker. IEEE Trans. Visual Comput. Graphics **23**(3), 1235–1248 (2017)
10. Li, Y., Majumder, A., Lu, D., Gopi, M.: Content-independent multi-spectral display using superimposed projections. Comput. Graph. Forum **34**(2), 337–348 (2015)
11. Jones, A., et al: An automultiscopic projector array for interactive digital humans. In: ACM SIGGRAPH 2015 Emerging Technologies, pp. 6:1–6:1 (2015)
12. Amano, T., Ushida, S., Miyabayashi, Y.: Viewpoint-dependent appearance-manipulation with multiple projector-camera systems. In: ICAT - EGVE 2015, Eurographics Association, pp. 101–107 (2017)
13. Murakami, K., Amano, T.: Materiality manipulation by light-field projection from reflectance analysis. In: International Conference on Artificial Reality and Telexistence and Eurographics Symposium on Virtual Environments, pp. 99–105 (2018)
14. Nayar, S.K., Peri, H., Grossberg, M.D., Belhumeur, P.N.: A projection system with radiometric compensation for screen imperfections. In: IEEE International Workshop on Projector-Camera Systems (2003)
15. Amano, T., Minami, K.: Structural color display on retroreflective objects. In: Proceedings of the 25th International Conference on Artificial Reality and Telexistence and 20th Eurographics Symposium on Virtual Environments, ICAT - EGVE 2015, Eurographics Association, pp. 37–44 (2015)
16. Amano, T., et al.: Appearance control for human material perception manipulation. In: Proceedings of the 21st International Conference on Pattern Recognition (ICPR 2012), pp. 13–16 (2012)

Scientific Posters

Holistic Quality Assessment of Mediated Immersive Multisensory Social Communication

Alexander Toet[1]([⊠]) [iD], Tina Mioch[1] [iD], Simon N. B. Gunkel[2] [iD],
Camille Sallaberry[1,3] [iD], Jan B. F. van Erp[1,3] [iD], and Omar Niamut[2] [iD]

[1] TNO Human Factors, Soesterberg, The Netherlands
{lex.toet,tina.mioch,camille.sallaberry,jan.vanerp}@tno.nl
[2] TNO ICT, The Hague, The Netherlands
{simon.gunkel,omar.niamut}@tno.nl
[3] University of Twente, Enschede, The Netherlands

Abstract. Communication through modern immersive systems that afford the representation of a wide range of multisensory (visual, auditory, haptic, olfactory) social and ambient (environmental) affective cues can provide compelling experiences that approach face-to-face communication. The quality of a mediated social communication experience (QoE) can be defined as the degree to which it matches its real-life counterpart and is typically assessed through questionnaires. However, available questionnaires are typically extensive, targeted at specific systems, and do not address all relevant aspects of social presence. Here we propose a general holistic social presence QoE questionnaire (HSPQ), that uses a single item for each of the relevant processing levels in the human brain: sensory, emotional, and cognitive, behavioral, and reasoning. The HSPQ measures social presence through the senses of spatial presence (= telepresence + agency) in the mediated environment and social interaction (= interaction + engagement) with the other persons therein. Initial validation studies confirm the content and face validity of the HSPQ. In future studies we will test the stability, sensitivity, and convergent validity of the HSPQ.

Keywords: Mediated social communication · Social presence · Quality of experience

1 Introduction

1.1 Towards Mediated Multisensory Social Presence

Humans have a social and personal need for communication to maintain their interpersonal relationships. In our digital age, human social interaction is often mediated. Given the inherent human need for affective communication to establish trust and mutual understanding, mediated social communication should afford the same affective characteristics as face-to-face communication.

Modern multisensory immersive technologies can provide highly realistic mediated experiences by presenting the user with vivid immersive and extensive representations

P. Bourdot et al. (Eds.): EuroVR 2020, LNCS 12499, pp. 209–215, 2020.
https://doi.org/10.1007/978-3-030-62655-6_13

of real or virtual spaces. Social interaction through shared and mediated immersive environments can closely approximate the experience of face-to-face meetings by eliciting a sense of *social presence*: the sense of being in the same space as - and having social interaction with - other individuals [1]). The sense of being in a mediated environment is known as the sense of *spatial presence* [2], and consists of two components: the feeling of being located in the mediated environment rather than in the immediate physical environment (*telepresence*) together with the feeling of being able to act within that environment (*agency*). The sense of having social interaction with another individual involves a sense of *intimacy* (the feeling of connectedness or engagement that communicators feel during an interaction [3]) and a sense of *immediacy* (the psychological distance between the communicators [3]). Hence, social presence is inherently bidirectional (involving a sense of mutual awareness).

To assess how successful a communication system is in providing its users a sense of social presence, we need instruments that quantify the quality of their experience (QoE [4]). In this study, we define the *quality of a mediated experience* as the extent to which the experience agrees with its unmediated counterpart. Telepresence is optimal when the user is not aware that the communication is mediated. Social presence increases with the availability and perceived quality of (multisensory) social cues (supporting the senses of intimacy and immediacy), the behavioral realism and the interactivity (supporting the sense of agency) of the communication system. Although many different definitions of QoE have been presented in the literature, there is an ongoing debate about the nature of this construct, and a robust holistic framework with validated associated quality measures is still lacking [4]. Questionnaires are the currently most widely used tools to measure (social) presence [1, 5, 6]. However, most existing questionnaires are targeted at specific systems while their items only tap into a subset of all factors that contribute to social presence [7]. As a result, their scope is limited, and they only provide incomplete information.

The way we experience our environment and the people therein involves different processing levels in our brain that all contribute to the subjective quality of the experience [8]. Therefore, we will first discuss a conceptual holistic framework that describes how multisensory stimulation affects our brain at different processing levels, and we will link these levels to relevant perceptual, affective, and cognitive outcomes. Then we will present an efficient holistic social presence QoE questionnaire (HSPQ) that includes a single item for each of these outcomes and we will discuss the results of initial validation tests. In our future work we will use the HSPQ for the development of a novel immersive multi-sensory communication platform that affords mediated affective communication by providing users an experience of social presence through synchronized bidirectional sensing, digitization, transmission and replication of auditory, visual, and tactile information.

1.2 A Holistic Framework for Multisensory Perception

In natural conditions we experience our immediate physical environment through direct sensory input, which is converted into neural signals in the central nervous system and transmitted up to the cortex, resulting in a continuous stream of perceptions. A system that artificially stimulates our senses in correct harmony by presenting the right (congruent, consistent) sensory cues associated with a familiar (natural) multisensory percept in the correct (appropriate spatiotemporal) way can evoke the illusion of a natural (unmediated) percept. In other words, for highly naturalistic sensory stimulation, our brain cannot distinguish whether a consistent multisensory holistic percept originates from our direct physical (real-world) environment or a mediated (possibly fabricated) one. Thus, technology that substitutes the (natural) sensory input from our physical environment by signals representing a different (e.g., sensed remote or even simulated virtual) environment, can in principle evoke the illusion of a direct (physical, unmediated) experience of that environment [9]. Schreuder et al. [10] presented a holistic conceptual framework that describes how multisensory environmental stimulation affects our brain at the sensory or perceptual, emotional, cognitive, behavioral and decision-making levels. In the next section we will first discuss the need for QoE measures, and we will give a brief overview of the state-of-the-art in this field. Then, in Sect. 2, we will present a new social presence questionnaire that directly links to the relevant outcomes at each of the relevant processing levels identified by Schreuder et al. [10].

1.3   The Quality of Mediated Immersive Experiences

Given the increasing availability of systems that afford mediated immersive social inter-actions between people, there is a need for metrics that efficiently and fully evaluate their QoE. Existing social presence questionnaires predominantly address the sensory components of mediated presence experiences. An exception is the Virtual Experience Test (VET [11]) that provides a more holistic measure of a mediated social presence experience by including affective, cognitive, active and relational dimensions in addi-tion to its sensory dimension. However, the instrument is designed for the development of virtual environments and games and is not sufficiently general for the evaluation of multisensory social communication systems. Also, the VET only measures the qual-ity of social interaction at the behavioral and reasoning levels, but not on the sensory, emotional, and cognitive levels.

Next to being holistic, relevant, sensitive and reliable, QoE measures for social presence should also be convenient and nonintrusive and generalizable across different communication systems [1]. Since there is currently no measure that meets all these criteria. the development of QoE metrics for social presence is still an ongoing effort [4]. In the next section we will present a social presence questionnaire based on items for each of the processing levels in the conceptual framework of Schreuder et al. The resulting tool will be efficient (it uses a concisely formulated single item to measure each relevant outcome) and holistic (it addresses all relevant outcomes), and therefore nonintrusive and generalizable. Then, in Sect. 3, we will briefly discuss some preliminary validation studies. The conclusions of this study will be presented in Sect. 4.

2   A Holistic Social Presence Measure

In this section we present a new holistic social presence questionnaire (HSPQ) that taps into each of the five relevant (sensory, emotional, cognitive, behavioral and deci-sion making) processing levels for multisensory environmental stimuli identified by

Schreuder et al. [10]. The HSPQ (Table 1) measures social presence through the senses of spatial presence (= telepresence + agency; 5 items) in the mediated environment and social interaction (= interaction and engagement) with the other persons therein. Since social interaction inherently involves a bidirectional exchange of physical and emotional signals, we maintain a distinction between the internal (*"own"*; 5 items) and external (*"the other"*; 5 items) assessment perspectives for this subscale of the HSPQ. Social presence is optimal when both spatial presence and social interaction are optimal. An optimal quality of spatial presence (= telepresence + agency) is achieved:

- at the sensory level, when system (QoS) parameters do not degrade the mediated representation (item 1: fidelity),
- at the affective or emotional level, when the mediated environment evokes similar emotions as its unmediated counterpart (item 2: consistency),
- at the cognitive level, when the mediated environment is experienced as natural (item 3: naturalness),
- at the behavioral level, when the mediated environment affords natural behavior without any limitations or restrictions (item 4: agency), and
- at the reasoning or decision-making level, when the mediated environment allows one to think in a similar way as in its unmediated counterpart (item 5: reasoning).

An optimal quality of social interaction is achieved:

- at the sensory level, when system factors do not affect the immediacy of the sensory impression that people have of one another (items 6 and 11: immediacy),
- at the affective or emotional level, when the mediation process does not degrade the feeling of intimacy (items 7 and 12: intimacy and engagement),
- at the cognitive level, when the mediation process does not affect the feelings of involvement between people (items 8 and 13: naturalness),
- at the behavioral level, when the system affords natural communication behavior without any limitations or restrictions (items 9 and 14: behavior), and
- at the reasoning level, when the fact that the communication between partners is mediated does not affect their reasoning and decision making (items 10 and 15: reasoning).

3   Validation

We performed a preliminary validation study to assess the content and face validity of the HSPQ.

Content validity was rated for each item by a panel of 10 experts, on a 4-point Likert scale (1 = *"not relevant"*, 2 = *"somewhat relevant"*, 3 = *"quite relevant"*, 4 = *"very relevant"*) [12]. The ratings were dichotomized (1, 2 = *"not essential"*; 3, 4 = *"essential"*) and the Content Validity Ratio was computed for each items as $CVR = (n_e - N/2)/(N/2)$, where n_e is the number of panel members that judge an item as *"essential"* and N is the total number of panel members [13]. The overall content validity of the HSPQ was quantified by the Content Validity Index (CVI), which is simply the mean of the CVR values over all items in the test. The CVR exceeds the critical level of 0.62 [13] for most items, except for items 3 (.22) and 5 (.33). The CVI was 0.85. Thus, the HSPQ and most of its items have a high content validity, while only two items (3 and 5) need further refinement.

Face validity was tested by a panel of 10 participants, who rated the clarity (ambiguity) of each item on a 10-point Likert scale (0 = "*I don't understand this item*", 10 = "*I understand this item*"). The interrater agreement was quantified through the intraclass correlation coefficient (ICC) with its associated 95% confidence intervals, based on a mean-rating ($k = 3$), consistency, 2-way mixed-effects model [14]. The ICC was 0.77 [0.56, 0.91] indicating good agreement between the different raters. On average, most HSPQ items scored above 8.0, except for items 2 (5.9) and 5 (6.5). Thus, it appears that these two items need to be reformulated.

Table 1. The holistic social presence questionnaire (HSPQ).

| | | Processing level | | | | |
		Sensory	Emotional	Cognitive	Behavioral	Reasoning
	Spatial presence	[1: fidelity] *I have direct contact with the environment (I see, hear, feel, smell the environment without any restrictions or distortions)*	[2: consistency] *My sensations agree with the environment (What I see, hear, feel, and smell matches the environment)*	[3: naturalness] *The environment appears natural*	[4: agency] *I can behave in a natural manner in the environment*	[5: reasoning] *I can think in the environment as in normal life*
Social presence	Internal ("*own*") perspective	[6: immediacy] *I have direct contact with the other person(s). (I see, hear, feel, smell the other person(s), without any restrictions or distortions)*	[7: intimacy] *I feel engaged with the other person(s)*	[8: naturalness] *The other person(s) appear natural to me*	[9: behavior] *I can interact with the other person(s) in a natural manner*	[10: reasoning] *The other person(s) affects my thinking as in normal life*
	External ("*other*") perspective	[11: immediacy] *The other person(s) appear to have direct contact with me (The other person(s) appear to see, hear, feel, smell me without any restrictions or distortions)*	[12: intimacy] *The other person(s) appear to feel engaged with me*	[13: naturalness] *I seem to appear natural to the other person(s)*	[14: behavior] *The other person(s) interact with me in a natural manner*	[15: reasoning] *I appear to affect the thinking of the other person(s) as in normal life*

4 Conclusions

We present a new holistic assessment tool for measuring the QoE of mediated social presence. The HSPQ uses a single item to tap into each of the relevant processing levels in the human brain: sensory, emotional, and cognitive, behavioral, and reasoning. The HSPQ measures social presence through the senses of spatial presence (= telepresence + agency) in the mediated environment and social interaction (= interaction and engagement with the other persons therein). The HSPQ distinguishes between the internal ("*own*") and external ("*the other*") assessment perspectives for the social interaction subscale of the HSPQ. Initial validation studies confirm the content and face validity of the HSPQ. We are currently refining the scope and formulation of some items in the HSPQ to further increase its content and face validity. Then, we will test its stability, sensitivity, and convergent validity in different mediated multisensory social communication settings. In our future work we will use the HSPQ for the development of a novel immersive multi-sensory communication platform that affords mediated affective communication by providing users an experience of social presence through synchronized bidirectional sensing, digitization, transmission and replication of auditory, visual, and tactile information.

References

1. Skarbez, R., Brooks, F.P., Whitton, M.C.: A survey of presence and related concepts. ACM Comput. Surv. **50**(6), Article 96 (2017)
2. Lombard, M., Jones, M.T.: Defining presence. In: Lombard, M., Biocca, F., Freeman, J., IJsselsteijn, W., Schaevitz, R.J. (eds.) Immersed in Media, pp. 13–34. Springer, Cham (2015). https://doi.org/10.1007/978-3-319-10190-3_2
3. Short, J., Williams, E., Christie, B.: The Social Psychology of Telecommunications. Wiley, New York (1976)
4. Möller, S., Raake, A.: Quality of Experience: Advanced Concepts, Applications and Methods. Springer, Cham (2014). https://doi.org/10.1007/978-3-319-02681-7
5. Grassini, S., Laumann, K.: Questionnaire measures and physiological correlates of presence: a systematic review. Front. Psychol. **11**, 349 (2020)
6. Youngblut, C.: Experience of presence in virtual environments. IDA Document D-2960, Institute for Defence Analysis, Alexandria, VA, USA (2003)
7. Hwang, H.S., Park, S.: Being together: user's subjective experience of social presence in CMC environments. In: Jacko, J.A. (ed.) HCI 2007. LNCS, vol. 4550, pp. 844–853. Springer, Heidelberg (2007). https://doi.org/10.1007/978-3-540-73105-4_93
8. Goldstein, E.B.: Sensation and Perception, 7th edn. Wadsworth Publishing Co Inc., San Francisco (2007)
9. Gallace, A., Ngo, M.K., Sulaitis, J., et al.: Multisensory presence in virtual reality: possibilities & limitations. In: Multiple Sensorial Media Advances and Applications: New Developments in MulSeMedia, pp. 1–40. IGI Global (2012)
10. Schreuder, E., van Erp, J., Toet, A., et al.: Emotional responses to multisensory environmental stimuli. SAGE Open **6**(1), 1–19 (2016)
11. Chertoff, D.B., Goldiez, B., LaViola, J.J.: Virtual experience test: a virtual environment evaluation questionnaire. In: IEEE Virtual Reality Conference 2010, pp. 103–110. IEEE Press (2010)

12. Waltz, C.F., Bausell, R.B.: Nursing Research: Design, Statistics, and Computer Analysis. F.A. Davis, Philadelphia (1981)
13. Lawshe, C.H.: A quantitative approach to content validity. Pers. Psychol. **28**(4), 563–575 (1975)
14. Shrout, P.E., Fleiss, J.L.: Intraclass correlations: uses in assessing rater reliability. Psychol. Bull. **86**(2), 420–428 (1979)

Conversation with Your Future Self About Nicotine Dependence

Gizem Şenel[1,2(✉)] and Mel Slater[1,2]

[1] Event Lab, Department of Clinical Psychology and Psychobiology, University of Barcelona,
08035 Barcelona, Spain
{gizemsenel,melslater}@ub.edu
[2] Institute of Neurosciences of the University of Barcelona, 08035 Barcelona, Spain

Abstract. Nicotine dependence continues to be one of the major contributors to the global disease burden, despite the wide variety of assessment and treatment techniques developed. Although VR has been used as an instrument to improve cue-exposure therapy techniques, the full extent of its power in the treatment of addictions has not been fully explored. In this paper, we utilize body-swapping, a VR specific paradigm, in order to facilitate a dialogue between the present self and the future self of the smoker about nicotine dependence. The experiment will compare the difference in Fagerström Test for Nicotine Dependence, Stages of Change, Future-Self Continuity Scale and Perceived Risks and Benefits Questionnaire scores before and after the dialogue between three groups, each named based on who the participant is talking with: Present Self, Future Self Smoking Cessation, and Future Self Still Smoking. We expect this new approach to lower nicotine dependence and lead to long-term healthy behaviour choices as well as pave the way for novel VR-treatment techniques.

Keywords: Virtual reality · Nicotine dependence · Future self-continuity

1 Introduction

Tobacco use causes more than 8 million deaths every year [1], and nicotine continues to be one of the most addictive substances that negatively impacts the health and wellbeing of society. SARS-CoV-2 has spread around the world since late 2019 [2], and it has been causing hundreds of thousands of deaths and significant suffering. Not surprisingly, considering that the negative progression and adverse effects of SARS-CoV-2 is likely to be associated with smoking [3], smoking cessation interventions have come into prominence [4] during the time of the pandemic.

Virtual reality (VR) has been used in the investigation, assessment and treatment of mental health disorders including anxiety, schizophrenia, eating disorders and substance use disorders [5]. Cue exposure therapy, the most widely used technique in VR for the treatment of nicotine dependence [6–8], aims to extinguish the association between substance-related cues and substance-use by repeated exposure to the craving and withdrawal inducing substance-related cues [9, 10]. Previous research has demonstrated that

© Springer Nature Switzerland AG 2020
P. Bourdot et al. (Eds.): EuroVR 2020, LNCS 12499, pp. 216–223, 2020.
https://doi.org/10.1007/978-3-030-62655-6_14

smoking cues presented in virtual environments elicit physiological responses and sub-jective craving to smoking [11], leading to neural activation in craving related brain regions [8]. Systematic literature reviews concluded an overall cue reactivity effect and a significant increase in craving when participants were presented with smoking-related virtual environments compared to virtual environments without smoking-related cues [12]. Other successful VR-based approaches include the task of crushing virtual cigarettes and combining VR-based coping skills training with Nicotine Replacement Therapy. Crushing virtual cigarettes in the VR environment, resulted in decreased nico-tine dependence scores of regular smokers in four weekly sessions [13], while combining VR coping skills training with Nicotine Replacement Therapy reduced the number of cigarettes smoked and enhanced smoking cessation rates compared to the traditional Nicotine Replacement Therapy [14].

Despite the amount of research and the techniques that have been developed to utilize VR to enhance the probability of smoking cessation, nicotine dependence still poses a serious challenge for many smokers. One of the problems to overcome in quitting smoking lies in the difficulty for individuals to realize the long-term harmful effects of smoking [15]. As the harm is incremental and long-term, the risks are easy to overlook and underestimate [16, 17]. This tendency to devalue future outcomes compared to immediate rewards is called *delay discounting* or *temporal discounting*. When presented with an intertemporal choice involving monetary gains, individuals tend to discount the value of monetary gains that are temporally further away. This discount effect is much stronger for health outcomes [18, 19], implying a general underestimation of the value of long-term health decisions. It is further shown that smokers have higher temporal discounting compared to non-smokers [20, 21]. This effect has been shown to reverse as the number of cigarettes smoked decreased [22]. Moreover, imagining a positive autobiographical future event, episodic future thinking, has been shown to reduce cigarette smoking and temporal discounting [23].

It is known that our perception of our potential future selves including hopes, fears, goals and threats, affect our current self-image and work an as incentive for future behaviour [24]. For instance, the results of a survey in which the data was obtained 23 years apart indicated that those individuals who demonstrated positive self-perceptions of ageing, lived on average 7.5 years more compared to those who did not have positive perceptions of aging [25]. The decision-making process for the future self resembles more the decision-making process for others, which is different from the decision-making process for the present self [26]. The temporal distance between present and future selves was found to cause individuals to make observer-like attributions towards the future self, which can be shifted to an actor-like attributions of the future self when the focus is on the thoughts and feelings, rather than actions [27]. Neuroimaging studies have found that current self vs future self ratings elicit activation in the rostral anterior cingulate cortex, the same area activated during the self vs other judgements, and individual differences in this activation can predict temporal discounting [28].

The future self-continuity model suggests that sharing similarities between present self and future self, seeing future self more vividly and positively, influences the intertem-poral decision-making process by encouraging people to make decisions today rather than tomorrow for a better future [29]. Consistent with this model, when people interacted with their old age rendered versions in virtual reality, temporal discounting rates dropped for a money allocation task by investing more money for retirement funds [30]. On the other hand, lack of future self-continuity influenced decision making, leading people to make more unethical choices [31]. Meanwhile, vivid perception of the future self is related to decreases in delinquent choices and cheating [32] and understanding the emotional consequences of choices [33]. Future self-continuity also contributes to the enhancement of long-term health and exercise behaviour [34]. Promising results from these studies emphasize the possible usage of future-self continuity model, but applications of this model in the field of addiction disorders can still be expanded by incorporating virtual reality.

Virtual reality can provide realistic representations of people (avatars) and an interaction space that can change the perception of the participant, such as feeling illusory ownership over their virtual hands and limbs [35], transferring ownership to an opposite sex virtual body [36] and when embodied in an avatar of a child's body, overestimating the size of the virtual objects and associating with child-like attitudes [37, 38]. The ownership over the virtual body can cause changes in the behaviour of the participant. For example, being embodied as a virtual representation of Lenin has been shown to increase presence in a scenario related to Russian Revolution [39] while being in a virtual body of Einstein improves cognitive performance [40]. On the other hand, the behavioural and perceptual change is not only limited to virtual experience, but it can still affect real life. In a racial bias experiment, light-skinned participants showed an immediate decrease in their implicit racial bias scores after being embodied in a dark-skinned virtual body [41] and this change was sustained for at least one week [42]. When participants had a conversation about a personal problem and offered themselves self-counselling by swapping between two virtual bodies, one looking like themselves and another resembling Sigmund Freud, their mood improved [43], and their perception of change and help increased [44]. The body-ownership illusion was stronger, when the embodied Freud body moved synchronously with their own movements. The overall effect was stronger when they provided their own solutions to their personal problem while embodied as Freud rather than listening to scripted answers from a pre-programmed Freud.

The research described in this paper proposes that utilising the future-self continuity model in the VR body-swapping paradigm can give insights about the motivation behind smoking as well as possible health consequences and can leverage the individual's own problem-solving skills to help their nicotine dependence. Although there are many digital applications for health [45, 46], here we only concentrate on an immersive approach using virtual reality.

The main goal of this study is to explore the virtual experience of having a conversation with the future self and the influence of this on possible changes in nicotine dependence scores, stage of smoking and perception of risks and benefits related to smoking. We expect to find that after having conversation with the future self who stopped smoking, participants will have higher future self-continuity scores compared to other conditions, as earlier research suggested vivid and positive perception of future self can increase future self-continuity [29]. In addition, it was suggested by the previous study that future self-continuity improves long-term health behaviour [34]. Hence, a body-swapping conversation with the future self can be expected to increase health behaviour, improving in the stages of change scale of smoking and modulating perceived risks and benefits of smoking.

2 Methods

2.1 Experimental Design

A between-groups experimental design has been designed and is currently partially implemented for this study to assign participants into one of 3 different groups: "Future Self Smoking Cessation" (FSSC), "Future Self Still Smoking" (FSSS), "Present Self" (PS) by counterbalancing their nicotine dependence scores. In each condition, participants will talk about their nicotine addiction and will engage in self-counselling by swapping between two avatars. The first avatar, who will define the problem about nicotine dependence to start the conversation, will be the present self. The appearance of the second avatar, who will respond, will be different depending on the assigned condition: the future self who stopped smoking (FSSC), the future self who continues smoking (FSSS) or the present self (PS). The age-rendered avatars in future self (FSSC and FSSS) conditions will look very similar, but the skin of the avatar in the FSSS condition will have a more pale looking skin tone. Also, the avatars will differ in smoking status, as smoker and non-smoker.

2.2 Procedure

This experiment will consist of three sessions. In the first session, participants will be asked to complete questionnaires such as the Fagerström Test for Nicotine Dependence [47], Stages of Change [48], Perceived Risks and Benefits Questionnaire [49] and Future Self Continuity Scale [50]. Next, the experiment will be introduced and an online interview will take place to build problem definition about nicotine dependence. Participants will also send their frontal face photos without glasses to the experimenter for the generation of their avatar Headshot plug-in and SkinGen features of the Character Creator 3.3 software will be used to generate these 3D avatars (see Fig. 1). After the generation of the Present Self avatar, that takes a couple of minutes, skin and hair features of the avatar will be changed for the generation of the Future Self avatars. The FBX (film-box) files of these avatars will be exported to the Unity3D to create asset bundles that will be directly transferred to the Oculus Quest application. During the second session, participants' voices will be recorded for five seconds, and they will be assigned two avatars, one for their present self, and one for their assigned condition. After the avatar assignment, participants will enter into their lookalike avatar that is in a sitting position. The pre-recorded instructions will explain that they should look at the mirror in their left side, allowing them to see their virtual body and increase embodiment, and move their arms while looking at the mirror and down towards their body. The avatar for the assigned condition will be sitting in front of them. The conversation will start by the participant expressing their problem statement about nicotine dependence. Afterwards, the participant will swap the body and listen to the explanation of the problem from the future self or lookalike avatar and give a free form response. After this the bodies will be swapped again, they will be back in their own self-representation lookalike avatar and this time, will listen to the response on the assigned condition. During the future-self conditions, the voice of the participant will be processed in real time to a lower pitch by using the SoundTouch Audio Processing Library to sound more like an aged voice. The conversation will take as many swaps as required, until the participant has decided to conclude. After this session, they will complete body-ownership and presence questionnaires along with Future-Self Continuity Scale. The final session of the experiment will occur one week after the second session. Participants will complete questionnaires including Fagerström Test for Nicotine Dependence, Stages of Change, Perceived Risks and Benefits Questionnaire and Future Self Continuity Scale.

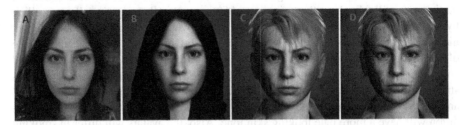

Fig. 1. Avatar generation process. (A) Face photo of the participant. (B) Present self avatar. (C) Future self smoking cessation avatar. (D) Future self still smoking avatar.

3 Expected Results

As a result of conversation with the future self, we expect to see increased future self-continuity scale scores for both future self conditions, while the scores for the present self condition is expected to stay the same. The increased future self-continuity is expected to decrease the temporal discounting, which would lead to a more realistic perception of the risks of smoking and benefits of quitting smoking. This updated perception of the effects of smoking is expected to increase the scores in the Perceived Risks and Benefits Questionnaire for all the participants. As positive experiences increase future self-continuity, a greater effect size is anticipated for the participants of the Future Self Smoking Cessation condition. Depending on the effect size and individual differences, we suspect some participants to make the transition into the next smoking status in the Stages of Change and have decreased scores in Fagerström Test for Nicotine Dependence.

4 Discussion and Conclusion

In conclusion, nicotine dependence continues to be a public health issue that is affecting millions of people every day. Temporal discounting is one of the reasons that makes quitting smoking harder for people with nicotine dependence. Increasing future self-continuity leads to a decrease in temporal discounting. Even though VR-integrated assessment and treatment tools for nicotine dependence have been effectively introduced, the main focus has been on using cue-reactivity methods in virtual environments. The appearance of the embodied avatar and body-ownership illusion result in changes and alterations of behaviours, attitudes and perceptions of the user. In addition, having conversation with one's self by swapping bodies with the virtual avatar of Freud has been found to improve mood. This research aims to approach the problem of VR-integrated assessment and treatment of nicotine dependence, by incorporating the body-swapping paradigm and the future self-continuity model. In this novel approach, conversation with the future self is expected to change the perception of the risks of smoking and benefits of not smoking to more realistic levels. The results will show whether the effect size is strong enough to make changes in the smoking status and nicotine dependence scores.

References

1. WHO Homepage (2020). https://www.who.int/news-room/fact-sheets/detail/tobacco
2. World Health Organization: Novel coronavirus (2019-nCoV): situation report, 13 (2020)
3. Vardavas, C., Nikitara, K.: COVID-19 and smoking: a systematic review of the evidence. Tob. Induc. Dis. **18** (2020). https://doi.org/10.18332/tid/119324
4. Berlin, I., Thomas, D., Le Faou, A.-L., Cornuz, J.: COVID-19 and Smoking. Nicotine Tob. Res. ntaa059 (2020). https://doi.org/10.1093/ntr/ntaa059
5. Freeman, D., et al.: Virtual reality in the assessment, understanding, and treatment of mental health disorders. Psychol. Med. **47**, 2393–2400 (2017). https://doi.org/10.1017/S00332917 1700040X
6. Lee, J.H., et al.: Experimental application of virtual reality for nicotine craving through cue exposure. Cyberpsychol. Behav. **6**, 275–280 (2003). https://doi.org/10.1089/109493103322 011560
7. Lee, J., et al.: Nicotine craving and cue exposure therapy by using virtual environments. Cyberpsychol. Behav. **7**, 705–713 (2004). https://doi.org/10.1089/cpb.2004.7.705
8. Moon, J., Lee, J.-H.: Cue exposure treatment in a virtual environment to reduce nicotine craving: a functional MRI study. Cyberpsychol. Behav. **12**, 43–45 (2009). https://doi.org/10.1089/cpb.2008.0032
9. Heather, N., Bradley, B.P.: Cue exposure as a practical treatment for addictive disorders: why are we waiting? Addict. Behav. **15**, 335–337 (1990). https://doi.org/10.1016/0306-460 3(90)90043-W
10. Heather, N., Greeley, J.: Cue exposure in the treatment of drug dependence: the potential of a new method for preventing relapse. Drug Alcohol Rev. **9**, 155–168 (1990). https://doi.org/10.1080/09595239000185211
11. Bordnick, P.S., Graap, K.M., Copp, H.L., Brooks, J., Ferrer, M.: Virtual reality cue reactivity assessment in cigarette smokers. Cyberpsychol. Behav. **8**, 487–492 (2005). https://doi.org/10.1089/cpb.2005.8.487
12. Pericot-Valverde, I., Germeroth, L.J., Tiffany, S.T.: The use of virtual reality in the production of cue-specific craving for cigarettes: a meta-analysis. Nicotine Tob. Res. **18**, 538–546 (2016). https://doi.org/10.1093/ntr/ntv216
13. Girard, B., Turcotte, V., Bouchard, S., Girard, B.: Crushing virtual cigarettes reduces tobacco addiction and treatment discontinuation. Cyberpsychol. Behav. **12**, 477–483 (2009). https://doi.org/10.1089/cpb.2009.0118

14. Bordnick, P.S., Traylor, A.C., Carter, B.L., Graap, K.M.: A feasibility study of virtual reality-based coping skills training for nicotine dependence. Res. Soc. Work Pract. **22**, 293–300 (2012). https://doi.org/10.1177/1049731511426880

15. Murphy-Hoefer, R., Alder, S., Higbee, C.: Perceptions about cigarette smoking and risks among college students. Nicotine Tob. Res. **6**, 371–374 (2004). https://doi.org/10.1080/146 22200412331320770

16. Arnett, J.J.: Optimistic bias in adolescent and adult smokers and nonsmokers. Addict. Behav. **25**, 625–632 (2000). https://doi.org/10.1016/S0306-4603(99)00072-6

17. Masiero, M., Lucchiari, C., Pravettoni, G.: Personal fable: optimistic bias in cigarette smokers. Int. J. High Risk Behav. Addict. **4** (2015). https://doi.org/10.5812/ijhrba.20939

18. Chapman, G.B.: Temporal discounting and utility for health and money. J. Exp. Psychol. Learn. Mem. Cogn. **22**, 771–791 (1996). https://doi.org/10.1037/0278-7393.22.3.771

19. Chapman, G.B., Elstein, A.S.: Valuing the future: temporal discounting of health and money. Med. Decis. Making **15**, 373–386 (1995). https://doi.org/10.1177/0272989X9501500408

20. Kollins, S.H.: Delay discounting is associated with substance use in college students. Addict. Behav. **28**, 1167–1173 (2003). https://doi.org/10.1016/S0306-4603(02)00220-4

21. Bickel, W.K., Yi, R., Kowal, B.P., Gatchalian, K.M.: Cigarette smokers discount past and future rewards symmetrically and more than controls: is discounting a measure of impulsivity? Drug Alcohol Depend. **96**, 256–262 (2008). https://doi.org/10.1016/j.drugalcdep.2008.03.009

22. Yi, R., Johnson, M.W., Giordano, L.A., Landes, R.D., Badger, G.J., Bickel, W.K.: The effects of reduced cigarette smoking on discounting future rewards: an initial evaluation. Psychol. Rec. **58**(2), 163–174 (2008). https://doi.org/10.1007/BF03395609

23. Stein, J.S., Wilson, A.G., Koffarnus, M.N., Daniel, T.O., Epstein, L.H., Bickel, W.K.: Unstuck in time: episodic future thinking reduces delay discounting and cigarette smoking. Psychopharmacology **233**, 3771–3778 (2016). https://doi.org/10.1007/s00213-016-4410-y

24. Markus, H., Nurius, P.: Possible selves. Am. Psychol. **41**, 954 (1986). http://dx.doi.org/10.1037/0003-066X.41.9.954

25. Levy, B.R., Slade, M.D., Kunkel, S.R., Kasl, S.V.: Longevity increased by positive self-perceptions of aging. J. Pers. Soc. Psychol. **83**, 261–270 (2002). https://doi.org/10.1037/0022-3514.83.2.261

26. Pronin, E., Olivola, C.Y., Kennedy, K.A.: Doing unto future selves as you would do unto others: psychological distance and decision making. Pers. Soc. Psychol. Bull. **34**, 224–236 (2008). https://doi.org/10.1177/0146167207310023

27. Pronin, E., Ross, L.: Temporal differences in trait self-ascription: when the self is seen as an other. J. Pers. Soc. Psychol. **90**, 197–209 (2006). https://doi.org/10.1037/0022-3514.90.2.197

28. Ersner-Hershfield, H., Wimmer, G.E., Knutson, B.: Saving for the future self: neural measures of future self-continuity predict temporal discounting. Soc. Cogn. Affect. Neurosci. **4**, 85–92 (2009). https://doi.org/10.1093/scan/nsn042

29. Hershfield, H.E.: Future self-continuity: how conceptions of the future self transform intertemporal choice: Hershfield. Ann. N. Y. Acad. Sci. **1235**, 30–43 (2011). https://doi.org/10.1111/j.1749-6632.2011.06201.x

30. Hershfield, H.E., et al.: Increasing saving behavior through age-progressed renderings of the future self. J. Mark. Res. **48**, S23–S37 (2011). https://doi.org/10.1509/jmkr.48.SPL.S23

31. Hershfield, H.E., Cohen, T.R., Thompson, L.: Short horizons and tempting situations: lack of continuity to our future selves leads to unethical decision making and behavior. Organ. Behav. Hum. Decis. Process. **117**, 298–310 (2012). https://doi.org/10.1016/j.obhdp.2011.11.002

32. van Gelder, J.-L., Hershfield, H.E., Nordgren, L.F.: Vividness of the future self predicts delinquency. Psychol. Sci. **24**, 974–980 (2013). https://doi.org/10.1177/0956797612465197

33. Loewenstein, G.: Out of control: visceral influences on behavior. Organ. Behav. Hum. Decis. Process. **65**(3), 272–292 (1996). https://doi.org/10.1006/obhd.1996.0028

34. Rutchick, A.M., Slepian, M.L., Reyes, M.O., Pleskus, L.N., Hershfield, H.E.: Future self-continuity is associated with improved health and increases exercise behavior. J. Exp. Psychol. Appl. **24**, 72–80 (2018). https://doi.org/10.1037/xap0000153

35. Slater, M.: Inducing illusory ownership of a virtual body. Front. Neurosci. **3**, 214–220 (2009). https://doi.org/10.3389/neuro.01.029.2009

36. Slater, M., Spanlang, B., Sanchez-Vives, M.V., Blanke, O.: First person experience of body transfer in virtual reality. PLoS ONE **5**, e10564 (2010). https://doi.org/10.1371/journal.pone.0010564

37. Banakou, D., Groten, R., Slater, M.: Illusory ownership of a virtual child body causes overestimation of object sizes and implicit attitude changes. Proc. Natl. Acad. Sci. **110**, 12846–12851 (2013). https://doi.org/10.1073/pnas.1306779110

38. Tajadura-Jiménez, A., Banakou, D., Bianchi-Berthouze, N., Slater, M.: Embodiment in a child-like talking virtual body influences object size perception, self-identification, and subsequent real speaking. Sci. Rep. **7**, 9637 (2017). https://doi.org/10.1038/s41598-017-09497-3

39. Slater, M., et al.: Virtually being Lenin enhances presence and engagement in a scene from the russian revolution. Front. Robot. AI **5**, 91 (2018). https://doi.org/10.3389/frobt.2018.00091

40. Banakou, D., Kishore, S., Slater, M.: Virtually being Einstein results in an improvement in cognitive task performance and a decrease in age bias. Front. Psychol. **9**, 917 (2018). https://doi.org/10.3389/fpsyg.2018.00917

41. Peck, T.C., Seinfeld, S., Aglioti, S.M., Slater, M.: Putting yourself in the skin of a black avatar reduces implicit racial bias. Conscious. Cogn. **22**, 779–787 (2013). https://doi.org/10.1016/j.concog.2013.04.016

42. Banakou, D., Hanumanthu, P.D., Slater, M.: Virtual embodiment of white people in a black virtual body leads to a sustained reduction in their implicit racial bias. Front. Hum. Neurosci. **10**, 601 (2016). https://doi.org/10.3389/fnhum.2016.00601

43. Osimo, S.A., Pizarro, R., Spanlang, B., Slater, M.: Conversations between self and self as Sigmund Freud—a virtual body ownership paradigm for self counselling. Sci. Rep. **5**, 13899 (2015). https://doi.org/10.1038/srep13899

44. Slater, M., et al.: An experimental study of a virtual reality counselling paradigm using embodied self-dialogue. Sci. Rep. **9**, 10903 (2019). https://doi.org/10.1038/s41598-019-46877-3

45. Martínez-Pérez, B., de la Torre-Díez, I., López-Coronado, M.: Mobile health applications for the most prevalent conditions by the world health organization: review and analysis. J. Med. Internet Res. **15**, e120 (2013). https://doi.org/10.2196/jmir.2600

46. Abdullah, A.S., Gaehde, S., Bickmore, T.: A tablet based embodied conversational agent to promote smoking cessation among veterans: a feasibility study. J. Epidemiol. Glob. Health **8**, 225 (2018). https://doi.org/10.2991/j.jegh.2018.08.104

47. Heatherton, T.F., Kozlowski, L.T., Frecker, R.C., Fagerstrom, K.-O.: The fagerstrom test for nicotine dependence: a revision of the fagerstrom tolerance questionnaire. Br. J. Addict. **86**, 1119–1127 (1991). https://doi.org/10.1111/j.1360-0443.1991.tb01879.x

48. Prochaska, J.O., DiClemente, C.C., Norcross, J.C.: In search of how people change: Applications to addictive behaviors. Addict. Nurs. Netw. **5**, 2–16 (1993). https://doi.org/10.3109/10884609309149692

49. McKee, S.A., O'Malley, S.S., Salovey, P., Krishnan-Sarin, S., Mazure, C.M.: Perceived risks and benefits of smoking cessation: gender-specific predictors of motivation and treatment outcome. Addict. Behav. **30**, 423–435 (2005). https://doi.org/10.1016/j.addbeh.2004.05.027

50. Ersner-Hershfield, H., Garton, M.T., Ballard, K., Samanez-Larkin, G.R.: Don't stop thinking about tomorrow: individual differences in future self-continuity account for saving. Judgment Decis. Making **4**(4), 280 (2009)

VR as a Persuasive Technology "in the Wild". The Effect of Immersive VR on Intent to Change Towards Water Conservation

Konstantinos Chionidis[✉] and Wendy Powell

Tilburg University, Warandelaan 2, 5037 AB Tilburg, The Netherlands
konstantino.chionidis@gmail.com,
W.A.Powell@tilburguniversity.edu

Abstract. The combination of VR with the correct psychological mechanism could become a powerful persuasion system to stimulate intent to change towards important environmental issues such as water conservation. However, very limited research has been reported on VR usage in this area. Therefore, we conducted a between-groups study to investigate whether the level of presence felt in a VR environment together with a trigger mechanism such as guilt could spark intent to change towards water conservation. Participants were exposed to a persuasive message about water conservation in one of three conditions: audio only, simple VR and visually rich VR. Forty participants completed the study "in the wild". The results showed that while intent to change increased in all three groups, both VR groups indicated lower levels of change than the audio only group. Additionally, a positive correlation, albeit small, was found between presence and cued recall along with presence and intent to change. These results furthermore showed that presence could play a role in behavior modification and intent to change.

Keywords: Virtual Reality · Water conservation · Persuasive system · Presence · Trigger mechanism · Memory · Cued recall · In the wild · Guilt

1 Introduction

Climate change is one of the numerous problems which society is facing, and water conservation is an important facet of the solution to this long term problem. Raising awareness of the problem is perhaps one of the first steps in almost any type of conservation effort and could be considered a prerequisite for any type of behavior change [3, 26]. Notwithstanding, there are various characteristics of environmental problems which hinder the raising of awareness such as the abstract nature of the issue or the fact that these issues have a gradual effect over time making them difficult to observe [9]. Hence, most people do not feel a responsibility to change despite knowing the existence of the problem [19].

This leads to the question of whether technologies such as Virtual Reality (VR) could play a role in the water conservation effort. VR is a highly interactive and realistic technology in and of itself, and when combined with other psychological tools it could become a powerful persuasive system to provoke various types of changes or outcomes

© Springer Nature Switzerland AG 2020
P. Bourdot et al. (Eds.): EuroVR 2020, LNCS 12499, pp. 224–233, 2020.
https://doi.org/10.1007/978-3-030-62655-6_15

in the users. Furthermore, the use and uptake of VR has grown substantially during the past few years and has been applied to many fields and areas of study due to the many advantages it offers. These advantages include greater control of environmental factors such as frequency, intensity, and quality [5] and its transparent replicability [14].

Changes in the attitude or behavior from the use of a persuasive system such as VR, could lead to different outcomes such as reinforcement, change or further shaping and defining of attitudes or actions [10]. These outcomes are therefore the result of focusing on the drivers or factors of human behavior to induce change. Fogg [6] defined a model of persuasive technology which identified three factors which could lead to behavior change: motivation, ability, and triggers. Additionally, as water conservation is an abstract concept, presence could play a role in behavior change. In the current experiment, the participants listened to an audio message which was reinforced by a VR environment in an effort to stimulate the feeling of presence and arouse intent to change.

2 Related Work

2.1 Use of Immersive Witness and Games Within VR

Of the few examples of VR usage within social change issues, most have focused on raising awareness of the problem. This is primarily done through the use of the technique of immersive witness. This technique takes a moral issue or concern for a distant issue and brings it directly to the participant so that it can be experienced through VR. This allows the participant to be temporarily connected both spatially and mentally through a feeling of presence to a place and more importantly to be immersed in an issue [16]. This temporary immersion creates an experience for the participant which could change their response and feelings. It has been argued that the feeling of presence could be considered as an effective tool through which a moral reaction can be obtained from a participant [8].

In the global marine conservation effort, a slightly different approach has been taken where instead of movies or lifelike environments for raising funds, games have been developed in VR [2]. While the use of different types of games to overcome psychological problems such as PTSD [21] or even some types of phobias is not new, what is interesting is the usage of VR to create a more intense lifelike experience for the participants. These games allow the participants to explore the undersea environment in a way they might not have been able to do so before and helps the participant to feel a sense of connection with the environment [2]. As the connection with the environment is built, the games act in an educational manner by providing information to the user and then indirectly creating greater awareness for the environmental issues. Built within the games are the main learning principles to help educate, create awareness, and more importantly stimulate change and action [2].

There have been very few studies completed on the use of VR in water conservation. One such study, by Hsu et al. [9], showed that an exaggerated feedback (EF) mechanism could be used to change behavior through negative reinforcement. The study used a VR game which provided the participants with negative feedback on their use of water. The strength of the negative feedback was then systematically increased to stimulate change in the behavior towards water conservation. The positive results did provide a direct link between the participants intention to change and the use of VR through negative reinforcement [9]. While this study provided interesting results concerning the negative feedback mechanism, it does not compare VR results with Non-VR results as does the current study, which leads to speculation on whether it was the message which was persuasive instead of the use of VR.

2.2   Presence Within a VR Environment

With the increasing use of technologies such as VR being directed towards influencing user's behavior, it is important that a holistic approach is taken when developing a persuasive technology. Relevant social psychological theories should be considered alongside a range of factors specific to VR technologies, such as presence. It could be thought that both aspects are mutually inclusive and that for a persuasive system to be successful both presence and social psychological theories should be finely tuned.

Presence could arguably be one of the most important of the three main aspects of a Virtual Environment (VE), the other two being the computational model or autonomy and the software or interaction [12]. Slater [23, 24] defined presence as the illusion one feels of being there in the environment. This illusion of being in the environment, if strong enough, can lead a person to automatically react to the environment when a perceived threat or action to them or near them is felt. This instinctive reaction happens although the person within the environment cognitively knows that both what is happening within the environment and that the environment itself is not real [23, 24]. Hence, presence could be considered to be the mediator which permits other psychological aspects such as emotions or feeling to be activated but that the illusion happens when the person in the VE no longer perceives the very existence of the medium [4]. Furthermore, it implies that presence could be considered to have a causal role in the experience with the VE as the feeling of presence is increased with arousal which in turn increases the emotional state of the participant [4]. Thus presence may play an important role in the use of VR as a persuasive technology.

2.3   A Persuasive Model to Influence Behavior

While, presence may play an important role in the persuasive model, Fogg, describes the three principle factors that influence behavior in his 2009 model for persuasive design, named the Fogg Behavior Model (FBM). The importance of this model has been highlighted by Mustaquim and Nystrom, who stated in their 2014 paper on design principles for persuasive systems that the FBM and its three principles should be acknowledged as the basis for all persuasive design principles. Although the well-known phenomena of cognitive dissonance states that cognitive discomfort will create a change in attitude, Mustaquim postulates that cognitive consistency is important because to motivate change, the urge for consistency should be strong enough [15].

Within the previously mentioned study by Hsu et al. [9], negative reinforcement was used and this could fall under the category of a trigger within the FBM. The negative feedback acts as a trigger the moment it is given to the participant. This trigger leverages the motivational element of mental pain which then in turn creates fear of repeated and stronger negative feedback, hence triggering change in behavior. Such negative triggers, including guilt, might be able to be leveraged within persuasive technology in order to trigger the desired attitude or behavioral change.

It has been shown that the feeling of guilt along with the typical reactions towards it make it a compelling tool for persuasive influence [17]. Therefore we designed a study to investigate the role of presence in VR when combined with a negative trigger (guilt) in order to provoke a change in attitude to water conservation. Specifically, the trigger mechanism used was a persuasive message given to the participants during the experiment in a similar way that commercial marketing companies use guilt to promote healthy food or to obtain donations to charities. O'Keefe [18] describes that the way it could be used, perhaps based on the cognitive dissonance viewpoint, is that first an issue where there exists a deviation between the users ideas or standards and their actions should be highlighted. Once that has been done the user will react in order to reduce this inconsistency or feeling of cognitive discomfort [18].

While it could be argued that the factor used in the present study could be either a motivation which later leads to a future trigger when the participant enters a bathroom environment or a trigger initiated by the message given and based on participants previous experiences of having being in a shower or bathroom. It is believed that trigger could be a better fit because all of the study participants are familiar with use of a shower or a bathroom environment and that the verbal message given to the participants in the study, together with the sound of running water in the environment, would leverage the previously existing element of motivation, causing a feeling of guilt, and therefore act as a spark.

2.4   Combining Presence and Memory Within a VR Environment

Although the trigger mechanism used is an important aspect of the experiment, the measurement of the participants self-reported sense of presence is a significant indicator when measuring the participants intention to change. When examining presence, it has been shown that it does play a role and could influence the outcomes or differences of a persuasive VR experience [27]. When combining presence with memory, an even stronger indicator is given for the success of a persuasive system. A review of the literature shows that there are discrepancies in the findings related to how presence is interpreted or correlated with memory. In some literature, it is theorized that the higher the level of presence the more details and data the participant will remember about the virtual environment such as objects, layout or messages [13]. From a different perspective, it has been suggested that if the user's cognitive capacity is fully focused and engaged in a VR environment, the user will have a lower level of recall pertaining to the content or details of their environment [7].

When measuring the effect of cued recall, a study completed by Bailey [1] tested whether participants could remember environmental information given to them while in a VR experience and then further pass this information on to a secondary person. However, contrary to the researcher's hypothesis, the results showed a negative correlation between the level of memory and the level of presence [1]. This implies that the high level of presence felt acts as an inhibitor to the ability to recall information that was given during the VR experience. This could be because high impact events could possibly overload memory capacity of the brain [11]. A possible secondary reason could be that high impact events could stimulate physiological arousal which in turn could influence cognitive processes [20]. However, it is probable that as usage of VR increases and becomes more commonplace, it will no longer be a novelty and possibly lessen the inhibition to recall information. This study extends Baily's original work by comparing VR to a non-VR condition allowing for a greater understanding of the true effect of VR.

3   Methods

We conducted a between-subjects study to investigate whether the level of presence felt in a VR environment together with a trigger mechanism such as guilt could spark intent to change towards water conservation. 40 participants, aged between 19–29, were exposed to a persuasive message about water conservation in one of three conditions: audio only (n = 13), simple VR (n = 14), and visually rich VR (n = 13). The only difference between the three conditions was the medium through which the participants would engage during the experiment. The participants were randomly assigned to one of the three different groups and all three groups listened to the same audio message which contained information about water conservation while the sound of running water could be heard in the background. At the end of the message there was a call to action where the participants were given information on how they could individually contribute to the conservation effort. This call to action, together with the rest of the message, was intended to create a sense of guilt and act as a trigger mechanism.

As the study was completed "in the wild" during a worldwide COVID-19 pandemic the simple VR and the visually rich VR groups were sent a smartphone Head Mounted Display (HMD) by post (Fig. 1).

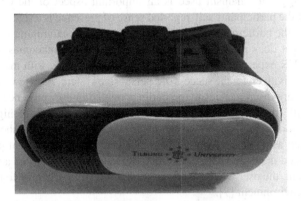

Fig. 1. Smartphone VR headset used to display the VR environments

The Android Package File (APK) which could be used on an Android phone, together with the online questionnaires were sent by email in parallel. The simple VR environment consisted of a shower scene which could be seen from a first person Point of View (POV) while the richer environment had the same shower but also had a full bathroom for a richer environment (Fig. 2).

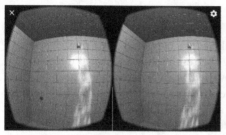
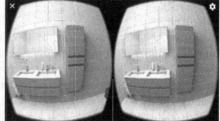

Simple VR environment   Richer VR environment

Fig. 2. The VR environments used in the two different VR condition

The participants filled in a total of four questionnaires post the consent and biographical form, of which two were non-standard (water survey pre and post experiment and memory test) and the fourth was the 1994 Witmer & Singer v3 presence questionnaire. It is important to note that to determine whether the message and the medium were able to elicit a modification in the participants intent to change, a series of questions were asked to the participants before they completed the experiment. These indicated the participants feelings towards water conservation along with asking them to quantify their actual usage of water in two of their most commonly daily completed activities: taking a shower and brushing ones teeth. Post the completion of the experiment, the participants were then asked the same questions except that the questions were slightly modified to ask the participants intended future length of time to complete the previously mentioned activities. To calculate this measure, the difference between each question was measured, i.e. for each positive change in a response, one point was given and then the total was summed up at the end. An overview of the experimental procedure for each condition can be seen in Table 1.

Table 1. Outline of the study procedure for the three experimental conditions

Experiment procedure			
Conditions	Audio only	Limited VR environment	Visually rich VR environment
Forms to be filled in before experiment	Consent/biographical form Water survey questionnaire	Consent/biographical form Water survey questionnaire	Consent/biographical form Water survey questionnaire
During experiment	Sit down in a chair with eyes closed	Wear HMD and asked to be supervised as they stand during experience	
Forms to be filled in after experiment	Memory test Water survey questionnaire	Memory test Presence survey Water survey questionnaire	Memory test Presence survey Water survey questionnaire

4 Results

A one-way ANOVA was conducted to evaluate the hypothesis that presence would stimulate a higher level of intent to change. The results showed a small effect size of $\eta 2 = 0.067$, $F (2, 37) = 1.295$, $p > 0.05$. However, when comparing the mean intent to change scores for the three conditions, differences between the groups can be identified (Table 2). The non-VR group had the highest mean score followed by the simple VR and finally the richer VR had the lowest score. The difference in the mean non-VR score and the fuller VR score was that of 1.94 points which is noteworthy considering the fuller VR had a mean score of 3.23 points.

Table 2. Intent to change scores for the three conditions

Group type	Mean score	Standard deviation	Skew	Kurtosis	Standard error
Non-VR	5.15	3.8	0.29	−1.38	1.06
Simple VR	3.64	2.98	−0.15	−1.05	0.8
Fuller VR	3.23	3.54	0.47	0.67	0.98

A Pearson's correlation coefficient was calculated between the participants self-reported presence scores together with their intent to change scores (Fig. 3). Presence scores were correlated with intent to change scores, $r(27) = 0.12$, $p > 0.05$. The scores were positively correlated, albeit weak and not significant.

Correlation between Intent to change and Presence

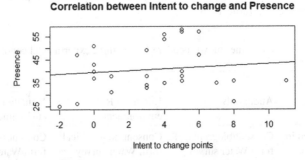

Fig. 3. Correlation between intent to change and presence scores

A second Pearson's correlation coefficient was calculated between the participants self-reported presence scores together with their memory scores (Fig. 4). These scores were correlated with the total memory scores, $r(27) = 0.26$, $p > .05$. This also indicates a small to medium effect size.

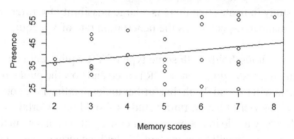

Fig. 4. Correlation between total memory scores and presence scores

5 Discussion

Limited investigation has been completed on the ability of presence in VR to simulate intent to change towards water conservation. Most of the VR work in conservation or other social change issues have been focused on raising awareness. Hence, this study could be seen as a step forward as it furthers this topic by not only measuring the relationship between presence and intent to change but also presence and cued recall, all of which was done in the wild.

While the study results are contrary with what was expected, there could be various underlying reasons which could have affected the outcome such as the experiment being conducted in the wild [25] during a worldwide pandemic, the media richness of the environment [22] or individual differences of the participants [10]. From a more theoretical perspective, it could have been due to the non-responsiveness of the participants to the behavior model used in the experiment [6], to the trigger mechanism of guilt [18], to the lower level of presence felt [4] or even a combination of all of these.

However, it is interesting to note a small positive correlation between both presence and memory and presence and intent to change. The fact that the effect size was small could be the reason that the non-VR group had a higher intent to change score than either of the two VR groups. Smaller effect sizes together with population variability generally require bigger sample sizes and using a larger sample size could add further insight in future research. It could be further hypothesized that had the level of presence been higher and the correlation been stronger, the two VR groups may have had higher intent to change scores than the non-VR group.

6 Conclusion

The results did not demonstrate that presence had a direct influence on the participants behavior in this experiment, however it did show that it could play a role in behavior modification and specifically intent to change. The recent Covid-19 pandemic has highlighted urgent need for a change in approach to threats to the environment, and these initial results suggest that high-presence VR could play an important role as a driver of behavior change.

This is important as very few studies have been completed in the wild during a worldwide pandemic when the majority of the people in many countries were experiencing some type of lockdown. While the impact of the COVID-19 pandemic will be felt in many fields, this study indicates that there is a large possibility for future research to be completed in this manner, especially as the penetration rate of VR equipment continues to grow.

As the number of households with some type of VR equipment continues to grow, the need for a better understanding of how VR is used and how the public reacts and feels about VR in the wild will expand. With this further understanding may come many future applications for VR as well. Finally, future studies should be undertaken to understand how VR can further play a role in not only water conservation but also in the many other climate change issues which will have an even greater long term impact than COVID-19.

References

1. Bailey, J., Bailenson, J.N., Won, A.S., Flora, J., Armel, K.C.: Presence and memory: immersive virtual reality effects on cued recall. In: Proceedings of the International Society for Presence Research Annual Conference, pp. 24–26, October 2012
2. Colleton, N., Lakshman, V., Flood, K., Birnbaum, M., Mc Millan, K., Lin, A.: Concepts and practice in the emerging use of games for marine education and conservation. Aquatic Conserv: Mar. Freshwater Ecosystem 26(Suppl. 2), 213–224 (2016)
3. De Groot, J., Steg, L.: Morality and prosocial behavior: the role of awareness, responsibility, and norms in the norm activation model. J. Soc. Psychol. 149(4), 425–449 (2009). https://doi.org/10.3200/SOCP.149.4.425-449
4. Diemer, J., Alpers, G.W., Peperkorn, H.M., Shiban, Y., Mühlberger, A.: The impact of perception and presence on emotional reactions: a review of research in virtual reality. Front. Psychol. 6, 26 (2015)
5. Emmelkamp, P.M.: Technological innovations in clinical assessment and psychotherapy. Psychother. Psychosom. 74(6), 336–343 (2005)
6. Fogg, B.J.: A behaviour model for persuasive design. In: Persuasive, 26–29 April 2009
7. Fox, J., Bailenson, J., Binney, J.: Virtual experiences, physical behaviors: the effect of presence on imitation of an eating avatar. Presence: Teleoperators Virtual Environ. 18(4), 294–303 (2009)
8. Gregory, S.: Immersive Witnessing: From empathy and outrage to action. Witness (2016). https://blog.witness.org/2016/08/immersive-witnessing-from-empathy-and-outrage-to-action/. Accessed 31 Jan 2017
9. Hsu, W., Tseng, C., Kang, S.: Using exaggerated feedback in a virtual reality environment to enhance behaviour intention of water-conservation. Educ. Technol. Soc. 21(4), 187–203 (2018)
10. Kober, S., Neuper, C.: Personality and presence in virtual reality: does their relationship depend on the used presence measure? Int. J. Hum.-Comput. Interact. 29, 13–25 (2013)
11. Lang, A., Newhagen, J., Reves, B.: Negative video as structure: emotion, attention, capacity, and memory. J. Broadcast. Electron. Media 40, 460–477 (1996)
12. Lin, J.W., Duh, H.B.L., Parker, D.E., Abi-Rached, H., Furness, T.A.: Effects of field of view on presence, enjoyment, memory, and simulator sickness in a virtual environment. In: Proceedings IEEE Virtual Reality 2002, pp. 164–171. IEEE, March 2002
13. Mania, K., Chalmers, A.: The effects of levels of immersion on memory and presence in virtual environments: a reality centered approach. CyberPsychol. Behav. 4(2), 247–264 (2001)
14. Morina, N., Ijntema, H., Meyerbröker, K., Emmelkamp, P.M.: Can virtual reality exposure therapy gains be generalized to real-life? A meta-analysis of studies applying behavioral assessments. Behav. Res. Therapy 74, 18–24 (2015)

15. Mustaquim, M., Nyström, T.: Designing persuasive systems for sustainability-a cognitive dissonance model (2014)
16. Nash, K.: Virtual reality witness: exploring the ethics of mediated presence. Stud. Doc. Film **12**(2), 97–100 (2018). ISSN 1750-3280
17. Oinas-Kukkonen, H., Harjumaa, M.: A systematic framework for designing and evaluating persuasive systems. In: Oinas-Kukkonen, H., Hasle, P., Harjumaa, M., Segerståhl, K., Øhrstrøm, P. (eds.) PERSUASIVE 2008. LNCS, vol. 5033, pp. 164–176. Springer, Heidelberg (2008). https://doi.org/10.1007/978-3-540-68504-3_15
18. O'Keefe, D.J.: Guilt as a mechanism of persuasion. In: The Persuasion Handbook, Developments in Theory and Practice, pp. 329–344 (2002)
19. Parker, J., Sams, D.: Eco-feedback technology's influence on water conservation attitudes and intentions of university students in the USA: an experimental design. In: Leal Filho, W., Sümer, V. (eds.) Sustainable Water Use and Management. GET, pp. 169–184. Springer, Cham (2015). https://doi.org/10.1007/978-3-319-12394-3_9
20. Reeves, B., Nass, C.I.: The Media Equation: How People Treat Computers, Television, and New Media Like Real People and Places. Cambridge University Press, Cambridge (1996)
21. Rizzo, A., et al.: Virtual reality as a tool for delivering PTSD exposure therapy and stress resilience training. Mil. Behav. Health **1**(1), 52–58 (2013)
22. Rockmann, K.W., Northcraft, G.B.: To be or not to be trusted: the influence of media richness on defection and deception. Organ. Behav. Hum. Decis. Process. **107**(2), 106–122 (2008)
23. Slater, M.: Immersion and the illusion of presence in virtual reality. Br. J. Psychol. **109**(3), 431–433 (2018)
24. Slater, M., Usoh, M., Steed, A.: Depth of presence in virtual environments. Presence: Teleoper. Virtual Environ. **3**(2), 130–144 (1994)
25. Steed, A., Friston, S., Lopez, M., Drummond, J.: An 'in the wild' experiment on presence and embodiment using consumer virtual reality equipment. IEEE Trans. Vis. Comput. Graph. **22**(4), 1406–1414 (2016)
26. Van der Werff, E., Steg, L.: One model to predict them all: predicting energy behaviours with the norm activation model. Energy Res. Soc. Sci. **6**, 8–14 (2015)
27. Villani, D., Riva, F., Riva, G.: New technologies for relaxation: the role of presence. Int. J. Stress Manag. **14**(3), 260 (2007)

Virtual Reality Experiential Training for Individuals with Autism: The Airport Scenario

Agata Marta Soccini[(✉)], Simone Antonio Giuseppe Cuccurullo, and Federica Cena

Computer Science Department, University of Torino, Turin, Italy
{agatamarta.soccini,simoneantoniogiuseppe.cuccurullo,
federica.cena}@unito.it

Abstract. One of the common traits of individuals with Autism Spectrum Disorder (ASD) is the inclination to perceive unknown situations and environments as a source of stress and anxiety. It is common for them to tend to avoid novel experiences -including traveling to new places- and therefore an environments like an airport can be overwhelming. Virtual Reality can be a functional tool to provide ASD users with a training system that allows them to experience the airport process, even several times, before facing the real life experience. We hereby present the scenario in which our investigation takes place, the system we developed, and a draft of the evaluation of the training technique.

Keywords: Virtual Reality · Neurodiversity · Autism · Experiential training · Airport simulation · Mixed reality

1 Introduction

Autism Spectrum Disorder (ASD) is a complex neurodevelopmental disorder characterized by deficits in social communication and interaction, accompanied by restrictive and repetitive behaviors or interests. Since ASD affects individuals in different ways, it is considered a spectrum condition. Some autistic people, for example, may have learning disabilities and cognitive issues, while others have full intellectual abilities [5]. Moreover, people with ASD are in some cases overwhelmed by environmental features that are, instead, easily managed by neurotypical individuals [11,12].

A majority of people with ASD may perceive as stressful all kinds of unknown situations and thus tend to avoid novel experiences [14], often preferring deterministic situations and rigid and repetitious routines [14]. As consequence, they are less likely to explore new places, and more likely to revisit well-known locations [16]. Indeed, this heavily affects the travelling experience. Most of these issues can be addressed by means of a meticulous planning of the tour, in order to prepare the user to tackle all the steps related to the travel experience [4].

© Springer Nature Switzerland AG 2020
P. Bourdot et al. (Eds.): EuroVR 2020, LNCS 12499, pp. 234–239, 2020.
https://doi.org/10.1007/978-3-030-62655-6_16

Several studies show that Virtual Reality (VR) is a useful tool for improving social skills, cognition, and functioning in autistic individuals, through a specific experiential training [2,3,6,17].

Following these results, we developed a VR application to support people with ASD minimize the level of stress and anxiety while travelling, and therefore rise autonomy and comfort. For this purpose, we give the chance to experience the situation before it happens, underline the difficulties and the solutions. In particular, we focused on the travel experience in an airport, since there may be an excess of sensory stimuli that make the circumstance daunting. This is an ongoing work, and the current paper describes the main motivation, the goals of the project and the implementation.

2   Related Work

Users with ASD show a positive attitude towards new technologies mainly because of the predictability of the interaction [10], including VR, as shown in the following studies. Kandalaft [6] investigated the feasibility of a training intervention in VR on high-functioning users with ASD focused on enhancing social skills, cognition, and occupational functioning. Significant increases in real life were found post-training. Similarly, providing several selected scenarios in VR helps autistic children adapt to new environments and contain anxiety [13]. Some works exploit Virtual Reality for training specific skills needed to travel on buses using serious games paradigms in VR [1,15]. Regarding flights, Miller suggests the efficacy of a training in VR to teach basic air travel skills to young children diagnosed with autism [8].

In general, it is uncommon for airports to offer pre-planned visits of the structure, even if several airports offer specific info material for ASD travelers. Among others, the airport of Dublin visually describes the different parts of the building and provides tips on how to face all the different situations, together with some general rules to follow during a trip[1]. Also in Italy, Caselle Airport, in Torino[2] as well as Milan Malpensa and Linate Airports[3] offer a similar support, offering a textual and visual description of all the steps to follow in order to take a plane.

To the authors' knowledge, the closest approach to VR for training ASD flight travelers in airports is proposed by the Airport of Boise, in Idaho, USA[4]: focusing on children, they provide a solution where users can watch a 360° video in order to explore the structure they will go through, from the check-in to the boarding phase.

---

[1] https://www.dublinairport.com/at-the-airport/help-and-support/travelling-with-autism.

[2] https://www.aeroportoditorino.it/autismo.

[3] https://www.milanomalpensa-airport.com/en/passenger-guide/special-assistances/autism-project.

[4] https://www.cityofboise.org/programs/stories/virtual-reality-at-the-boise-airport.

In this scenario, a VR solution seems perfectly suitable: users can move freely into scenes, interact with objects and perform actions as if they were in a real life situation. Based on this consideration, we propose a VR system to learn the important steps to be done in an airport, leading their own experience in the virtual environment.

3 Description of the Project

The project is a joint collaboration between the Computer Science Department at University of Torino and the Adult Autistic Center of the Local Health Agency of the City of Torino. In the past few years, the Department developed and validated several technological solutions dedicated to the autonomy of ASD users especially in transportation, and recently investigated the use of VR. As mentioned, travelling can be challenging for people with ASD, especially in contexts like airports or stations, where the excess of multi-sensory stimuli might be perceived as overwhelming.

We developed a virtual scenario in which users reach the airport, go through a specific process, like all travellers have to, and reach the aircraft. We defined the steps following the indications from the flyer of the Airport of Torino Caselle, in Italy[5]. In particular the steps are: entrance, check-in, security checks, duty free shops, gates and waiting rooms, plane boarding. A 360° view of the check-in desks is represented in Fig. 1, while in Fig. 2 we can see a view of the security check area. The simulations is a generic representation, valid for a number of airports, as we describe general steps that users have to follow to board.

The system was designed in Maya2020[6] and developed in Unity2019.4.3f1[7] to run on an Oculus Quest[8]. We found that head mounted display the most suitable option among the commercial solutions, because of the six degrees of freedom, the lack of wires, and the headphones-free spatial audio.

We plan to test the prototype with some patients of the Adult Autistic Center in order to assess the usability and acceptability of the solution, as well as the efficacy of the intervention in increasing people autonomy and lowering stress. The experimentation will involve 10–15 participants, of all genders, all adults, with ASD. The first step will consist in a usability test: the participants will be wearing the head mounted display and familiarize with the controllers. We will use as a baseline the data of a similar population of neuro-typical users in the same conditions. The way we quantify the acceptance values will be through a User Experience questionnaire [9] and collecting responses on a Lickert scale. The analysis of the single ASD data set will confirm the expected acceptability of the experience, while a compared data analysis will give us an insight on the difference of acceptance rate of neuro typical and atypical users.

---

[5] https://www.aeroportoditorino.it/en.
[6] https://www.autodesk.com/products/maya/overview.
[7] https://unity.com/.
[8] https://www.oculus.com/quest.

Fig. 1. 360° view of the check-in area of the airport

Fig. 2. View of the security check area of the airport

As a next step, to quantify the efficacy of the training in VR, we will run some sessions in a time slot of two weeks. Half of the users will do the training and half won't, so the outcome of the final performance will underline the significance of the training. As metrics, we will be focusing on a check of the successfully performed tasks, together with a subjective report on the sense of comfort. We will start from the Kirkpatrick Evaluation Model (based on Reaction, Learning,

Behavior, Results) where the calculation of the single factors will be re-adapted to our scenario, according to specific topics to which ASD are more sensitive [7,18].

4   Discussion and Conclusions

In the current paper, we underlined why travelling might be a source of anxiety or confusion for people with autism, and identified the airport as a potentially disturbing scenario. To prevent a negative experience in real life, we propose a Virtual Reality training system that ASD users can benefit of, before facing the actual task.

As an outcome, the general appreciation of the use of technologies by ASD users let us believe they will enjoy this virtual experience. We also expect that, after the training, they will be prepared to manage a trip into an airport with all the necessary skills. Still, the experimentation has not been done yet.

Some issues might appear: users in general, and ASD users in particular, may not be keen on wearing a head mounted display for long periods, for example more than 10 min per session. We therefore need to implement tasks that can be resolved in a short time. A delicate topic related with this technology solution are intrinsic in the concept of simulation. The transfer of skills from virtual to real must be shown to be successful, as simulators might be unhelpful or even counter-productive in the training for the real task.

As a development of the training process, in the different training sessions, the objects in the environment might be recombined or changed of location, in case the users feel confident in facing more complex adventures, in terms of novelty. Also, we start proposing a scene with no characters, but adding some avatars might be part of the steps of the training, as they are often source of stress and unexpected noise. While the current project involves VR, we are planning to develop different paradigms of mixed or augmented reality (XR) applications with similar training goals.

References

1. Bernardes, M., Barros, F., Simoes, M., Castelo-Branco, M.: A serious game with virtual reality for travel training with autism spectrum disorder. In: 2015 International Conference on Virtual Rehabilitation (ICVR), pp. 127–128. IEEE (2015). https://doi.org/10.1109/ICVR.2015.7358609
2. Didehbani, N., Allen, T., Kandalaft, M., Krawczyk, D., Chapman, S.: Virtual reality social cognition training for children with high functioning autism. Comput. Hum. Behav. **62**, 703–711 (2016)
3. Gregory, K., Kate, K., Jonathan, W., Frederick, L., Edward, F.: An exploratory analysis of increasing self-efficacy of adults with autism spectrum disorder through the use of multimedia training stimuli. Cyberpsychol. Behav. Soc. Netw. **23**, 34–40 (2020)
4. Hamed, H.M.: Tourism and autism: an initiative study for how travel companies can plan tourism trips for autistic people. Am. J. Tourism Manag. **2**(1), 1–14 (2013). https://doi.org/10.5923/j.tourism.20130201.01

5. Hobson, R.P.: Autism and the Development of Mind. Routledge, Abingdon (1995)
6. Kandalaft, M.R., Didehbani, N., Krawczyk, D.C., Allen, T.T., Chapman, S.B.: Virtual reality social cognition training for young adults with high-functioning autism. J. Autism Dev. Disord. **43**(1), 34–44 (2013)
7. Law, E.L.C., Roto, V., Hassenzahl, M., Vermeeren, A.P., Kort, J.: Understanding, scoping and defining user experience: a survey approach. In: Proceedings of SIGCHI, CHI 2009, pp. 719–728. Association for Computing Machinery, New York (2009). https://doi.org/10.1145/1518701.1518813
8. Miller, I.T., Wiederhold, B.K., Miller, C.S., Wiederhold, M.D.: Virtual reality air travel training with children on the autism spectrum: a preliminary report. Cyberpsychol. Behav. Soc. Netw. **23**(1), 10–15 (2020)
9. Narciso, D., Bessa, M., Melo, M., Coelho, A., Vasconcelos-Raposo, J.: Immersive 360° video user experience: impact of different variables in the sense of presence and cybersickness. Univers. Access Inf. Soc. **18**(1), 77–87 (2019). https://doi.org/10.1007/s10209-017-0581-5
10. Putnam, C., Chong, L.: Software and technologies designed for people with autism: what do users want? In: Proceedings of the 10th International ACM SIGACCESS Conference on Computers and Accessibility, Assets 2008, pp. 3–10. ACM, New York (2008). https://doi.org/10.1145/1414471.1414475
11. Robertson, A.E., Simmons, D.R.: The relationship between sensory sensitivity and autistic traits in the general population. J. Autism Dev. Disord. **43**(4), 775–784 (2013). https://doi.org/10.1007/s10803-012-1608-7
12. Robertson, C.E., Baron-Cohen, S.: Sensory perception in autism. Nat. Rev. Neurosci. **18**(11), 671 (2017). https://doi.org/10.1038/nrn.2017.112
13. Sait, M., Alattas, A., Omar, A., Almalki, S., Sharf, S., Alsaggaf, E.: Employing virtual reality techniques in environment adaptation for autistic children. Procedia Comput. Sci. **163**, 338–344 (2019)
14. Simm, W., et al.: Anxiety and autism: towards personalized digital health. In: 2016 CHI, CHI 2016, pp. 1270–1281. Association for Computing Machinery, New York (2016). https://doi.org/10.1145/2858036.2858259
15. Simões, M., Bernardes, M., Barros, F., Castelo-Branco, M.: Virtual travel training for autism spectrum disorder: proof-of-concept interventional study. JMIR Serious Games **6**(1), e5 (2018). https://doi.org/10.1007/s10803-012-1544-6
16. Smith, A.D.: Spatial navigation in autism spectrum disorders: a critical review. Front. Psychol. **6**, 31 (2015). https://doi.org/10.3389/fpsyg.2015.00031
17. Strickland, D.: Virtual reality for the treatment of autism. Studies in Health Technology and Informatics, pp. 81–86 (1997)
18. Tcha-Tokey, K., Loup-Escande, E., Christmann, O., Richir, S.: A questionnaire to measure the user experience in immersive virtual environments. In: VRIC 2016. ACM, New York (2016). https://doi.org/10.1145/2927929.2927955

A Machine Learning Tool to Match 2D Drawings and 3D Objects' Category for Populating Mockups in VR

Romain Terrier[1,2(✉)] and Nicolas Martin[2]

[1] Univ Rennes, INSA Rennes, Inria, CNRS, IRISA, Rennes, France
[2] Institute of Research and Technology b<>com, Cesson-Sevigne, France
{romain.terrier,nicolas.martin}@b-com.com

Abstract. Virtual Environments (VE) relying on Virtual Reality (VR) can facilitate the co-design by enabling the users to create 3D mockups directly in the VE. Databases of 3D objects are helpful to populate the mockup and necessitate retrieving methods for the users. In early stages of the design process, the mockups are made up of common objects rather than variations of objects. Retrieving a 3D object in a large database can be fastidious even more in VR. Taking into account the necessity of a natural user's interaction and the necessity to populate the mockup with common 3D objects, we propose, in this paper, a retrieval method based on 2D sketching in VR and machine learning. Our system is able to recognize 90 categories of objects related to VR interior design with an accuracy up to 86%. A preliminary study confirms the performance of the proposed solution.

Keywords: Drawing recognition · Virtual Reality · Machine Learning

1 Introduction

Virtual Reality (VR) offers an immersive and interactive environment, and has been explored to support the design of complex products [11] by, for example, enabling the users to create 3D mockups directly in the virtual environment. A solution to easily create a mockup in VR is to provide a database of 3D common objects. Indeed, in early stages of the design process, there is no need to use a range of representations for the same concept of product (e.g., a desk chair, an operator chair, and an executive chair). Providing a database of 3D common objects implies the user to search and to select the objects using VR interface. Nevertheless, manual search in these database can be inefficient and time-consuming. In this paper, we propose a solution mixing Machine Learning (ML) techniques and a natural user's interaction (i.e., 2D drawings) to find 3D objects to populate a mockup in VR. The novelty lies on the use of ML techniques

---

R. Terrier and N. Martin—Contributed equally to this research.

© Springer Nature Switzerland AG 2020
P. Bourdot et al. (Eds.): EuroVR 2020, LNCS 12499, pp. 240–246, 2020.
https://doi.org/10.1007/978-3-030-62655-6_17

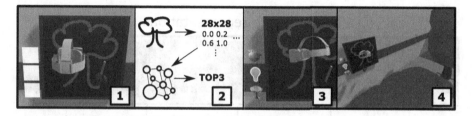

Fig. 1. (1) The user sketches. (2) The image is resized and interpreted by the ML model which gives the three best correspondences. (3) The corresponding vignettes are displayed. (4) The user selects the vignette of the object which is then instantiated in the virtual environment.

that accept various sketched representations of the concept in input leading to a unique 3D common object for all those variant representations (Fig. 2). The aim of the contribution is to facilitate the retrieving interaction of a unique 3D object while taking into account the variability of 2D sketch representations (e.g., various chair sketches for one 3D chair). The user's interactions with our tool are entirely performed in VR. In this way, our tool is able to enrich VR applications dedicated to design.

2   Related Works

In the literature, several tools have already been proposed. A first retrieval tool [9] proposes to extract descriptors of 3D models contained in a database by generating 2D views of the 3D models. The database is made of multiple classes containing multiple 3D models. For example, the class chair contains several different chairs. The tool use a single 2D sketch to match several 3D models of the same categories. The tool is not implemented in VR and do not focus on matching a single class to the sketch.

A second tool [3] focuses on matching the "best views" of 3D models and 2D sketches. The tool is able to extract 2D views of the 3D models contained in a database. Based on the 2D sketch of the user, the ML techniques provides the best corresponding 3D models and the appropriate orientation of the 3D models according to the sketch. As the previous tool, this solution is not implemented in VR and do not focus on matching a single class to the sketch.

A third tool [4] is implemented in VR. It enables the user to draw in 3D and to retrieve the most corresponding 3D models in a database of the same class (e.g., a chair). The tool extracts multiple descriptors of the 3D drawing by projecting the 3D drawing onto twelve 2D views and then compares the descriptors of the 2D views with descriptors of the 3D models. The tool is able to take into account the variations of the 3D models of the same class. For example, a user is able to draw a rocking-chair in 3D and the tool displays the various 3D chairs that best match the 3D drawing. Nevertheless, this solution does not match the need of the early design stage that require common objects for the mockup instead of variations of the same object's class.

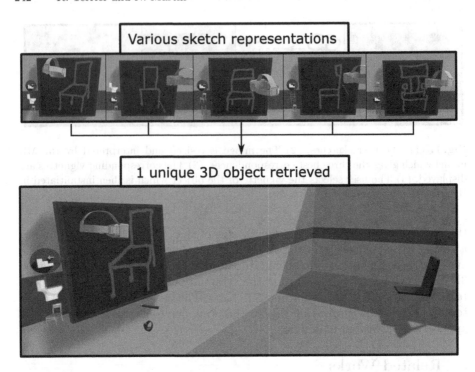

Fig. 2. Different 2D sketches of a same concept (e.g., a chair) are recognized as a same category. Thus, one same 3D object is instantiated for different 2D representations.

The recognition of sketch category using ML methods seems promising. The training of ML models can be defined as building systems capable of learning from data to achieve something without being explicitly programmed [1] (e.g., speech-to-text). This approach has gained popularity in recent years [8] thanks to research breakthroughs [7]. In more details, using supervised methods, the training of ML models intends to infer the function (i.e., $P(Y—X)$) between the input data (i.e., sketch; X) and the output data (i.e., sketch categories; Y) [7]. In others words, ML models aims to map the sketch and the corresponding categories are to automatically classify the drawing. In this way, after training, the models should be able to recognize, in real time, the current category of the drawing without asking the user for the label.

3   Design and Implementation

3.1   Sketch Category Recognition - A Machine Learning Approach

The Quick, Draw! Dataset provided by Google was used to train our model to recognize categories from sketchs [5] (50 million drawings across 345 categories of hand-drawn images). The 90 categories appearing to be the most relevant for

VR interior design have been selected. For each category, 5000 drawings were randomly selected: 60% were used for training, 20% for validation and 20% for testing.

Pre-processing. The intensities of the drawings have been normalized in the range [0.0, 1.0] and resize to 28×28 pixels.

Network Structure. The architecture of the model was composed as follows: 2 convolution layers, each followed by batch normalization, ReLU activation and max pooling layer. The top of the model was composed of 2 dense layers (ReLU activation) interspersed with dropout layers and a final dense layer with a softmax activation.

Training Details. To train our network, the learning rate was fixed to 0.0001. An optimizer Adam [6] was used and a categorical cross-entropy was defined as loss function. The training was performed using Keras [2] with a Tensorflow [10] backend.

Recognition Performance. The performance of the trained model was evaluated on Top-1 accuracy[1] and Top-3 accuracy[2]. On the testing dataset, the trained model was able to reach a Top-1 accuracy of 70% and a Top-3 accuracy of 86%.

3.2   VR Implementation

The virtual environment (VE) is designed in Unity3D. To immerse the user, an Occulus Rift HMD and its controllers are used in the VE and to interact within it. The VE is composed of a virtual blackboard, a virtual pen, three user interface (UI) slots for thumbnails predictions next to the blackboard and a position in the VE to instantiate 3D objects. The database is integrated in Unity3D and contains 90 unique 3D objects. The retrieval process of the 3D object among the 90 items database is designed in four steps.

First, the user draws the 2D simplified representation of the object on a virtual blackboard in the VE. Once the draw is completed, the user starts the recognition phase by triggering a controller button (Fig. 1-1).

Second, the new 2D texture of the blackboard containing the 2D drawing is extracted and transformed into JSON in order to be send to the Python module using a network socket. Upon receipt of the message on the socket, the trained model resizes the 2D texture into a 28×28 one and predicts the 3 most likely categories (Fig. 1-2). The prediction is sent back through a network socket in order to be used in the Unity3D environment.

Third, the thumbnails of the three predictions are displayed next to the virtual blackboard (Fig. 1-3).

---

[1] Top-1 accuracy: the answer with the highest probability must match the expected answer.

[2] Top-3 accuracy: any of the three answers with the highest probabilities must match the expected answer.

Finally, the user selects the thumbnail corresponding to the 2D drawing and the associated 3D object is then instantiated in the VE (Fig. 1-4). If no thumbnail is corresponding, the user is able to clear the blackboard or to complete the current 2D drawing before lunching the recognition step once again.

4   Preliminary Evaluation

The preliminary evaluation aims to check that the recognition performance with users is of the same order as that obtained with data from Google Quick, Draw!.

4.1   Material, Participants and Measures

The evaluation is based on the implementation of our tool in Unity3D. The participants holds an head-mounted display (HMD), Occulus Rift, to be immersed in VR. The Occulus' controllers enable the interaction between the participant and the objects in the virtual environment. The virtual environment is composed of a virtual black board and a virtual pen. The participants use the virtual pen to draw in 2D on the blackboard. The controllers are displayed in VR and their positions are mapped to the participants' hands. Three slots are situated next to the virtual board to display the results of the predictions. At their initial state, the three slots are white indicating that no prediction has been performed.

Two participants[3] (one female - 33 years old, one male - 30 years old) took part in the preliminary evaluation. Concerning the VR experience, one had more than fifty uses of VR and the other had less than three uses of VR. None of them was paid for the evaluation.

Objective measures were used to evaluate the performance and are related to the appearance of the class associated with the drawing among the Top-3 of the predictions displayed to the user. The trial is considered as validated if the class appears in the Top-3 and as validated if the class doesn't appear in the Top-3.

4.2   Protocol

The preliminary evaluation is composed of two parts: the tutorial (25 trials) and the experiment (30 trials). The aim of the tutorial is to teach the user how to use the tool. At each step, the user have to performed trials which consists in taking the virtual pen, drawing the object given by the examiner on the blackboard, validating the drawing, and selecting the picture that depicts the object drawn. Each drawing depicts one of the ninety categories that the model is able to recognize. The objects given to the participant are different in the experiment than in the tutorial. During the experiment, the objects given to the participants are different than during the tutorial.

---

[3] Due to the COVID-19 pandemic and related lockdown, the evaluation could only be carried out on two participants.

4.3   Results

To measure the performance of the recognition model in VR conditions, the percentage of drawings correctly classified is evaluated.

For the first participant, the Top-3 performance rate is 76.67%. For the second participant, the Top-3 performance rate is 96.67%.

4.4   Discussion

The results obtained during the training verification tests, with 5000 drawings per category from sketches from the *Quick, Draw!* Database, reach a Top-3 performance of 86%. The recognition performance with users during our preliminary study is approximately equal to those with the drawings of the database *Quick, Draw!*. However, the evaluation is run with a small not representative sample of participants. These results therefore express a trend rather than a generality and need to be studied further to be validated.

To improve the performance, the model could be trained with more drawings by category to take even more into account the variability of the drawings.

It would be interesting to assess the usability of the tool in the context of creating a virtual mockup and with a larger sample of participant.

However, some limits can be pointed out. 90 categories of sketches was selected from the Quick, Draw! Dataset [5] and some other categories could be interesting for design in VR. Thus, in future works, the addition of new categories should be explored, by enabling the users to add a new 3D object and to sketch multiple examples of this object. Lastly, it could be more efficient to provide a drawing space directly situated in front of the user's location instead of drawing on a fixed blackboard.

5   Conclusion

We propose a VR solution for an efficient 2D sketch recognition taking into account the variability of representations for a same concept. This solution enables the user to draw in VR and, immediately after, to select one conceptual matching to populate the mockup with the corresponding unique 3D object.

Acknowledgments. This study was carried out within b<>com, an institute of research and technology dedicated to digital technologies. It received support from the Future Investments program of the French National Research Agency (grant no. ANR-07-A0-AIRT).

References

1. Bell, J.: Machine Learning: Hands-On for Developers and Technical Professionals. Wiley, Indianapolis (2014)
2. Chollet, F., et al.: Keras (2015). https://keras.io

3. Wang, F., Kang, L., Li, Y.: Sketch-based 3D shape retrieval using convolutional neural networks. In: 2015 IEEE Conference on Computer Vision and Pattern Recognition (CVPR), pp. 1875–1883. IEEE (2015)
4. Giunchi, D., James, S., Steed, A.: 3D sketching for interactive model retrieval in virtual reality. In: Proceedings of the Joint Symposium on Computational Aesthetics and Sketch-Based Interfaces and Modeling and Non-Photorealistic Animation and Rendering - Expressive 2018, Victoria, British Columbia, Canada, pp. 1–12. ACM Press (2018)
5. Google: The Quick, Draw! Dataset.: googlecreativelab/quickdraw-dataset (2017). https://github.com/googlecreativelab/quickdraw-dataset. original-date: 2017-05-09T18:28:32Z
6. Kingma, D.P., Ba, J.: Adam: A Method for Stochastic Optimization. arXiv:1412.6980 [cs], December 2014. http://arxiv.org/abs/1412.6980
7. LeCun, Y., Bengio, Y., Hinton, G.: Deep learning. Nature **521**(7553), 436–444 (2015)
8. Lee, J.H., Shin, J., Realff, M.J.: Machine learning: overview of the recent progresses and implications for the process systems engineering field. Comput. Chem. Eng. **114**, 111–121 (2018). https://doi.org/10.1016/j.compchemeng.2017.10.008. https://linkinghub.elsevier.com/retrieve/pii/S0098135417303538
9. Lei, H., Luo, G., Li, Y., Lin, S.: 3D model retrieval based on hand drawn sketches using LDA model. In: 2016 6th International Conference on Digital Home (ICDH), pp. 261–266. IEEE (2016)
10. Abadi, M., et al.: TensorFlow: Large-Scale Machine Learning on Heterogeneous Systems (2015). http://tensorflow.org/
11. Wang, P., et al.: A comprehensive survey of AR/MR-based co-design in manufacturing. Eng. Comput. **36**, 1715–1738 (2020). https://doi.org/10.1007/s00366-019-00792-3

Performance Design Assistance by Projector-Camera Feedback Simulation

Taichi Kagawa$^{(\boxtimes)}$ and Toshiyuki Amano(iD)

Wakayama University, Wakayama, Japan
{s206314,amano}@wakayama-u.ac.jp

Abstract. In this paper, we propose a simulation method for a projector-camera system that aims to design assist for the installation art using a projector-camera feedback system. The simulator requires a precise estimation of the optical response between the camera and the projector via the projection target. For this requirement, we model the optical response with a non-linear projector response model and Light Transport matrices. Experimental results show our proposed simulator successfully reproduced the behavior of the pixel feedback animation that is a illumination projection used un-stable condition in addition to the static appearance manipulation.

Keywords: Spatial augmented reality · Projector-camera system · Light transport matrix · Installation art

1 Introduction

In recent years, the illumination shown by projection mapping has attracted a lot of media attention. Research on projection mapping has been intense. Most of its fundamental techniques were established in 2001 as augmented reality by Raskar et al. [1]. Since then, various projection techniques, such as super-resolution, defocus compensation, and high dynamic range projection, have been proposed. Amano and Kato [2] proposed a successive appearance manipulation technique (appearance control) that controls the actual appearance of the images by optical feedback using a projector and a camera. There has been considerable applied research on appearance control; its application includes visual assistance for dichroic color vision and myopia, material appearance manipulation, optical illusion, and installation arts.

For the installation art application, a projection technique called "pixel feedback animation" (PFA) that intentionally oscillates and saturates the projector-camera feedback system to generate attractive flickering and patterns is proposed. In 2015, Amano performed an installation art of a tapestry "Gekko" made in Nishijin textile in collaboration with a traditional Japanese craftsman, Hiroto Rakusho (Fig. 1). In this installation art, the PFA technique and an appearance manipulation in a stable state that alters apparent color or contrast were used for the augmentation by illumination projection. In 2016, this projection technique was also applied to a statue at the Nihonbashi Mitsukoshi Main Store (Fig. 2). The statue was difficult to create a three-dimensional (3D) model of the

© Springer Nature Switzerland AG 2020
P. Bourdot et al. (Eds.): EuroVR 2020, LNCS 12499, pp. 247–252, 2020.
https://doi.org/10.1007/978-3-030-62655-6_18

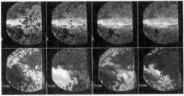

Fig. 1. Installation art of a tapestry (left), PFA (right) (Bubble (upper) and Reflection (lower))

Fig. 2. Installation art on the statue Magokoro

statue because of its height (11 m) and complicated shape. Moreover, it was necessary to maintain a bright lighting environment during the display owing to the sales floor. Thus, general projection mapping on the statue was problematic. By contrast, appearance control and PFA production does not require a shape model. Another one is it can be applied even in a bright environment.

Although installation arts using appearance control and PFA have the aforementioned advantages, there are two issues in its design. First, the projector–camera system needs to be in an unstable state to generate projection patterns that change with time for PFA; hence, it is difficult to predict its behavior. Second, the behavior of PFA significantly depends on the reflection characteristics of the art object and the environmental lighting. It is necessary to adjust the projection parameters on the actual object at the exhibition venue to achieve the desired PFA; this adjustment is often time consuming. For example, "Bubble" is caused by an extreme increase in the value of the image processing intensity in the contour enhancement process. Meanwhile, "Reflection" is generated in the brightness equalization process by setting the image gain lower than normal and considerably increasing the image processing intensity. However, it is impossible to determine the performance parameters in advance because the impression of the performance can be significantly affected by slight changes in the environment. Hence, the aim of this study is to realize a projection design in a remote environment, such as a laboratory or office, as well as the optical and geometrical response between the projector and the camera.

2   Pixel Feedback Animation

Figure 3 shows the projector–camera feedback system used for appearance control. The system optically changes the object's appearance to the reference R, which is given by the image processing of C_{est}. This is a natural appearance that is estimated from the relationship between the captured image and the projection image. Such manipulation

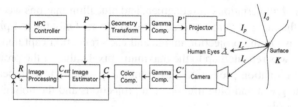

Fig. 3. Projector-camera feedback system [2]

can be successfully performed in real-time because C_{est} is estimated during projection for the appearance manipulation. PFA is caused by setting excessive parameters when applying image processing in the system. In PFA, the projection behavior depends on the reflection characteristics, such as specular and diffuse reflection on the projection surface, and these characteristics cause a strong reflection and scattering of the projection light on the art object. The reflections affect neighboring pixels and cause bleeding on the captured image. Additionally, the optical response of the actual equipment is non-linear owing to the saturation and dark noise of the captured image. Therefore, it is difficult to predict the behavior of the system by simple reflection measurement using uniform color projection. Thus, it is necessary to project onto the actual art object several times to find the parameters that achieve the desired effect. In this study, we propose a projector–camera system simulator that involves a projector–camera response to accurately predict the captured image.

3   Projector-Camera System Simulator

In this study, we replaced the optical and geometrical responses between P and C in Fig. 3 with the aforementioned projector–camera response model, and constructed a simulator for the projector–camera feedback system. We also modeled a projector–camera response via a projection target by separating the direct reflection and global illumination components. The former was modeled using the projector response table, whereas the latter was modeled using light transport matrix. The light transport matrix and response table were measured using the following three steps:

In Step 1, we measured the light transport matrix [3]. Light transport matrices describe not only the optical relationship of geometrically corresponding pixels between the projected image and the captured image but also the relationship among surrounding pixels. Therefore, we can model the bleeding of the projected light, which is one of the causes of PFA. However, the light transport matrix is sometimes darker than the actual result because the measurement of the light transport matrices with [3] does not include dark elements below the threshold owing to noise reduction in each light transport matrix. Although this thresholding has a slight difference in each single captured image, this small error can accumulate in the simulation of the solid pattern image projection. Hence, we separated the direct reflection components from light transport matrices and obtained the direct reflection components separately.

In Step 2, the direct reflection components were obtained. The correspondence between the pixel values of the projected image and the captured image was measured.

First, the images of all variations of red, green, and blue illuminations were projected by a projector, and the images were captured using a camera. Only the red-pixel value was increased step-wise in the projection image and each reflection captured using a camera. This process was repeated up to the maximum pixel value of the projection image. When the red illumination projection was completely captured, we repeated the same procedure for the green and blue illumination projections and then obtained responses $D_k^r(\boldsymbol{p_k}), k \in \{r, g, b\}$.

In Step 3, pixel mapping between the captured image and the projection image was obtained using a gray code pattern projection as a prior calibration. As the pixel mapping showed a pixel correspondence between the projection image and the captured image, we obtained the direct reflection components at each light transport matrix from the relationship. Afterward, we replaced these direct components with 0 to remove the direct reflection components from the light transport matrices T_k^r, T_k^g, T_k^b.

$$C_k = T_k^r \boldsymbol{p_r} + T_k^g \boldsymbol{p_g} + T_k^b \boldsymbol{p_b} + D_k^r(\boldsymbol{p_k}), k \in \{r, g, b\} \tag{1}$$

where c_k and p_k are vector representations of the captured and projected images, respectively. Through these procedures, the image captured by the system was estimated from the pixel map indicating the correspondence between the projector and camera pixels, with the light transport matrix describing the tendency of indirect reflection and the array holding the direct reflection component.

4 Result

4.1 Simulation Environment

In the experiment, we used the Nishijin textile shown in Fig. 4 (left). The textile has beautiful patterns created using various materials, such as dyed yarn and gold and silver foils. The woven structure of the foil can cause brightness saturation and light bleeding. Hence, we placed it on a desk in a dimmed environment and set up the experiment environment as shown in Fig. 4 (right). In this situation, the projector projected illumination onto the projection target from above, and the camera focused down on the target from the same location as the projector. The ground truth PFA images were also captured with this projector-camera system.

Fig. 4. Nishijin textile to be measured (left) and Experimental setup (right)

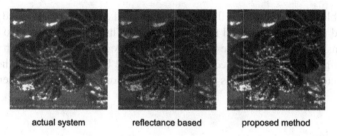

actual system   reflectance based   proposed method

Fig. 5. Comparison image of the projection results of monochrome conversion

4.2   Evaluation of Static Appearance Manipulation

We compared the simulation results of the manipulation that makes the scene appear monochrome. Each result was expanded to compare the methods (Fig. 5). Based on the comparison, our system reproduced colorful spike noise that occurs in the misalignment of the pixel mapping, as shown in Fig. 5. When the images were manipulated by the actual system, a sub-pixel order of misalignment between the projected pixel and the captured pixel occurred. It produced a pseudo-color in the reflectance estimation, and its error accumulated and produced spiky noise in the projection image. It cannot be estimated with the surface reflectance used in [3].

4.3   Evaluation of Pixel Feedback Animation

Our proposed method was evaluated for bubbles, one of the performance issues described in Sect. 1. The PFA was measured from 0 to 50 frames to compare its frame-by-frame behavior. Figure 6 shows the change in bubbles for each method as three frames elapsed from frame 17. The time has passed towards the bottom of the image. In the whole image, some bubbles that were not reproduced by the reflectance-based method and our method were generated. To compare the changes in PFA over time, the sizes of the bubbles were compared using each method. The growth was compared by the change in the diameter

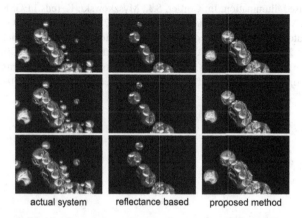

actual system   reflectance based   proposed method

Fig. 6. Comparison of projection results of "Bubble"

of each bubble. The results show that the mean error of the reflectance-based method is 32.31%, and that of the proposed method is 5.57%. This result is related to the use of the light transport matrix. Because this system can reproduce blur, the growth process of bubbles is similar to that of a projector–camera system. Using this method, the behavior of the projector–camera system is reproduced by contour enhancement when a bubble grows.

4.4 Discussion

We confirmed the static appearance manipulation is successively reproduced. Since it enabled the estimation of the spike noise caused by the misalignment of pixel mapping, our simulator can be used for authoring using static appearance manipulations. In contrast, it still needs improvement for the pixel feedback animation simulation. We are focusing on the thresholding of Light Transport matrices for its investigation, but the reason is not clear at this moment. However, the impression of the simulation results is not much different from the actual projection. Therefore, we believe our simulator can be a useful authoring tool for the installation based on the projector-camera feedback.

5 Conclusion

In this study, we proposed a projector–camera response model that employs light transport matrices with projector response functions. Our model reproduced illumination leakage and flickering. With these characteristics, the unstable state behavior of the PFA can be correctly reproduced. However, it remains the problems on the detail that could not be reproduced in the simulation of the PFA. In the future, we will try to achieve a more accurate simulation by investigating this mechanism.

References

1. Raskar, R., Welch, G., Low, K.-L., Bandyopadhyay, D.: Shader lamps: animating real objects with image-based illumination. In: Gortler, S.J., Myszkowski, K. (eds.) EGSR 2001, pp. 89–102. Springer, Vienna (2001). https://doi.org/10.1007/978-3-7091-6242-2_9
2. Amano, T., Kato, H.: Appearance control using projection with model predictive control. In: Proceedings of 20th International Conference on the Pattern Recognition, ICPR (2010)
3. Miyagawa, I., Arai, H., Taniguchi, Y.: Efficient acquisition of light transport matrix using push broom-type projector illumination. ITE Trans. Media Technol. Appl. 3(1), 30–39 (2015)

Author Index

Printed in the United States
By Bookmasters